Persistent Pastoralists
Peter Rigby

For my two families:
Zebiya and Kimuli; and Toreto,
Katau, Papaai Koisenge, and
Yieyio Ng'oto Toreto.
Ore oloany oltoilo loo'ltung'anak, nelo
aning' ooloo'lmeneng'a.

Persistent Pastoralists

Nomadic Societies in Transition

Peter Rigby

Zed Books Ltd.

Persistent Pastoralists was first published
by Zed Books Ltd., 57 Caledonian Road, London,
N1 9BU in 1985.

Copyright © Peter Rigby, 1985

Cover design by Jacque Solomons
Cover photo by Richard Cross © 1985 Contemporary
Historians. Used with permission
Photographs courtesy of the author
Printed by The Pitman Press, Bath

British Library Cataloguing in Publication Data

Rigby, Peter
  Persistent pastoralists: nomadic societies in transition.
  1. Nomads — Africa, East
  2. Herders — Africa, East
  I. Title
  305.8'9676   GN658

  ISBN 0-86232-226-X
  ISBN 0-86232-227-8 Pbk

US Distributor: Biblio Distribution Center,
81 Adams Drive, Totowa, New Jersey 07512

Contents

My younger brother, Katau ole Koisenge.

Dancing during mutai "home feast" after olpur meat feast in the forest.

My cross-cousin Mandero (second from left) with my younger brother Toreto (second from right) and unmarried girls (intoyie, during ceremonial dance.

Acknowledgements

Some of the research upon which this book is based was supported by research grants from the University of Dar es Salaam and Temple University, Philadelphia, for which I am deeply grateful.

It is impossible to mention the large number of people in East Africa and elsewhere without whose help and encouragement the work embodied here could not have been carried out. I owe most to Olpayian Koisenge and his family, particularly Toreto ole Koisenge, Katau ole Koisenge, and Yieyio Ng'oto Toreto, who took me into their home and made me a son and a brother. But virtually the whole Ilparakuyo community and diaspora in Tanzania knew of my presence, and I could not have proceeded without their tacit consent.

I am also indebted to my colleagues and students at the University of Dar es Salaam, Temple University, Philadelphia, and elsewhere, for stimulating discussion, criticism, and encouragement, particularly Drs. A.O. Anacleti, Henry Bernstein, John Galaty, Alan Jacobs, Sam Kajumba, Ivan Karp, Gary Littlejohn, Daniel Ndagala, Thomas Patterson, and Marja-Liisa Swantz; as well as Ndugu M.L. ole Parkipuny, Melkiori Matwi, Simeon Mesaki, and Jonas Ruben Wanga in East Africa and Peter Biella, Richard Cross, and Naomi Kipury in Philadelphia; and Robert Molteno, Roger van Zwanenberg, and Anna Gourlay in London; and many others too numerous to mention. Finally, but most importantly, this book could never have been written without the encouragement, stimulus, and support of my wife Zebiya and my daughter Kimuli, who put up with my frequent absences from the *enkang'* in Dar es Salaam, and frequent invasions of kinsmen and age-mates from a vast array of other Ilparakuyo and Maasai *inkang'itie*.

* * *

Grateful acknowledgement is made to Cambridge University Press for permission to reproduce the materials appearing in Chapters 3, 4, and 5.

These are based upon articles which were originally published as follows:

Chapter 3:   Peter Rigby, "*Olpul* and *entoroj*: the Economy of Sharing among the Pastoral Baraguyu of Tanzania", in Équipe écologie et anthropologie des sociétés pastorales (eds): *Pastoral Production and Society,* Cambridge/New York: Cambridge University Press (1979).

Chapter 4:   Peter Rigby, "Time and Historical Consciousness: the Case of Ilparakuyo Maasai", *Comparative Studies in Society and History,* Vol. 25, No. 3, July 1983, pp. 428-56. Cambridge University Press, Cambridge and New York.

Chapter 5:   Peter Rigby, "Pastors and Pastoralists: the Differential Penetration of Christianity among East African Cattle Herders", *Comparative Studies in Society and History,* Vol. 23, No. 1, January 1981, pp. 96-129. Cambridge University Press, Cambridge and New York.

Peter Rigby

Preface

This book is an attempt to develop a historical materialist critique of the nature and relevance of certain contemporary theories in social and cultural anthropology which claim to address problems of "development", "social change", and socio-economic transformation. The critique is conducted not merely at the level of abstract theorization, but in the context of understanding the politico-economic transformation of particular pre-capitalist social formations in eastern Africa. Although deriving from an extensive study among a particular section of pastoral Maasai, the Ilparakuyo of Tanzania, the book is emphatically not a "traditional" ethnographic text in the sense of a comprehensive description (if that were even possible) of a particular "society". It therefore has implications for pastoralist studies in other regions of Africa, the Middle East, central Asia, Latin America; in fact, wherever pastoralists still exist. It should also be of both theoretical interest and some practical significance as a critique of some of the assumptions underlying capitalist "development" strategies in East Africa and elsewhere in the underdeveloped world.

Despite the complexity and somewhat esoteric nature of the various theoretical arguments involved, the following essays should thus be of use to students of the social sciences in general, as well as to non-specialists who are interested in a radical view of a branch of those sciences which has had, and still has, considerable (and often detrimental) influence upon the lives of many of our fellow countrymen in East Africa and elsewhere. These may appear to be somewhat grandiose claims; but it is difficult to exaggerate the dangers that may be generated when the practitioners of social science interact with those who design "development policies", particularly those policies which can seriously affect the lives of large numbers of people who are both oppressed and exploited in increasingly effective ways, and who have few avenues of response and retaliation.

Of the many-stranded, and often over-specialized, lines of thought emerging in contemporary social and cultural anthropology, two are the most important for our particular purposes. The first is known as "applied" or "development" anthropology; the second is "Marxist" anthropology. Both are well represented and illustrated in the increasingly important field of "development studies" among the numerous pastoralist social formations still functioning in many of the more "inhospitable" regions of the world, often referred to as semi-arid or arid areas. The choice between these two competing, even contradictory, theoretical problematics may well have crucial implications for the future of pastoral peoples and the viability of their social formations, as well as for the discipline of anthropology itself.[1] While the demise of the latter may not be a reason for mourning, and for some might be a positive cause for rejoicing, the fact that some of the theories generated by anthropology's more "bourgeois" forms are now implicit in discussions of "development strategies" cannot be swept under the carpet. Since I am largely concerned in the rest of this book with the task of "re-embedding" the anthropology of pastoralism as a specialized and unique element in a radical and comparative political economy, and hence as a contribution towards contemporary revolutionary theory and practice, it is appropriate at this point to look at the implications of the one kind of anthropology for the other, in however brief and unsatisfactory a form.

Perhaps in keeping with the origins of applied anthropology in the juxtaposition of social science and the colonial administration (read "imperialism"), contemporary development anthropology is, on the whole, practised primarily in an "interdisciplinary" context. As the result of a desperate effort to make it "technically relevant" to the other members of the "team" (development economics, agronomy, pasture management, to mention a few), anthropology is reduced to its lowest common denominator by making it provide what it is theoretically incapable of providing. As Marc Augé astutely notes:

> Nowadays the notion of interdisciplinarity may be taken to tally fairly exactly with the areas in which each discipline is incomplete and lacking in confidence, and it may therefore be said to be at the cross-roads of intellectual confusions. Interdisciplinarity is the proud title we give to the anxiety from which the different disciplines suffer. (1982: 111)

This is true even if, as Augé adds, this anxiety is itself productive of a new awareness that reality does not necessarily correspond to the boundaries of each discipline!

In such a debilitating context, the only valuable function of applied or development anthropology becomes politically (and economically) impossible. To achieve some theoretical coherence, these "anthropologies" would have to conform to Roger Bastide's (1971) definition which takes

> applied anthropology to be an anthropology of application, and one that would include within its field of vision, and in the construction of its intellectual field, the "subjects" as much as the "objects" of this application, the "developers" as much as the "developed". (Augé 1982: 94)

Instead, by its very inability to develop a truly reflexive and critical theoretical stance, anthropology in relation to contemporary development studies and strategies has often become an apologetic for the contradictions of increasing exploitation, which are the inevitable consequences of neo-colonial domination.

But if this is the case, why not let anthropology dig its own grave and bury itself quietly, without the need for a requiem? I have already suggested one reason why we cannot take this position. There is a second and more important reason, which is one of the main subjects of this book. But if anthropology is to be reabsorbed into a critical political economy and is not simultaneously to disappear, it must demonstrate its relevance for real transformations (revolutions?). A merely moral and ethical, and hence ideological, self-critique of the kind offered by "Africanist historiography" in response to colonial historiography is not enough (Temu and Swai 1981). Even the radical philosophies of such political practitioners as Nkrumah, let alone the ideological constructions of Senghor and other advocates of *négritude*, fail in this regard. As Paulin Hountondji (1976) points out, their philosophical critiques remain at the ideological level:

> The passionate quest for an identity denied by the colonizer, but with the underlying idea that one of the elements of cultural identity is indeed "philosophy", the idea that all culture rests on a particular, permanent, and metaphyisical substratum. (Quoted in Augé 1982: 85)

But as Hountondji also sees, and Augé as anthropologist approves, the "person of the militant and that of the analyst are complementary but not confused" (ibid: 85-6). If anthropological theorization *per se* is thus not "a guide to action, a theory of revolutionary or counter-revolutionary practice", it nevertheless remains true that "every radical (moral, political) critique of anthropology leads to an *epistemological enquiry*, or ought to do so" (Augé 1982: 97, 93, my emphasis).

That there is something worth saving through the reintegration of anthropology with a comparative political economy based upon the problematic of historical materialism is attested to by the work of such key figures as Worsley, Godelier, Meillassoux, Mafeje, Bonte, Bourgeot, and others, many of whom are discussed in the pages that follow. But this reintegration entails that anthropology must abandon its positivist commitment to a "specificity completely dependent on that of its *object*", whether the latter be "African societies", "primitive societies", or "pastoral societies". For these "objects" themselves are the spurious contructs of anthropologists (or historians), based upon assumptions about the "uniformity and legibility" of such societies; assumptions that are rightly rejected by "those who are being observed, once they have a chance to speak" (Augé 1982: 82). Furthermore,

> Hountondji therefore holds that cultural anthropology and ethnology must owe their existence as separate disciplines, *vis-à-vis* sociology in particular,

"to this arbitrary division of the human collectivity between two types of society that they claim, with no proof at all, to be fundamentally different" (quoted in Augé 1982: 82).

It will be seen that the notion of "pastoral praxis" which I develop in this book is crucial to my understanding of the penetration of classless pastoral social formations in eastern Africa (what Bonte has called "non-stratified social formations": 1977) by commodity relations and peripheral capitalism and the consequent emergence (or relative non-emergence) of classes. This is a specifically non-philosophical, non-metaphysical, notion, closely akin to that suggested by Hountondji's concept of a group's "practical ideology". Lest my later development of the *coherence* of the idea of pastoral praxis and its integral theory (or "ideology") be misconstrued as a statement if an "ethnophilosophy" (cf. the work of Galaty of "ethnosociology" and "ethnoeconomics" referred to later), a conceptualization I reject as strongly as Hountondji and Augé, let me immediately ally myself with what Augé rightly describes as the "really subversive nature" of Hountondji's concept of "practical ideology" (Hountondji 1983: 178-9):

> What strikes one first as being a group's practical ideology (in the singular) is never just its *dominant* practical ideology. Instead of hastily extending it to all the group's members, instead of naively taking it at face value, instead of forging a philosophical theory out of it that is presumed to have the support of the entire community, the prudent analyst will strive to uncover behind the surface unanimity, the whole gamut of non-dominant ideologies or, at any rate, relations at a tangent to the dominant ideology.

What I am trying to get at in the notion of pastoral praxis, and am still in the process of developing, is a *dialectical relation* between various ideological elements (one of which is "dominant") and the constantly changing imperatives of the material base of pastoral existence, invariant only in the sense that the physical nature of the major means of production (the herd) remains the same, as do the exigencies of transhumance, the commitment of labour, etc. In this manner, I agree with Augé when he concludes from Hountondji's work:

> In thus relativising the irreducibility of intercultural differences, and in postulating the existence of intercultural differences and of relations of force and domination, all of which have been marked to a greater or lesser degree by an idiom presupposing unanimity, Hountondji is subscribing to an anticulturalist project that does clearly go some way towards defining and justifying a form of intellectual optimism. (Augé 1982: 86)

II

It may be seen from the issues discussed above that the approach I take in this book implies a theoretical shift towards what has been labelled "Marxist" in recent collections of conference papers on the problems of pastoralist development (e.g. Galaty and Salzman, eds.: 1981). In fact, it is the story of that shift, and a theoretical statement of its necessity. But where Salzman, as an anthropologist who identifies himself as an "empiricist", is intrigued by the fact that Bourgeot (a Marxist) is *not* an economic determinist, and Schneider (a non-Marxist) *is* (Salzman 1981: 163), the reader who manages to struggle through the following pages should feel no such surprise. The reasons for this are elaborated in the Introduction (Chapter 1). Although most of the other essays which constitute the succeeding chapters of this book are based on materials published elsewhere or circulated in one form or another over the past seven or eight years, a) their differential accessibility, and b) their theoretically developmental nature as expressed in their roughly chronological order, have prompted me to take seriously the suggestion of a number of friends, colleagues, kin, and affines that I publish them together. The reasons for this decision are also elaborated in the Introduction, which deals basically with what I consider to be two of the most important recent theoretical contributions to the study of pastoralist political economy (Bonte and Hedlund). This does not imply that I do not consider many other contributions and approaches of great significance and value.

Each of the subsequent chapters, written at various times over a period of six years, four of which were spent in intermittent "fieldwork" among Ilparakuyo, stands on its own as a study of some aspect of Ilparakuyo "society" and its historical and contemporary relationships with other Maasai sections, other East African pastoral social formations, and the broader political economy of East African nation states. But linked together, they also represent a set of theoretical, methodological, and personal transformations which, in the opinion of some of those who have seen them, throw some light not only upon the particular problems of pastoralists and their interpretation, but also upon the central issues of the relation between theory and praxis in the social sciences. It is for this reason that, apart from editorial changes, cross-references, and additional explanatory footnotes, these essays have been left in their original form.

This is not the place to enter the complex debate on the concept of "praxis". My usage of it is derived basically from Marx's multi-faceted concept; but this in itself is subject to an enormous amount of debate (e.g Lefebvre 1968: 25-57; cf. Hoffman 1975; etc.). The point of departure for this debate is, classically, Marx's "Theses on Feuerbach" (Marx 1845 [1975]: 421-3), the most famous of which is, of course, the 11th thesis: "The philosophers have only *interpreted* the world in various ways; the point is to *change* it." As Hoffman rightly points out, this does not mean that we must *stop* interpeting it (1975: 30-1 and *passim*). Although *praxis* is the Greek (and German) word for the English word "practice", the latter does not represent the Marxist (or any other revolutionary or philosophical) usage of the term (Bernstein 1971: ix-xiii, and *passim*). Suffice to say here that for Marx, *praxis* transcends idealism, positivism, and vulgar materialism in that, "Through praxis, thought is reunited with being, consciousness with sensuous or physical nature, the mind with spontaneity" (Lefebvre 1968: 57).

Although every chapter deals with specific structural and historical aspects of Ilparakuyo and Maasai social formations, each begins with an attempt to grapple with some of the theoretical issues involved in their interpretation. These critical explorations embody a theoretical journey, the "shift" I have already mentioned, a journey which I try to elaborate and extend in the Introduction, but which also becomes apparent in the reading of the chapters themselves. This theoretical odyssey, however, is inseparable from my own personal journey "into" Ilparakuyo and Maasai language, culture, and pastoral praxis, and a deepening appreciation of the terrible odds they have encountered and still face in an increasingly exploitative world dominated by international capitalism.

Despite the enormity of these odds, it will also become apparent that my Ilparakuyo kinsmen, friends, and age-mates have taught me not only to understand the resilience of a way of life, but have also instilled in me a determination to fight against the tide of global and local forces of exploitation that continues to threaten the struggle for freedom of all oppressed peoples. In other words, my journey towards an understanding of the contemporary and historical Ilparakuyo social formation and culture has freed my thinking from the domination of restricted and ultimately alienating forms of anthropological theory and has enabled me to grasp, at least partially, the essential need for the dialectic of theory and praxis which lies at the heart of historical materialism. It is my contention in this book that, without this realization, neither anthropology nor any of the other social sciences will, or have any reason to, survive.

For purposes elaborated in the Introduction, the succession of chapters does not follow strictly the chronological order in which they were written, but the overall trend is a temporal one. And, as already noted, the material included in this book does not provide a comprehensive statement of the detailed structures of Ilparakuyo local communities, such as the "kinship system", marriage patterns, neighbourhood organization, dispute settlement, and so forth; these must await a future publication. What is presented here is an overall view of some elements of Ilparakuyo and Maasai historicity, their relationships with other peoples, their encounter with colonialism, neo-colonialism, and Christianity; and certain key institutions which ensure the reproduction and viability of these social formations, all within the context of a developing theoretical problematic which, it is suggested, provides the only path to any real understanding of them and the inseparability of theory and praxis.

III

Ilparakuyo (sing. Olparakuoni) are a historically distinctive section of the pastoral Maasai, within the overall cultural grouping of the Maa-speaking peoples of Tanzania and Kenya whose common language, *Olmaa*, is also known descriptively as *enkutuk oo 'lMaasai*, "the mouth (language) of the Maasai". They are also known in the literature as "Baraguyu" (Beidelman 1960, and *passim*) or "Parakuyu" (Berntsen 1979, and *passim*)[2] and as "Wakwavi" by coastal and some other Bantu-speaking peoples, also rendered "Kuafi" (Krapf 1860); these last two terms, whatever their origin, are totally rejected by Ilparakuyo. They have further been classified as "Iloikop" since the period of earliest missionary contact and colonial penetration (Krapf 1860; Johnston 1885; Baumann 1894; etc.), a designation also adopted by Jacobs (1965a, and *passim*) but seriously questioned by Berntsen (forthcoming).

Some contemporary pastoral Maasai refer to Ilparakuyo as "Ilumbwa", a term associated with "Wahumba", or "Wahumha", by which they are known by most central Tanzanian Bantu-speakers amongst whom they live. Other Tanzanian and Kenyan Maasai accept the Ilparakuyo designation of themselves, but in the form of "Ilparakuo" (sing. also Olparakuoni; fem. pl. Imparakuo, sing. Emparakuoni) which means literally, "people very well off in terms of livestock". Such terminological problems are by no means peculiar to this social formation, and are discussed in somewhat more detail in Chapter 4. But it should be noted here that all these designations are relative to time and space, and are not "fixed" and historically stable categorizations. I have decided, in consultation with my closest kinsmen and friends, particularly Toreto ole Koisenge and Melkiori Matwi, to retain the forms Olparakuoni/Ilparakuyo throughout this book.

Notes

1. There are numerous commentaries on the failure of the social sciences, for example, in investigating the historical factors involved in the disastrous Sahel drought and famine of 1969-74; but this is not the place to examine these commentaries in detail. This is clearly a case in which social science interventions on behalf of "development strategies" based upon capitalist economic theory have probably had a more destructive effect on the pastoral social formations in the area than the original ecological causes (cf. Bourgeot 1981: 116-7, 123-6). A "solution" based upon "range management" geared to an entire "ecosystem", a solution that ignored the economic and political conditions underlying the famine, has been "destructive of an already precarious equilibrium which has always existed ... within traditional pastoral production – an equilibrium between the objectives of consumption and the possibilities of production." (Bourgeot 1981: 124 ; cf. Comité Information Sahel, 1974, for two examples of what a critical and Marxist analysis can contribute; cf. Augé 1982: 96, 122-3.)

2. The prefixes Il- and Ol- are masculine plural and singular respectively. Berntsen follows the convention of dropping the initial prefix, hence "Parakuyu" (as well as "Maasai"). At the risk of inconsistency, I have retained "Maasai" throughout since it is a term generally accepted in the literature, but use the prefixes for Ilparakuyo, since other Maasai *sections*, such as Ilpurko (i.e. Purko), are often referred to using the plural prefix at least, particularly in the more recent literature.

1. Introduction

"Isipat eng'ari, meng'ari irrekiei."
"Truths are shared, customs are not" (Ilparakuyo/Maasai
proverb).

The history and sociology of the Maa-speaking peoples is a rapidly growing
field to which scholars from among Ilparakuyo, pastoral Maasai, and other
sections of the "culture area" are contributing increasingly, particularly in
such areas as the unravelling of the intricate linguistic, ritual, and symbolic
structures of the age-set organizations, marriage institutions, and other
characteristic elements of these social formations; but also towards a
theoretical and practical understanding of the processes of politico-
economic transformation which, as we shall see, take somewhat unique
forms in these societies. Many of these scholars, some of whom are actively
engaged in the critique or implementation of "development programmes",
are referred to and cited in what follows. But before I outline the form of the
present set of essays, I must digress briefly to indicate the relationship between Ilparakuyo studies, other pastoral studies in general, and other
Maasai studies in particular.

Although all the Maa-speaking peoples display an overall similarity of
language, culture, and social organization derived from a common but complex historical past, the vast areas they inhabit, both contemporarily and
even before major disruptions by colonial penetration, particularly in
Kenya, result in a great deal of diversity between various sections, and even
within them. This diversity is manifested at a number of different levels, constantly changing throughout the known and increasingly apparent histories
of these social formations. For example, ecological conditions in the areas
they occupy vary a great deal, as do the historical conditions of colonial
penetration, the emphases given to alternative elements in the major forces
and means of production, the details of production relations, the organization of labour, and hence the types of political-economic transformations
taking place. Variation is also manifested in the ideological emphases given
to structural elements, such as descent and kinship, the age-set system, and
the role of prophets or religious leaders in the different sections and sub-

units of the overall area. This variation produces a major theoretical problem in interpretation, as will become apparent.

More systematically, we may state that the historical, material, social and ideological conditions of production, reproduction, and transformation of different sections of the Maa-speaking peoples are extremely diverse. Further aspects of this diversity and similarity between Ilparakuyo, Maasai, and other pastoral social formations in Tanzania are discussed in Chapter 6.

The difficulties in generalizing about specific structural elements from one section of the Maa-speaking peoples to another are repeated, on a lesser scale, within the sections larger in terms of population or geographical dispersal. Ilparakuyo, occupying as they do "interstitial" areas within and between the various agricultural and agro-pastoral societies amongst whom they live, are divided into two broad politico-ritual areas, the northern and eastern, and the southern and western. Although I have had considerable contact with Ilparakuyo from the south-western area during my residence among the Wagogo (Rigby 1969a, and *passim*), and there is considerable movement of population between the areas, I have lived intensively only in local communities in the north-eastern sections. While there is fair reason to suggest that this "division" of Ilparakuyo is of the "amoeboid" type, resulting in the replication and hence identity of two "viable units" characteristic of some pastoral formations (e.g. Dyson-Hudson 1966: 259-69), for Karimojong; cf. Bonte 1976: 194), I hesitate even to generalize comprehensively from one sub-section to the other.

This diversity in the details of the relations of production and hence the organizational forms and emphases given to structural elements is not merely the result of wide dispersal and variations in ecological and other historical and material conditions of production; it is also linked to another critical issue. Contrary to the common anthropological propensity to isolate "pure types" of societies to study as units independent of their historical, material, and cultural surroundings, *none* of the social formations discussed in this book are able to survive *totally* upon the products of their herds. Although committed primarily to a pastoral regime, and constantly renewing their goal to subsist entirely upon their herds, the members of all these societies know, and have always known as far as historical memory allows, that they must obtain agricultural and other produce from their agricultural, agro-pastoral , and hunting and gathering neighbours, by barter, purchase, or other means. This knowledge, in fact, lies at the heart of an elaborate symbolic and mythological system which provides the "background" to the origins of their historical consciousness (cf. Galaty 1982; see Chapter 4 below). The interdependence thus generated between pastoral and non-pastoral formations is also historically documented for most sections of pastoral Maasai, even during periods of highest "success" in pastoral production, but particularly so in times of drought, epidemic, or other natural and political disaster (e.g. Muriuki 1974 for pastoral Maasai/Kikuyu relations; cf. Hedlund 1979; Chapter 3 below). The relations of production and the conditions of reproduction of these social formations, both material and ideological, while displaying an internal coherence, must also include their relations with other pastoral and non-pastoral neighbours; none of them are, or ever have been, discrete "tribes" or "ethnic groups".[1]

Given these facts, the discussion of various aspects of the Ilparakuyo social formation presented in most of the following chapters includes more or less detailed comparisons with other Maasai sections, other pastoral and agricultural formations, and their interrelationships. But I hasten to add that the formulations I arrive at are weakest in this area, and much more work is required.[2] Furthermore, although a number of the studies presented here deal with elements of the penetration of capitalism and the increasing domination of capitalist relations of production in the overall context in which these social formation are located, what is achieved is merely an opening glimpse of what needs to be done. It therefore seems in order for me to concentrate here on an elaboration of some of the major theoretical issues which arise from this context, both to place the studies themselves and to relate them to projected efforts to broaden the context of analysis. But first a brief statement on where my research in pastoral social formations began, and how the incipient theoretical and practical journeys took root.

II

During my attempts to grapple with the problems of the social and economic organization of the Wagogo people of central Tanzania (Rigby 1969a, 1967b, 1967c, 1968a, 1968b, 1977a, and *passim*), I felt a deep yet only partially articulated dissatisfaction with the theoretical models available at the time in anthropology and sociology. This led me from the beginning to examine in considerable detail the problematic now generally known as "structuralism", the anthropological founding father of which is, of course, Claude Lévi-Strauss. Although Schneider (1971: 111) categorizes my earlier book on the Wagogo (1969a) as being "plainly in the structural functional tradition" while noting that "in general Rigby is more economically sophisticated than the tradition from which he derives (Radcliffe-Brown, Fortes, *et al*.)", Kuper (1973: 22) is probably more accurate in placing it as an attempt to apply the theoretical framework he calls "neo-structuralism" in an African situation. I make this point here for two important reasons.

First, as I indicate at a number of points in the following chapters, the structuralist problematic represented for me at that time an important attempt to deal reflexively with the basic epistemological problems bedevilling functionalist anthropology. Functionalism had of course been under attack from various quarters for a long time: for example, by those anthropologists concerned with "social change", "conflict theory", and so on.[3] But most of these onslaughts were launched from the same empiricist and positivist base as the theoretical position they were trying to dislodge, with little or no impact upon epistemological issues or the problem of the relationship between theory and practice. Structuralism offered at least the appearance if not the reality of epistemological reflexion (cf. McKeon 1981).

Second, continuing efforts to establish a definite if somewhat tenuous *rapprochement* between structuralism and Marxism, particularly in French anthropology, added the possibility of dissolving the ahistoricism of structuralist analysis as well as the chance of an approach to the problems of dialectic and praxis. Perhaps unfortunately, and despite Lévi-Strauss's own attempts to reconcile the structuralist and Marxist problematics (e.g. Lévi-Strauss 1963: 23, 95, 324-45; 1967) and the work of Althusser, Garaudy, Godelier, and others, developments in structuralism itself have virtually destroyed any hopes of a fruitful marriage for the reproduction of a structuralist-Marxist anthropology (see, for example, Diamond, 1974, 1980; Sève 1972; Scholte 1972, 1980; Goodfriend 1978). Thus when I state in Chapter 3 that "a structuralist methodology becomes indispensable" for an understanding of the institutions of *olpul* and *entoroj* in Ilparakuyo society, the comment must be read in the light of a continuing process of theoretical development: i.e., this Introduction and what follows in later chapters.

Throughout the period of my efforts to expand the horizons of structuralist analysis in the direction of history and praxis, I was also deeply concerned with the problems of politico-economic transformation in pastoral societies and the fallacies and contradictions of capitalist "development" in the under-developed world. This concern is clearly related to the issues of praxis in anthropology and the social sciences in general, although I did not at the time refer to them as such (Rigby 1966, 1967a, 1969b, 1971a, 1976a, 1977a). Thus while noting, for example, that "the 'Arusha Declaration' (Nyerere 1968) states clearly and unequivocally that if some development goals are to be achieved in a reasonable time, rural development must be given greater emphasis than urban/industrial development" and that "consistent with this [Tanzanians must] eschew heavy reliance upon capital, from whatever source, and squarely place the future of Tanzania upon the ability of the rural population to produce more" (Rigby 1969b: 49), I lacked the theoretical tools to establish the real rather than the apparent causes of underdevelopment. My initial concern for praxis in the social sciences, however, is another factor that led me inevitably to my present position. I now look in some more detail at the genesis and elements of this position.

III

There is no doubt in my mind that my membership in a "Third World" African country and my determination to teach anthropology (or sociology: there is no disciplinary distinction in most African universities) where I had done most of my research have both been major factors in my arriving at my present theoretical stance, quite apart from a commitment to the discipline and expanding familiarity with critical political economy and historical materialism. As I have already acknowledged, many students and colleagues, not only at the University of Dar es Salaam, but also at the other universities in which I have worked in East Africa, Britain, Canada, and the United States, have also been fundamentally instrumental in making me aware of critical issues of theory and methodology and their interdependence with praxis.

But above all, my relatively unusual intellectual and emotional absorption into Ilparakuyo society has been the dominant influence in the process of my theoretical and practical enlightenment. It is for this reason that I have included the rather rambling and sometimes anecdotal essay in Chapter 2, which represents the beginnings of this journey. In later chapters, I reflect upon subsequent episodes of this journey which, of course, has no intellectual terminal other than my ultimate disappearance from the Ilparakuyo scene! With the advantages of hindsight, a number of critical issues and criticisms arise, and may be appropriately considered here.

Soon after I had become associated with an Ilparakuyo community through my adoption into one particular family and homestead, two events occurred which were crucial to what follows. First, although I was teaching full-time at the University of Dar es Salaam, I decided that I should get involved in the specific and obvious problems of socio-economic transformation which were besetting this and other similar communities. This would entail more systematic "research" than I had originally envisaged in my association with, and absorption into, the affairs of my Ilparakuyo family and its ties with other domestic groups, both locally and in the far-flung diaspora of the Ilparakuyo section as a whole. Second, the Tanzanian Ministry of National Culture and Youth, in collaboration with the Academy of Finland, began in 1975 to organize a "participatory research" project in the same area, part of the West Bagamoyo District of the Coast Region in Tanzania, a project that included the pastoralists in the community to which I was already attached (cf. Swantz 1977, 1981, and *passim*; Anacleti 1981; etc.). When this project, which was to become the Jipemoyo Project,[4] finally got under way in the middle of 1976, I was asked to become an informal academic adviser to its operations in the area, particularly in relation to Ilparakuyo, and an unofficial liaison with the Department of Sociology at the University of Dar es Salaam.

The intractable problems of elaborating a "participatory research" design have been extensively discussed elsewhere (cf. Swantz 1977; Anacleti 1980; Paakkanen 1981) and, inevitably, the problematic in its bourgeois form comes to grief in its *reductio ad absurdum* (e.g. Moser 1981). Only one element of the debate need concern us here. From the outset, one Tanzanian member of the Jipemoyo team, Mr Kemal Mustafa, consistently and correctly adopted the view that, since Tanzania's goals were socialist and not capitalist development, the theoretical foundations of the project should be squarely based upon the historical materialist problematic.

I had previously been associated with Mr Mustafa while he was a graduate student at the University of Dar es Salaam, and our ongoing co-operation in the Jipemoyo project enabled us to sustain a theoretical dialogue that proved, certainly from my point of view, invaluable. It may be said without too much distortion that our original positions upon theoretical issues can be described as representing attempts to approach a very similar position from different directions. Thus I, while journeying from the subjective idealism of bourgeois phenomenology through Schutz, Habermas and others and its Weberian ancestry towards a more critical position, could note in 1977 that:

> A Marxist phenomenology would contain the two procedural elements: 1) interpretation and translation of the 'real world' of everyday life through the intersubjective situation in which the social scientist is involved, which illuminates the common and elemental link between knowledge and interest, and 2) the translation in turn of the knowledge produced into action by theoretical reflexivity

and conclude that "knowledge obtained through processes of mere observation or data collected upon the unsound assumption of ontological objectivity is ultimately alienated knowledge" (see Chapter 2, p.46). Mustafa, on the other hand, sounded at the same time a more Althusserian note (1977: 47):

> one of my aims . . . is to contribute towards the development of [a] general theory of society by concentrating in particular on the development of a materialist phenomenology. The historical materialist analysis of ideology and consciousness provides the basis for the integration of bourgeois phenomenology into a materialist problematic. However, the end is not to develop a materialist phenomenology *per se*, but rather . . . to enrich the systematic totality of the historical materialistic anaylsis as a whole by developing its theoretical scope.

From these beginnings, then, during which I had already begun to search in Marx's writings, particularly the *Grundrisse*, for the elements of a historical materialist interpretation of the Ilparakuyo social formation in which I was already involved, a theoretical problematic increasingly critical of structuralist concerns began to emerge. I then began the necessary task of establishing a critical notion of mode of production, social formation, and their transformations: the elements, in other words, of a comparative political economy grounded in historical materialism. In this task, the seminal work of the French Marxist anthropologists, "structuralist" and non-structuralist, particularly the influence of Meillassoux, Godelier, Terray and their associates, as well as subsequent developments in the work of

Bonte, P-P. Rey, Bourgeot, and others, played a dominant role. As a result, the theoretical power of certain basic elements in Althusser and Balibar's interpretations of the historical materialist problematic is unavoidable, and is frequently evident in what follows (cf. Kahn and Llobera 1981: 274-7, and *passim*).

IV

The comparative development of the concepts "mode of production" and "social formation" in recent Marxist anthropology has followed several parallel but not mutually exclusive paths. To this already complicated state of affairs has been added the further and totally spurious problem of the "contradiction" or "opposition" between "modes of production theory" and "world system theory", as if they were entirely different problematics. While the origin of this "problem" is understandable, given the disparate roots of the concepts themselves, its effects are more confusing than illuminating.

The nature of this continuing debate has been admirably traced in a number of recent publications (e.g. Bloch 1975; Hindess and Hirst 1975, 1977; Godelier 1977; Amin 1976, 1980; Seddon 1978; Clammer 1978; Wolpe 1980; Kahn and Llobera 1981) and in the pages of several journals, both in English and in French. From this complex of material I must extract only those threads which are of immediate concern in this study.

The "modes of production controversy" (Foster-Carter 1978a) is, therefore, historically derived from a number of different sources. The publication of an English version of the *Formen* in 1964, edited and introduced by Eric Hobsbawm (Marx 1964), and the later appearance of a full English translation of Marx's *Grundrisse* (1973), constituted a major inspiration for the debate, leading to one particular strand in the conceptualization of distinct modes of production. Another critical element, as I have already noted, was Althusser and Balibar's "reading" of *Capital I* (1968, English trans. 1970). Then again, the already mentioned claim of the Lévi-Straussian structuralists to a place in the Marxist tradition was a further factor in attempts to "reintegrate" the body of anthropological knowledge into the theories of historical materialism (Lévi-Strauss 1963; McKeon 1981), or vice versa.

At any rate, in the field of pastoral studies, Pierre Bonte's seminal work on the use of models derived from the *Formen*, particularly the concept of the "Germanic" mode of production, was perhaps the most significant (e.g. Bonte 1974, 1977, 1981, and *passim*). The impact of these studies upon what follows is amply evident, although my analysis does differ from his in a number of ways. But several questions arise from this approach, and a brief discussion of them may throw some light on issues raised in subsequent chapters.

The basic issue around which all these questions revolve is this: does

15

the application of the concept of the Germanic (or other) mode of production to East African pastoral social formations really illuminate and lead to explanation not only of their *form*, but also their actual and potential *transformation*? We can deal with the achievements of this basic theoretical procedure, which leads on naturally to a consideration of the articulation of modes of production, only after its major weaknesses have been mentioned.

The core concept in the utility of the Germanic mode of production is its categorization of the *domestic* and *community* levels of the relations of production and their *articulation*, and it is here that both its strength and weakness lie. For on the one hand, in his historical formulation Marx erroneously introduces the notion of "individual property" which is not applicable, as is amply demonstrated in this book, to these East African formations; yet on the other hand, he sees clearly the *real* nature of the community relations of production, which Bonte calls the "communal form of production" (1977: 176), and hence the *conditions* for the reproduction of the social formation, as being embedded essentially in *ideological* institutions such as those of kinship, age-set organization, and ritual (Marx 1973: 845-6; see Chapters 3 and 6 below).[5]

What Marx does not provide us with in the *Grundrisse*, however, is a sound historical materialist base upon which to construct a *theory* of these ideological institutions; for this, we have to turn to Marx's later work in all *three* volumes of *Capital*, as well as to Althusser and Balibar's reading of Volume I. It is because Bonte does not do this systematically that some weaknesses arise in his theorization of the relations of production in East African pastoral social formations, although he does attempt to use the concept of "fetishism" from *Capital I* (Bonte 1977: 180-2; cf. 1975 and 1981). And although Bonte does provide us with a powerful model of transformation in these societies (1977, 1981), amongst whom the *commoditization* of livestock does give rise to the fetishization of cattle concomitant with incipient class formation (cf. Marx 1973: 513), his analysis lacks a sense of the historicity which is an integral part of the ability of these formations to reproduce themselves. I address some of these issues again, both later in this Introduction and in Chapters 4 and 5.

But these are minor difficulties when compared with the enormous advances in our understanding of "non-stratified" East African pastoral social formations and their transformation achieved through the use of the Germanic mode of production concept and the entailed notion of the articulation of this with other, most specifically the capitalist, modes of production (cf. Wolpe 1980; Foster-Carter 1978a, 1978b). The first element in this basic achievement has been to free the anthropology of East African pre-capitalist social formations from the burden of bourgeois categories and concepts, such as "property", "ownership", "capital", "profit", the "buying", and "selling" of livestock and women, and numerous other clichés such as the "cattle complex" and "patriarchy". These issues are dealt with in various contexts in the following chapters; but it is important to note that in raising them, I am not flogging a dead horse. A great deal of contemporary writing in economic anthropology is still either consciously involved in the non-debates between the "substantivists" and the "formalists" (e.g. LeClair and Schneider 1968), firmly committed to one side or the other, at least by intent if not in practice (e.g. Schneider 1970, 1979; cf. Godelier 1972, 1977: 17-22; Clammer 1978: 4-6), or unconsciously the victim of dominant bourgeois categories of thought by the unwitting application of such categories to pre-capitalist social formations (e.g. Llewelyn-Davies 1978, forthcoming).[6] This is particularly true of analyses of pastoral societies.

To return to the illumination derived from the use of the historical materialist concept of the Germanic mode of production in the study of these societies, it will become apparent from what follows that not only does this procedure enable us to *explain* such apparent anomalies as the so-called "cattle complex" and the "conservatism" of Ilparakuyo and Maasai (Chapters 3 and 6; cf. Bonte 1981: 32-42), it also allows us to *differentiate*, in terms of the articulation of the relations and forces of production, between pastoral, agro-pastoral, hunting and gathering, and agricultural communities in their pre-capitalist forms and their *reactions* to capitalist penetration and its accompanying ideological trappings such as Christianity (or Islam), the bourgeois justification of wage employment even to the point of forced labour, and the commoditization of the relations of production (Chapters 5 and 7; cf. Bonte 1981: 24-5). The analysis of these processes for Ilparakuyo Maasai is far from deep in this book; indeed, it represents only a beginning and will be taken up in future publications. But a further discussion of some of the specific theoretical issues involved in them is not out of place here.

V

As I have already noted, the power of the mode of production concept enables us to understand and theorize the nature of the domestic and communal levels of the relations of production and their articulation in each specific instance. It also allows us to differentiate between different manifestations of the same mode of production (i.e., the Germanic) on the *basis* of the differences of the forces and major means of production, *without* capitulation to a final determinism by the development of productive forces or any other techno-ecological determinism. The position I have consistently tried to adopt in the following essays is succinctly summarized by Bonte:

> On the one hand, the mode of production, as a specific concept of a form of social and economic organization, defines a law of development of the productive forces, not only in relation to the variations in the level of labour productivity, but in the very *nature* of the productive forces, in this case in the degree of specialization in herding [emphasis added]. On the other hand, it

17

contains the sum of variations of relations of production compatible with the reproduction of the structure of these relations of production – a complex structure, itself dominated by the form in which the surplus is realized – not merely an historical development of this structure, but an actual structural feature of the mode of production. This means that the concept of mode of production rests upon a specific articulation of productive forces and relations of production which constitutes the economic determination. (The latter cannot be reduced to determination in the last instance by either the productive forces or the relations of production.) (1981: 43)

By relating the differences in the very "nature" of the productive forces to variations in the labour process and the concept of labour (Bonte 1981: 23-5) and hence the specific social formations in which the Germanic mode of production may be manifested (pastoral, agro-pastoral, agricultural), we may simultaneously distinguish between the forms in which the community level of the relations of production will appear (descent and kin-group, age-set organization, the state), as well as the ways in which transformation of the society will occur, though autonomous developments coupled with articulation with other modes of production. But although I am entirely in agreement with Bonte that, in East African "non-stratified" pastoral formations with which we are concerned, the community levels of the relations of production and hence reproduction are inseparable from the ideological domain (*pace* Marx in the *Formen*, above), I cannot accept his conclusion that "Among Nilotic pastoralists, the real existence of the community or community 'in-itself' is religious in nature . . . " (Bonte 1981: 34).

This difference of opinion arises out of two basic issues: first, as I state in a number of places in the body of this book, I do not believe that the concept of "cattle fetishism" is useful in the analysis of these formations, *until* commoditization of livestock takes place. Second, and following on from this, my interpretation of the Ilparakuyo and Maasai material indicates that religious ideas and ritual practices are subsumed by the age-set and kinship organizations, not the other way around. The latter, although ideological in nature, function as relations of production and are inseparable from pastoral praxis, again with the exception only of the role of the great prophets (*iloibonok kituaak*), a role *already* transformed during the 19th Century as a result of colonial and capitalist penetration (Chapter 5). I do not deny that "the particular characteristics of capitalist alienation of labour have obscured the fact that there are other forms of the alienation of labour common to pre-capitalist societies" (Bonte 1981: 38), but the nature of this latter alienation does not lie in the fetishism of cattle among Ilparakuyo and Maasai (cf. Godelier 1977: 49-51). It seems that the spectre of the "cattle complex" is still evident in this kind of interpretation, which lacks historicity and hence comparative value.

I suggest therefore that Bonte confuses the dominance of the ideological aspect of the mode of production in these pastoral social formations with the dominance of religion (1981: 31), which is an institutional concept and hence out of place in a rigorous notion of mode of production. As a result of this conflation, there are a number of anomalies in Bonte's analysis. While giving an excellent account of how age-set structures may be transformed (Bonte 1974, 1978, 1981: 44-5), he fails to relate the ideology of age-set organization as an integral aspect of the community relations of production and hence of pastoral praxis and its reproduction to the whole complex of religious and symbolic practices revolving around these structures, isolating instead the role of the great prophets from the age-set organization and concluding erroneously that

> the dominance of *religious* structures in Nilotic societies can be explained by the fact that these structures not only define the communal form of production, but also, and above all, the social form of surplus production. (Bonte 1981: 45, emphasis added)

Hence his discussion of the rise of the great Maasai prophet (*oloiboni kitok*) Mbatyany during the 19th Century also lacks historical context, as does his otherwise superb comparison of the egalitarian Nilotic pastoral formations with the hierarchical, patriarchal system of the Bahima pastoralists of the Ankole state and its implications for class formation, the position of women, and the state (1981: 47-50).

Bonte's overall conclusion (1981: 41) that "the contradiction between the unequal accumulation of livestock among the autonomous domestic groups and the equal access of these groups to collective resources [determines] the laws of transformation of the productive system" in these East African pastoral formations is startlingly correct, and I return to these issues later (Chapters 5-7). But to give his overly "structuralist" model of transformation a dynamic historicity, we must go beyond the somewhat static theorization of a specific mode of production to the problem of the articulation of modes of production with peripheral capitalism and the world system.

VI

Representing within the historical materialist problematic a pendulum swing away from the structuralist tendencies of Bonte's analysis is Hedlund's important study of "peripheralization" among the Ilkaputiei section of Kenya Maasai (1979). I use the idea of a "pendulum swing" judiciously, for although Hedlund and Bonte appear to be unaware of each other's work, by failing to develop as rigorous a notion as Bonte's of the dominant pre-capitalist mode of production represented by the Maasai social formation, Hedlund's analysis of its articulation with peripheral capitalism is weakened, and he too, for reasons other than those outlined above, lapses into another form of ahistorical generalization. But his study represents a considerable achievement, not only because it addresses the crucial problem of what he terms the "basic contradiction" in the Maasai pastoral formation, and we must examine it a little further.

Where Hedlund is dealing with the specific aspects of the transformation of the Ilkaputiei of Massai into a "periphery" (1971, 1979: 28-34), his historical analysis is impeccable. It is a superb demonstration of the continuity between colonial exploitation on the one hand, and the encouragement of commodity production, class formation, and ultimate impoverishment of a "marginal" pastoralist social formation by an independent government committed to capitalist "development" goals on the other, aided and abetted by such institutions as the International Development Association of the World Bank, the United States Agency for International Development, The Swedish International Development Agency, and West German agencies. The short-term interests of both local (national) and international capital in this most peripheral of peripheries are admirably served by the encouragement of so-called "group ranches" associated with individual land tenure, the latter *demanded* by the international agencies promoting these developments through agricultural credit programmes. The fate of increasing impoverishment for large numbers of Maasai pastoralists and the fact that "the tendency towards concentration of wealth is an inbuilt part of the logic of the development of group ranches" (Hedlund 1979: 33) is irrelevant to the interests of capital at whatever level, except insofar as these processes serve their exploitative interests.

Hedlund correctly rests his analysis upon a notion of the articulation of modes of production. For example, he notes (1979: 32) that "the comparative affluence" that individual members of the group ranches were able to attain in a relatively short period "was mainly the result of their ability to draw resources from two asymmetrically linked modes of production", i.e. those embedded in the peripheral capitalist formation of the nation-state on the one hand, and still a part of the pre-capitalist Maasai formation on the other. He establishes further that the most important result of the process of peripheralization is "the exploitative relationship between . . . the emerging underdeveloped capitalist and the pre-capitalist modes of production co-existing within the periphery" (Hedlund 1976: 16). He also emphasizes admirably such critical details as the fact that during the disastrous 1960-1 East African drought, the more "developed" areas of Kenya Maasailand suffered *more* severely in terms of livestock casualties than the "comparatively underdeveloped areas" (1979: 29), and that the transition from a pre-capitalist mode of production to a "peripheral capitalist mode of production" involves not only a weakening in the ability of the social formation to reproduce itself, but also a deterioration in the forces of production themselves – tools, technical knowledge, the very science of pastoral praxis (1979: 15-16). But above all, Hedlund's discussion of the relatively high productivity of pastoral labour as opposed, for example, to subsistence agricultural labour, its variability in bad seasons, and its link to the levelling effect upon the unequal distribution of the means of production in bad or drought seasons (1979: 18-19) is a major contribution to the study of

Maasai and other pastoral social formations and their transition.

It is, however, precisely because Hedlund does not sufficiently theorize the pre-capitalist mode of production as manifested in these East African pastoral societies that the patterns and correlation upon which he bases his initial model arc inconsistent and, ultimately, cyclical and hence ahistorical. At one moment he correctly categorizes the "hump backed Zebu" and all livestock as "the most important means of production", as well as the "most prestigious" (1979: 17); at the next he is talking about "livestock that are unnecessary as producers or means of subsistence" as a "form of surplus, mainly used for social activities" and constituting a "specific form of ceremonial fund", a reference to Wolf's category of surplus in peasant societies (Hedlund 1979: 19; cf. Wolf 1966: 7-9). While this may be true, how can the major means of production constitute a "surplus" or a "fund"?

Then again, the core of his model of the pre-capitalist Maasai social formation and its dominant mode of production is based upon a process of "continuous hierarchization", the development of "patron–client" relationships, and hence a "stratification process" frustrated only by some "social and ecological factors" (1979: 20-1). While this model is probably true of Ilkaputiei Maasai in the middle of the 20th Century, the correlations upon which it is based, such as the contention that "through intermarriage, women and cattle tend to circulate between households of similar economic status" and that where such transactions occur between rich and poor households their importance in "reducing basic economic differences is limited as the amount of livestock involved in this kind of marriage transaction is limited compared to the number transferred between wealthy families", are clearly the *consequence* of long years of colonial domination, land alienation, and the penetration of commodity relations; they do not emanate from the pre-capitalist mode of production itself. While Hedlund is obviously dealing with the impact of these very factors from the late 19th Century on, and probably much earlier (cf. 1979: 23, 28), he fails to relate them to his model of the "pre-capitalist system" which, as a result, appears formalistic and lacking in itself any historical dynamic which is not cyclical and hence "structuralist" in a particular way.

IMPORTANT

The sloppy theorization of the pre-capitalist mode of production of the Maasai social formation thus leads Hedlund into a number of anomalies ironically similar to those already pointed out in Bonte's more formally structuralist analysis. The role of the ideological in the reproduction of the Maasai social formation is recognized (1979: 21-2), but it is again restricted to religious forms. Hedlund does not seem to realize that when he correctly identifies the functioning of age-set relations as the basis for the community relations of production (pp. 22-6), he is talking about ideological relations as well, since age-set organization just as much as kinship organization emanates from the dominant ideological domain, a dominance determined by the very nature of the Germanic mode of production manifested in the pre-capitalist Maasai social formation itself.

If Hedlund had realized this, he would have avoided such ostensibly accurate but ultimately anomalous statements as the following:

> Relations of production as well as the political and ideological superstructure are to a large extent *embedded in* the age-class system, a rigid hierarchy of male age-classes, each with a strictly defined socio-political status. (1979: 22, emphasis added)

Here the age-set system seems again to take on an ontological status of its own, different from the relations of production and the political and ideological superstructure which are "embedded in it", and thus assumes a primordiality and *sui generis* form usually ascribed by anthropologists to kinship systems. He would also have avoided such obvious errors as the attribution without evidence of ulterior motives to junior elders when he has clearly demonstrated the economic "rationality" of their decisions;[7] and he would have certainly refrained from inventing the notion that "social control of senior warriors by means of force, traditionally the most important control mechanism, was established within the structure of the age–class system through a complex of alliances, *ol-piron*", when he is clearly discussing *ritual* control, since the senior warriors also have their *olpiron* elders, the senior elders (see Chapters 3 and 6), by no means a weak force in Maasai society.

But the point is made: through the over-formalization of the pre-capitalist mode of production, the transformations generated by Bonte's otherwise excellent model become structural transformations and lack a sufficient measure of historicity; by an under-formalization of the same mode of production, Hedlund's historical study lacks critical depth because the contradictions of the present are projected back onto the past, the pre-capitalist formation, resulting in a similar loss of historicity for very different reasons. Neither criticism denies the outstanding and seminal contributions of both studies to our understanding of East African pastoral formations and their history, and the issues raised by them must form the basis of future studies in this area and, by implication, other pastoral formations as well.

VII

I have spent some time on a discussion of the major theoretical contributions of Bonte and Hedlund as representing admirably the current state of advanced theory in the field of pastoral studies. Together with the earlier parts of this Introduction, they provide a context for a reading of the material in the body of this book, particularly the later chapters (4–7). It remains for me to add that the task of categorizing the nature of the mode or modes of production manifested in the pre-capitalist Ilparakuyo and Maasai social formations is by no means complete. But it is an essential task if we are to understand the historical processes characteristic of these social formations, both before and after the penetration of colonial domination and peripheral capitalism seen as a process of increasing articulation with the antagonistic elements of the ongoing expansion of capitalist primitive accumulation on a global scale. For the theoretical problematic of historical materialism which can encompass this task, we must turn to a fuller utilization of Marx's insights in the final sections of *Capital*, Volume I, and the relevant sections of Volumes II and III, as well as the work of Wolpe, Rey, Meillassoux, and numerous others, some of whom have been referred to in this Introduction.

This is a task which takes us beyond the scope of this book. What is offered here is a preliminary exercise in mapping out the potentially revolutionary intellectual and emotional journeys which must be undertaken if we are to develop a true integration between theory and practice in anthropology, and in relation to such social formations as those of Ilparakuyo, Maasai, and other East African pastoralists. We, together with all the peoples of the "Third World", must be engaged in a struggle for survival against the specific forms of domination and exploitation which began with the rise of capitalism to its present global scale from the 16th Century until the present. The studies presented in this book are offered as a small contribution to anthropology and to that struggle.

Notes

1. The "internal" diversity of reliance upon pastoral and agricultural produce is also documented for several social formations classified as "pastoral": for example, the Jie and Karimojong of north-eastern Uganda (Gulliver, 1955; Dyson-Hudson 1966, and *passim*) which are more correctly classified as "agro-pastoral".
2. Despite the propensity of anthropologists to present functionally "coherent" studies of isolated "tribes" or "ethnic groups", those scholars who have taken account of historical factors have, on the whole, managed to avoid the deepest pitfalls of the approach: for example, Southall 1953; Leach 1954; Smith 1960; and more recently, Thornton 1980.
3. A good example of a relatively "organized" attack upon functionalism was the so-called "Manchester School", led by Max Gluckman; but because it lacked a rigorous alternative problematic, the debates raised by it were ultimately futile from an epistemological point of view (cf. van Teeffelen, 1978).
4. The range of meanings covered by Kiswahili "*jipemoyo*" are difficult to define simply in English, largely because *moyo* means so many different things in different contexts. The project name embodies the subjunctive form of *jipa moyo!* which basically denotes the exhortation, "take heart", "pluck up courage!", or, more literally, "give yourself heart!".
5. It should be noted that this formulation of the Germanic mode of production is reminiscent of the concept of "domestic groups", their development cycle, and

their articulation with the wider community (e.g., Goody 1958, 1976; Fortes 1958; Sahlins 1972; cf. Gulliver 1955; Rigby 1969a). However, "reminiscent" is the operative word here, for the Marxist problematic imbues the analysis with distinctive qualities lacking in these other formulations, however much the latter were influenced, as indeed they were, by unacknowledged historical materialist formulations.

6. It should be noted that Llewelyn-Davies' use of the *philosophical* and legal notions characteristic of bourgeois capitalist society differs from the attempt by the "formalists" in economic anthropology consciously to use the concepts of bourgeois political economy in the explication of pre-capitalist social formations, such as in the work of Schneider (1970, 1979, and *passim*; cf. Goldschmidt 1981).

7. Hedlund claims that

> changes of traditional status positions are generally opposed by the junior elders and they have *consequently rejected* formal education in the use of modern technology [sic] as these might threaten their political and economic dominance. (1979: 25, my emphasis)

If this is the case of Ilkaputiei, they must be somewhat of an anomaly, for although they reject *formal* education, Ilparakuyo and other Tanzanian Maasai sections gladly accept and use most extensively and skilfully "modern technology" in the form of veterinary medicines and services to ensure the health and increase of their herds (see Chapter 6).

2. Critical Participation, Mere Observation, or Alienation?

"*Menang'aroi oltung'ani te njata nagol.*"
"A man cannot be thrown by a stout stick" – people cannot be "objectified" like things.

I have been doing what is conventionally known as "fieldwork" among Ilparakuyo of West Bagamoyo District for just over one year; the number of days I have actually spent "in the field", however, add up to just over two months. Owing to the exigencies of my other duties, the longest single period I spent in the area in which Ilparakuyo live was two weeks, this being almost immediately followed by a further week. All the rest of the trips I managed to make to the area have averaged two or three days each.[1]

I make this initial statement for more than merely introductory purposes. The first reason for being so explicit is wholly negative: it could be considered unfortunate, to say the least (and it certainly does to me if not to you), for someone to have the temerity to present a paper under the title I have chosen or, for that matter, under any other title relating to the Ilparakuyo.

There are, however, some positive reasons for which I am bold enough to pursue my chosen topic, and I feel I must enumerate at least some of them before I proceed. Superficially, some of these reasons may appear merely incidental, others more soundly "theoretical"; I attempt, among other things, to demonstrate that any such absolute distinctions are not valid. But first I must outline some of these "positive" elements in my all too brief fieldwork.

Perhaps the most important is that I am, and have been for some time, a relatively full (if largely absentee) son and member of an Ilparakuyo homestead (*enkang'*). Furthermore, my younger Olparakuoni brother (*olalahe lai*) is a full (and more frequently present) member of my homestead in Dar es Salaam, which is also the periodic venue for gatherings of Ilparakuyo *ilmurran* (young men) and junior elders (*ilpayiani*) who may happen to be visiting Dar es Salaam for a day or two from the home area. This fortunate eventuality lessens the participatory gap caused by my work-enforced exile from my Ilparakuyo environment.

My descent and affinal status in this particular *enkang'* has its roots in much earlier circumstances, in the days when I was of the *ilmurran* age-grade, and which need not detain us here. But it could be said with some accuracy that I am among those researchers who chose their specific area of research upon the grounds of an adoptive affinity and kinship rather than for strictly "scientific" reasons; for personal interest rather than exclusively in the pursuit of knowledge. Although, of course, my predominant sociological interests in the development of pastoral societies also led me there. This point may seem inconsequential at the moment; I trust its full significance will appear later.

Another preliminary point must be made: throughout my period with Ilparakuyo, and most particularly when I have been at Kwamsanga, I have not asked a single "formal" question, except those relating to language or the identification and use of basic cultural objects. The questions I have asked have all arisen entirely out of the social context in which I happened to be at that moment; although I have, on occasion, attempted to tilt the discussion in one direction or another.

This statement may, indeed probably will, horrify some research workers; they would probably ask me what I had been doing with all my valuable time, particularly during my all too brief visits to the village, if not following at least a formal question guide. To this I would reply that the most formally structured periods of my time have been spent in learning, or rather being taught, *enkutuk oo'lMaasai* or *Olmaa*, the language of Ilparakuyo. This extension of their everyday experience is quite legitimate in any context, since this is the first thing Ilparakuyo expect me to do, given my intentions – of which they are aware. So, tedious as it may be for them, they stretch their patience for me. "But", my interlocutor might respond, "you are not a linguist but a sociologist." Goaded by this, I would have to say, let me give you some examples of what I *have* been doing with my time with Ilparakuyo.

I have walked through the bush in the middle of the night with a group of *ilmurran*, after an *olpul* meat feast where the warriors had danced and sung of their exploits and their cattle, listening to songs that could never be sung in or even near any Ilparakuyo homestead. I have helped hold an *olmurrani* at the climax of his shaking trance (*agor* or *apush*) lest he hurt himself, only to see him calm himself soon after. I have sat for many hours with elders (*ilpayiani*) drinking gallons (literally) of beer, listening to them discuss almost everything: sex, morality, politics, religion, the weather, the qualities and quantities of beer, marriage, death, birth, and each other's iniquities, usually joking. We have explored in these discussions the characters of the *iloibonok* religious leaders and lesser diviners, the behaviour of the current generation of the *ilmurran* and the (quite acceptable) "extramural" infidelities of the elders' various wives, and so on. But above all, cattle, usually a topic of joyful if serious exchange, which have recently brought great sorrow and sadness.

After beer, perhaps carrying five or ten litres of it home for the journey and the morrow, six or seven of us senior warriors and elders, taking a shortcut in the dark, have sometimes got lost in seemingly limitless fields of Kwere maize, where every stalk seemed 15 feet high in the almost inpenetrable darkness; but we always found our way home eventually.

My brother and I have walked 16 miles or so in blazing sun in search of our father's homestead, which had been abruptly and forcibly shifted several miles from its original site while we were away in Dar es Salaam. During this burning journey, we were sometimes refused drinking water at some Kwere homesteads, even when there was obviously some available.

We have slithered down the impossibly slippery slopes of streams and river banks, both individually and collectively, sometimes in the company of a motorcycle: we *had* to get to the Ilparakuyo homestead on the other side or sleep in the bush in the rain. We have followed stray cattle through the forest at 5 a.m., only to find our elder brother, who had come from the other cattle camp, also on their trail; he had been so the whole of the previous afternoon and night without food or water.

We have frequently arisen at dawn to drag the carcases of one, two, or even three dead animals from the cattle byre where they had fallen during the night. We have slept with the sound of ox-bells and the stamping and urinating of cattle a few feet from our cars, sometimes to be awoken in the middle of the night by *ilmurran* who, quite rightly, maintained it was too cold to sleep, and who suggested that we should roast some maize. During ensuing nocturnal conversations I have heard perhaps about a meeting (*enkiguena*) of *ilmurran* which had taken place that day while I was talking and drinking with the elders, and about which I would have heard absolutely nothing in any other circumstances; or I merely have been amused by the story of the latest clandestine amatory exploits of friends and acquaintances. Once we were awoken at midnight when our father was away and only the women, brothers, other *ilmurran* and myself were present, to discover that someone had attempted to sleep with one of our sisters or wives without "showing himself", only to be ignominiously routed by the homestead dogs and to be heard crashing away at high speed in the dark undergrowth – pursued, not by the dogs, but by a good deal of half angry and half humorous invective.

I have also seen the joy of an old man with his sons and discovered, without any probing questions, how many others had died and who now would perhaps have been older than his eldest. I have felt the warmth of friendship and affection from two brothers, *ilmurran*, one of the senior the other of the junior sub-grades, who took me many miles away from our place to stay in their homestead, and have seen their sorrow and felt their pain when they told me how their father had lost more than 300 head of their herd of over 1,100 cattle during a short period of a few months. The senior *olmurrani* nevertheless told me of his plans to marry a second wife, the daughter of a homestead next to ours, and how many cattle had been given in bridewealth and how many remained to be exchanged, including "fines" dating from misdemeanours committed by relatives of his father's generation.[2] We met again a few days later when he was driving the second herd to his in-laws' homestead some 13 miles from his own; and the story of the marriage transaction was completed when he visited me in Das es Salaam some weeks later.

I have learned above all the richness of human beings as individuals who happen to be Ilparakuyo, and thereby face particular problems, have particular experiences, and thus have particular qualities that give them a dynamism and energy seldom matched in any culture in the world. I have become intellectually and emotionally bound up with their lives so inextricably that physical separation cannot destroy these ties. All this and, of course, a great deal more, I have carefully written down, intepreted from our intersubjective experiences in their multifarious contexts; but this is not the collection of random, subjective experiences. I have "discovered" something of the structure and identity of this community, and I give brief outline analyses of these structural aspects of Ilparakuyo society later. But in order to serve as a transition from what I have already said, which may be thought by some to be unduly anecdotal, I must provide a tentative theoretical and methodological justification for my activities.

II

Grounded firmly in my working and living with Ilparakuyo, I have been groping towards understanding through what might be called a Marxist phenomenology. Some will undoubtedly label what I have to say as "bourgeois eclecticism", radical or otherwise (cf. Harvey 1974: 104). As I have said elsewhere, eclecticism is a derogatory epithet only to someone who professes adherence to a "pure" religion, and this I certainly do not.

Labelling aside, phenomenological sociology, or rather the phenomenological method in sociology, was born of an attempt to reconcile a dualism, just as phenomenology arose in the philosophy of Husserl to re-establish "the *specifically practical significance* of the sciences ... through the revival of pure theory" in the classical sense (Habermas 1970: 40, emphasis added). In the phenomenological sociology, or perhaps one should say psychology of Vierkandt (1949: 241-4), for example, there is an attempt to "synthesize individualism and universalism", or combine "the collective consciousness of Durkheim ... with Simmel's formalism" (Aron 1957: 19-20): that is, to resolve the dualism in Tönnies' theory of *gemeinschaft* and *gesellschaft* in social forms.

Interestingly, there appears a recognition of an "intuitive element" in the understanding of social phenomena in these earlier examples of phenomenological sociology, for Aron notes (1957: 25) that one of the chief ways in which phenomenology such as Vierkandt's was used in practice was "To abstract the pure types (of social forms) by intuition, without having recourse to generalization from individual instances. It is in this way that community, the very essence of social life, is defined." It is, of course, also one of its main weaknesses; but more of that later.

The fundamental problem with which modern phenomenological methodology tries to deal is the dualism implicit between theoretical propositions about an "objective world" on the one hand, and the basic everyday "reality" of an intersubjective world on the other. The classical distinction between Being and Time, or the Cartesian dualism of Mind and Matter, have not yet been entirely escaped in the epistemology of the natural sciences, largely because until very recently, they have successfully been able to ignore epistemological problems entirely and have been content with a more or less naive positivism. This is because the "specious objectivity" which science has bestowed upon itself is not grounded in a scientific epistemology at all, but is still largely entrapped by the ontological assumptions of classical theories (Habermas 1966: *passim*). The natural sciences, whatever they claim, still retain their philosophical distinction between ontology and epistemology, the former postulating the problem of "how things are"; the latter being concerned with the issues of how we know anything, or more specifically, how we know what sort of world it is we live in and what sort of creatures are we that we can know something (or perhaps nothing) of this matter" (Bateson 1973: 284).

Perhaps the crucial point is that for the natural sciences it does not matter if they retain the "kind of ontology (uncritically derived) from the traditional concept of theory", and the positivism and empiricism which result from this adherence; for the social sciences any such naive ontological assumptions spell disaster. In fact, Habermas goes so far as to argue with, I think, considerable justification, that the methodological ignorance of the natural sciences protects them and enables them to

> earn the respect that is theirs by applying their methods imperturbably and
> without thought for their guiding interests . . . . This awareness of theirs has a
> safeguarding function, for at the self-reflective level the sciences lack the
> means of protection against the risks of a too clear view of the connection bet-
> ween knowledge and interests. (Habermas 1966).

Admittedly, the work of the great scientific philosophers who come from the "old" scientific tradition, and recent advances in the epistemology of the natural sciences, for example in the application of structuralist theories in mathematics, physics, biochemistry, etc., begin to dispel this "methodological ignorance" and epistemological naivety (e.g. see Piaget 1971; Monod 1970). Indeed, such developments seem to bear out the increasing convergence in methodology between the natural and social sciences, *not* because the social sciences are becoming "more scientific" in the sense of 19th Century scientistic rationality, but because science as a whole is escaping its ontological foundations (Schutz 1964).

In the social world, therefore, there is no ontological objectivity whatsoever; to posit it is a postivistic illusion. The social scientists' efforts to increase the scientific validity and respectability of their theories by recourse to the application of methods that have been so "successful" (in a predictive and manipulative sense) in the natural sciences, must therefore be seen not as an attempt to incorporate a scientific epistemology, but to impose an out-moded dualism between ontology and epistemology derived from classical and later positivist ideas of objective theory as embedded in a highly "limited scientistic consciousness of science" (Habermas 1970a: 53). The tragedy is that, both bourgeois sociology and many forms of the "Marxist problematic" approach, especially when they are concerned with the gathering of data, take precisely this positivist view of "scientific objectivity", thus destroying at the crucial point the relationship between knowledge and interest, or theory and practice. Thus some Marxists even praise bourgeois sociology for the very fact that it "has perfected methods of data collection which provide objective, reliable facts, mostly of a numerical order, upon which to base subsequent analysis". This is a contradiction in terms, for it is now almost universally accepted that social scientists (or any other scientists for that matter) do not, *cannot*, collect "facts" randomly accumulated for later analytical manipulation; the very process of "fact-finding" is guided and informed by theoretical (and hence epistemological) assumptions. Our grounds for rejecting the validity of such "random data collection resulting in basic facts" have already been stated: there are no ontological facts, at least in the social sciences, "out there", waiting to be collected. Every social fact collected by the social scientist (whether he be a temporarily employed census-taker or trained social scientist) is the result, and *only* the result, of an intersubjective experience between two or more individuals, communicating with each other through some common language; unless it be merely a matter of (literally) "counting heads", an operation which hardly provides data of social scientific interest.

Hence, although the Marxist sociologist claims to, and very often does, combine theory and praxis in his analysis and utilization of the data of social research, he more often than not ignores the problem of how those data are obtained and their relation to the intersubjective reality of everyday experience. At this point in the process of the production of knowledge, he is as equally, if not more, naive than his bourgeois counterpart in sociology or economics. He assumes that the social facts are "out there", waiting to be "collected" and delivered into his hands for analysis and interpretation. In so far as they are "competently collected", they can be used; "competence" here relates to the canons laid down by the rules of statistical procedure subsequently to be applied to these data. By this means, the Marxist sociologist assumes the "objective validity" of his facts, just as does the bourgeois sociologist; from there on they may part company in the analysis and interpretation of what they have.

It is my contention here that whatever conclusions our two personified sociologists, Marxist and bourgeois, may reach as a result of their activities (and these are frequently impressive), their results must be affected, if not distorted, by the assumption of objective validity of the data upon which they operate; these data in fact may bear little relation to the intersubjective social reality of the everyday world of which they purport to speak. As a consequence, any theory constructed from them must of necessity be flawed in some way, or still retain implicitly the false dualism between theory and practice which Marxism sets out explicity to demolish. Such a theory would therefore remain "alienated" from the social reality it purports to explain, and practice based upon it would be false. I am *not* saying here that statistical data collected in this fashion are irrelevant to sociological analysis and explanation. On the contrary, I am attempting to clarify the uses to which they may be put by exposing the epistemological and ontological assumptions that underlie their collection.[3] I now proceed to a critique of certain forms of what is often glibly called the "participant observation" method of data collection in the social sciences, of which I have myself hitherto held a relatively uncritical view. The intention again is not to demolish, but to clarify.

III

The very term "participant observation" implies the false ontological objectivity, derived from the natural sciences, which I have been trying so strenuously to dismantle. In the sociological context, it allows the logical possibility of being an "observer" without being a "participant" or a "participant" while not being an "observer"; both postulates are patently absurd. All participants (actors) must be observers in their own right, interpreting and analysing the situation, or else they would be unable to act or "participate"; similarly, all observers (social scientists?) must, if only by their very presence, participate (act?). Unfortunately, some social scientists have either ignored or deliberately denied these fundamental elements in any data collection process, as I shall show.

What presumably is meant by the term "participant observation" as a method of data collection, a much criticized method (e.g. discussion in Easthope 1974) ostensibly used by most social anthropologists and sociologists at one time or another, is that the "observer" writes down or otherwise records what he has gleaned from his participation in a particular social situation in the light of his "critical" scientific training. This being so, the "observer" is not merely "objectively" scrutinizing what is going on around him, but is involved as a "whole person", albeit a person with an interpretive equipment which is different from one not trained in his scientific discipline. Any subsequent interpretation of the data resulting from his participation is therefore "an interpretation of an interpretation", not an analysis of self-evident, ontologically objective "facts". As Schutz phrases it:

> The primary goal of the social sciences is to obtain organized knowledge of social reality. By the term "social reality" I wish to be understood the sum total

of objects and occurrences within the social cultural world as experienced by the commonsense thinking of men living their daily lives among their fellow-men, connected with them in manifold relations of interaction . . . . . From the outset, we, the actors in the social scene, experience the world we live in both as a world of nature and of culture, *not as private but as an intersubjective one*, that is, a world common to all of us . . . this involves intercommunication and language. (1970: 5-6).

In their misguided attempts to attain scientific respectability, instead of facing the intersubjective origin of their data as a necessary (and valuable) aspect of the epistemological foundations of the sociological enterprise, many bourgeois sociologists and social psychologists have attempted to devise techniques of "totally objective observation". In these, the social scientist becomes that peculiar anomaly, the "non-participant observer", rendered deliberately incapable of interacting simultaneously with the other individuals in the social situation as a human being for fear of contaminating his pure scientific objectivity. What those who adhere to such techniques do not realize is that, by "dehumanizing" themselves, they dehumanize man in general, the "object" of their study.

The *reductio ad absurdum* of this attempt is behaviourism. The iniquities, if not downright immorality, of this so-called methodology must be examined briefly, a) because it has strongly influenced data collection techniques in all the social sciences; and b) because a critique of it leads naturally to a discussion of language, and the close relations which exist between modern linguistics and the phenomenological method. Behaviourism, through its tight grip on academic psychology, has strongly influenced modern sociological concerns about objectivity and the techniques of observation, participant or not; hence, for example, the currency of the term "behavioural sciences" (cf. Borger and Cioffi 1970). To this extent it has a pernicious influence upon all the social sciences, since it attacks at the very roots of our data: at the point of their collection.

The two most prominent perpetrators of behaviourism are Watson, who coined the term in articles and books published from 1918 onwards, and Skinner, the most influential modern proponent of the doctrine in a series of books on his "experiments" (1953, 1957, 1972).[4] The main task of this pseudo-scientific methodology was to reject all concepts of consciousness and mind as being unscientific. Koestler neatly summarizes Watson's original intentions:

By "behaviour" Watson meant observable activities – what the physicist calls "public events", such as the motions of a dial on a machine. Since all mental events are private events which cannot be observed by others, and which can only be made public by statements based upon introspection, they had to be excluded from the domain of science. (1967: 19)

The behaviourist, in Watson's own words must exclude "from his scientific vocabulary all subjective terms such as sensation, perception, image, desire, purpose and even thinking and emotion as they were subjectively defined". (1928: 4)

The behaviourists, or "Skinnereans", seek to give what they call "causal" or "functional" explanations of behaviour; in this, they make no distinction between man and any other kind of animal. Furthermore, in order to achieve their scientific aims, they must dehumanize man: "Man, if necessary, must be seen as a machine" (Mennel 1974: 9). The reason given for this is frankly an appeal for the assumed methodology of the natural sciences to be applied to human behaviour as the only scientific method of analysing the latter. It is assumed that human beings "respond" to a given "stimulus" in a "conditioned" manner. All of these, "stimulus", "response" and subsequent "behaviour" are observable in sensory terms, and as such they are "facts" which "have a physical status to which the usual techniques of science are adapted, and they make it possible to explain behaviour as other subjects are explained" (Skinner 1953: 31).[5] What is more, the behaviourists go on (and this is the crunch), all this applies *pari passu* to human *verbal* behaviour, that is, language. Skinner explores this in his second book (1957) and finally extrapolates even further into the universal issues of human freedom versus determinism (1972).

There is neither time nor reason to go further into Skinnerean behaviourism; it has been subjected to a number of devastating and, I think, conclusive refutations and critiques (e.g. Chomsky 1959 and *passim*; Koestler 1967: 17-61, Mennel 1974: 9-13). The point I wish to emphasize is that it has had a profound effect upon the assessment of the validity of the "observation" part of participant observation techniques of data collection, *as well as* upon questionnaire methods in gathering statistical data. This may be glimpsed in the idea of a "closed question" as being a "verbal stimulus" to which there are assumed to be a limited range of "legitimate" or "relevant" responses; anything outside this range is rejected as redundant and therefore not amenable to further scientific interpretation and analysis. In other words, the kind of observation of human behaviour suggested by behaviourism, as well as the closed question – answer situation of questionnaire or question guide utilization, deny the creativity of both language and the intersubjective context of communication. Data obtained under such circumstances must therefore necessarily lack some of the most important properties of human experience: man is indeed reduced to a machine.

The concept of the "creativity of language" lies at the heart of modern theoretical advances in the study of linguistics: Chomsky's generative grammar. It is a scientific, analytical concept in this context, and does not refer directly to literary enterprise (although it does have something to do with it). "Why", asks Chomsky,

is it that all normal people have the capacity to utter new sentences which have never been spoken by themselves, nor very likely by anyone else? Why is the listener able to understand sentences never heard before? (Mennel 1974: 12)

Chomsky goes on:

> The idea that a person has a 'verbal repertoire' – a stock of utterances that he produces by 'habit' on an appropriate occasion – is a myth, totally at variance with the observed usage of language. (1967: 400, quoted in Mennel 1974: 12)

Generative or transformational grammar is manifested in the *competence* of the speaker of the language. Lyon's summarizes Chomsky's analysis as follows:

> Any psychological model of the way this competence is put to use in actual *performance* will have to take account of a number of additional facts which the linguist deliberately ignores in his definition of the notion of grammaticality ... Many of the sentences which the linguist regards as grammatical ... would never in fact occur "naturally" and, if constructed deliberately for the purpose of some linguistic element, will be difficult, and perhaps impossible, for actual native speakers to understand. (1970: 85)

I have quoted this passage because it leads directly back to our discussion of the phenomenological method and the related development of enthnometholodogy in the social sciences. There is a close correspondence between Chomsky's analysis of the "deep structure" of language and how it relates to linguistic "reality", and Schutz's phenomenology of social interaction. Cicourel succinctly notes: (1973: 33-4):

> Both Chomsky and Schutz stress the *intentions* of the speaker – hearers (not merely their 'stimuli' and 'responses') .... Schutz is concerned with the semantic component of social interaction. The linguist is not interested in focussing on interaction itself, but his statements can be extended logically to include conditions formulated by Schutz for understanding how social order or social interaction is possible'.

Or, we may add, how social reality is "constructed". (1973: 33-4; cf. Berger and Luckman 1971.) To translate this into "structuralist" language, the transformational structures of linguistic theory (cf. Piaget 1971; 74-96, and *passim*) are not merely *analogous* to the transformational structures of social forms in phenomenological theory, *they constitute an integral part of one another*. The intersubjectivity central to the "observation" of social interaction and the "creativity" of linguistic communication are merely different aspects of the same thing: neither is possible without the other, and a science of society is impossible without an understanding of both.

In order to clarify this, the argument must be taken a stage further. Chomsky's concept of linguistic competence stresses the monologic capability of the speaker. In order to extend this to the "intersubjective competence" of speaker and hearer, as does Cicourel, further elucidation is needed than that given by Cicourel. This is provided by Habermas in his theory of communicative competence. The details of how Habermas develops this theory are beyond the scope of this work but his position on the matter is succinct:

> (Chomsky's) thesis of monologuism assumes that the universal meaning components belong to the basic equipment of the solitary organism of speaking subjects. The thesis is incompatible with the proposition that semantic universals could also be parts of an intersubjectively produced cultural system. (Habermas 1970b: 133)

History and sociology are both interpretive sciences, if we are to agree with at least the general argument so far; but sociology must go beyond interpretation or translation; it is also a systematic science of action, producing monological knowledge. The transition from interpretation to action is brilliantly expressed by Habermas:

> The world of traditionally inherited meanings reveals itself to the interpreter only to the extent to which his own world thereby becomes transparent to himself at the same time. The man who understands the traditional meaning provides a link between the two worlds; he comprehends the factual content of what is handed down by applying the tradition to himself and his situation. If, however, the procedural rules thus combine interpretation with application, then the following explanation suggests itself; in revealing reality, interpretational research is guided by a concern for the maintenance and extension of possible intersubjective understanding which is necessary for the orientation of any symbolic interaction. Meaning is understood according to its structure with a view to a possible concensus of interacting individuals within the frame of a traditional or culturally patterned self-understanding ... a critical social science, however, is obviously not content with this; it tries in addition to discover which (if any) theoretical statements express unchangeable laws of social action and which, though they express relations of dependence, because they are ideologically fixed, are in principle subject to change. (1970a: 45-6)

It should be clear by now that my unequivocal stance upon the matter of the methodology of data collection and interpretation is that, as far as his limits take him, the social scientist's full participation both intellectually and emotionally in the day-to-day activities of any community, within the context of its language and culture, is indispensable to any *critical* understanding of the structures and processes he is trying to elucidate, and *ipso facto* the foundation any practice which may derive from such knowledge. Other techniques of data collection, however sophisticated and "scientific" they may sound, merely complement this; without it they may bear no relation to the reality of the community concerned, and would thus have no reality for knowledge of interest in the social sciences.

The route of my arrival at such a position has been at least partially clarified[6]. I feel I need not "defend" the phenomenological position I have taken against such critiques as those of Harvey (1972: 104-7) or Hindess (1972: *passim*). The synthesis with Marxist concepts of the inseparability of theory and *praxis*, which by now should also be initially evident, is made somewhat more explicit in the conclusion to this Chapter.

IV

In the following descriptions and interpretations of some "situations" from Ilparakuyo everyday experience, I make no apology for their "raw" "fieldnotes", quality; this "rawness" is intentional, for two reasons. The first is that they should be read in the light of what has gone before in this chapter and what I have said about theoretical and methodological issues, the reader then making the necessary interconnections in a do-it-yourself kit manner. The second is that, since this was originally a "working paper", it is illustrated with "working materials", not sophisticated pieces of polished analysis. The case material presented here, the context in which the data were recorded, and some of the interpretations should, in effect, stand illuminated by what I have already said, as well as providing in their turn illustration of some of the metholodogical points I have made in the previous sections.

One day in January, my father and I set out at about sunrise in search of local beer (*olmarua*) which, we had heard the previous night, was "not far away"; it had been brewed at the home of a Mkwere elder whose wife had a reputation for a reasonable brew. We passed by way of an Olparakuoni neighbour's homestead about half a mile away, to collect a five-litre plastic container in which we were to bring the beer home – in anticipation of some guests who were to join us later in the day (another reason for our unusually early departure). We would probably have taken the container to bring beer home anyway, irrespective of anticipated guests. At this neighbouring *enkang'*, the place of a prosperous and politically influential member of the Ilkidotu age-set, we drink fresh milk (*kule nailowa*) mixed with water, a sustaining but particularly thirst-quenching mixture called *enkarepus*; no curdled milk at that time of day.

Two topics arose in conversation: the effects on Ilparakuyo-Wakwere relations of the contemporary movement of both populations into *vijiji*; and the problem of accusations of vampirism (*mumiani*) and other rumours directed against some Ilparakuyo elders, my father, myself, and other members of our family. I deal with the latter in detail elsewhere; for the moment, the issue of Ilparakuyo – Wakwere relations in the context of current villagization measures.

On arrival at the place where we expected to find the beer, we were informed that it has not yet arrived from the brewer's homestead (it was now about 9 a.m.). Despite the fact that neither of us knew exactly where this homestead was, we proceeded undaunted, arriving unerringly at our destination like bee-eaters to the hive. Present at the homestead were the Mkwere elder, his wife, four or five other Wakwere women and, of course, the beer. The woman were preparing to carry the beer in relays, in large pots on their heads, to its eventual place of sale on the main road. We tasted the beer, which was good enough, and were told that it could not officially be sold until midday; this was "cultivating time".

On the way to the homestead, we had encountered another Mkwere elder, staggering under a load of newly-cut house-building poles towards the site of a new Kwere *kijiji* on the main road. We also came across freshly burnt down house sites set amidst fields of obviously fertile and prosperous potential; this my father noted with an edge of sadness in his voice. Three months earlier, he had been forcibly moved from his *enkang'*, having several of the buildings burnt down in the process. This concatenation of circumstances, and the fact that we were soon well into our first gallon of beer, generated the following conversation which I recorded, as verbatim as circumstances allowed, later in the day:

Olparakuoni elder (P.E.): So, you have to cultivate until noon, what about the problem of moving your houses to new *kijiji*? What don't you tell the government that you have to move first, and then cultivate new fields later? Or vice versa?

Mkwere elder (K.E.): We cultivate until noon, then move we have to, in our spare time. You people are rich [*watajiri*; note the use of this particular term] so you don't worry when you move [which is just not true: see other notes]. We poor ones, who rely on cultivation, if we don't grow our crops we will starve. We don't have cattle to sell in order to buy food.

P.E.   The trouble with you people is that you have never really liked us, yet you cannot do without us! Who do you get most of your money from when you brew beer like this?

K.E.   You people, of course.

P.E.   Where do you get your meat from?

K.E.   You, of course.

P.E.   Then why don't you like us? Now the government knows you don't like us, so they move us to one place and you to another. Surely you will lose by this?

By this time we had been joined by three Wakwere youths, one of whom was well known at our homestead, particularly when we were still at the old homestead, which was only about two miles away from this place. P.E. bought another gallon of beer, and while we all drank, he continued:

> We have lived together for a long time, have we not? We ask you to do things for us which we don't do ourselves, like cultivating, and you get money. Is this not good?

K.E. Yes, it is good because each of us had his own way of living, and we did things for each other. Take beer, for example; beer like this brings friendship between us, does it not?

P.E. Yes, it does indeed. Bring some more! Now look, at Lugoba, we Maasai paid to have water pumps built, the cattle dips made, and the pumps run, did we not?

K.E. Yes, you did.

P.E. Now they have moved us further away from them.

K.E. But some Maasai at Lugoba have not been moved; they sit there while we poor people get moved around.

The conversation then moved on to the reasons for the latter anomaly, an anomaly whose understanding is crucial for an overall analysis of the Ilparakuyo political economy – this will become apparent in later chapters. There is already enough material in this vignette of the situation for several interesting lines of inquiry and interpretation. Before our departure with our five litres of home beer, however, and having consumed three gallons amongst us, P.E. could not resist initiating the following exchange:

P.E. Now, you people really are cowards. Look at Peter here, he is my son, walks everywhere with me, and you say that because he comes to stay with me, his father, he and all of us must be *mumiani, wachinja-chinja*! [*Kiswahili*: blood-sucking killers.] Isn't that rather silly?

K.E. Of course it is, he is like my son also.

P.E. Even on our way here, two young girls ran away from us, and yet what were we looking for? People to kill? No, we were just looking for your miserable beer. Now we have a long way to return home and must leave.

The informality of the conversation set out here should not be taken to mean that issues of critical concern to the whole community were not discussed; they were. In several subsequent similar situations the same issues were raised, from which certain reliable "observations" may be made. Among other things: a) there was a spatial separation of Ilparakuyo and Wakwere going on as a result of pastoralists and cultivators being villagized separately; b) neither party particularly liked it, but; c) the cultivators were the most annoyed, or at least they were the most vocal about their annoyance; d) the reason ascribed for the separation could potentially heighten hostile relations between the two cultural groups:[7] and e) there are a multiplicity of other issues about the moves which are of purely internal concern to the Ilparakuyo community, but they would not be expressed in such a context and I do not deal with them here.

The overall interpretation I have listed above, which I first thought was heavily biassed by my involvement with Ilparakuyo, was later confirmed in a Dar es Salaam conversation with a senior government official who had been involved in the decisions leading to the plan. He told me that representatives of the cultivators had made strong protestations about the segregative tendencies inherent in the moves, and that several people felt it had been a mistake to dismantle the different elements that make up this complex community.

A reasonable tentative conclusion that may be arrived at is that Ilparakuyo and Wakwere look upon each other's economies and exchange relationships as complementary, if not other aspects of their societies and cultures, and that this view was, at least until recently, essentially correct. Any overall development plan could have at least taken this into account, but since it is hardly the kind of knowledge that would result from formal questioning, perhaps it did not come to the attention of the planners. A number of issues for further investigation clearly arise from this conclusion. Can such be called the result of "critical participation?"

V

The following data relate to the social structure and history of one particular homestead (*enkang'*) and its relations with others, some aspects of whose structures are thereby illuminated. The data also indicate some features of the overall structures of the Ilparakuyo community in this area. (cf. Beidelman 1960, *passim*) This *enkang'* lies some 13 to 15 miles from ours. Let us call the elder who is the head of this homestead Meteurr. He is of the senior level of the Ilkidotu (Ilmerisho) age-set, who are now junior elders (see Chapter 4). Here we note immediately a distinction between Ilparakuyo and pastoral Maasai residence patterns and domestic groups: Ilparakuyo *inkang'itie* do have a single head; Maasai local units do not (cf. Jacobs 1965a: *passim*).

My brother and I were invited to go to Meteurr's homestead by the two eldest sons, one of the senior sub-set of *ilmurran*, the other still a junior; I had not met their father at that time, nor did I know their relationship with ours or any other *enkang'*. I had come to know the brothers during one of the periodic dance sessions, several days or even weeks long, which the *ilmurran* have with the young unmarried girls (*intoyie*), usually (but not always) after an *olpul* meat feast. But through an age-set spokesman (*olaiguenani*) of the age-set, who is a personal friend of mine, the younger brother came to stay with us in Dar es Salaam in search of a cure for an apparently "incurable" cough. During his stay with us in Dar es Salaam we learned through the kind auspices of a medical friend that the case of the young *olmurrani* was not as serious as it appeared to be at first sight. After a two-week course of medication he was perfectly fit. Immediately he returned home, and knowing that I planned to be in the area for a couple of weeks in the near future, the two brothers began to make arrangements for our visit to their homestead; arrangements, I may add, purely in a social sense, since I had not been in that area before. The younger brother of the two was waiting for us at our homestead when we arrived for a stay in the *enkang'*, and remained with us until we had set a date to visit his place. We decided to do at least part of the journey by the local bus, which passes nearby in each direction once a day, since a direct-route walk in this area was both unpleasant and hazardous, with few Ilparakuyo *inkang'itie* in between; it was also raining nearly every day at the time.

After the first two miles of our six-mile walk from the nearest place the bus passes, we met Meteurr with two of his wives and a daughter on his way in the opposite direction, towards a nearby trading centre. He told us that his eldest son was away on a journey to Mvomero, for reasons which I discovered later that day. Ilparakuyo are great travellers, and this is one way in which news reaches all parts of the community very rapidly, a factor in their ability to retain such a strong identity. The elder said he would join us later in the afternoon.

By the time we had reached the homestead, I knew the names and relationships of the women who had been with Meteurr on the path, as well as others at the *enkang'*, since it was imperative that I should know whom to greet as "mother" (*yieyio*) and whom as "my wife" (*nakerai*, lit. "my child") and whom by name as "our sister": all this information was given to me to *educate me*, with not a single question of my part. I also learned that Meteurr had five wives, one of whom was a Mugogo and whose father, mother, and other kin were living as part of Meteurr's *enkang'*.

The elder returned early in the evening with his eldest son whom he had just met at the trading centre on his return from Mvomero. As the day and evening passed in conversation, I learned that our mother (at our place) was the elder full sister of Meteurr's second wife, and the kinship terms of address were established (in anthropological terms, the two brothers and we two were classifatory uterine parallel cousins). I also learned that Meteurr was the senior patrilateral (agnatic) parallel cousin of a neighbour of ours 13 miles away. As a result I knew why the two sons were such frequent visitors to "our place", and why the eldest was about to marry the daughter of another neighbour of ours at Kwamsanga. All sorts of things began to fall into place, including the history of movement and migration of Meteurr's *enkang'* and several others as well.

But I also stumbled upon something I did not really yet know about *our* family. I had heard vaguely that my younger brother, although married, had been betrothed to a second, Emparakuoni, girl (his present and first wife is a Mugogo). I now knew she was the daughter of a neighbouring *enkang'* to Meteurr's, and we were to visit there in the morning. The marriage itself was still a long way off.

After the evening meal and further general discussion, we retired. But not before I had realized from the conversation between ourselves, Meteurr, and his two sons, that "the food we Ilparakuyo have to eat these days, *ugali* [maizemeal porridge] and beans, is not really our food at all; this is because our cattle are dying so fast, we have had to send most of the herd away to a safer camp, and there is little milk at the *enkang'*." This issue came up again in a conversation the following morning, at the *enkang'* of our future father-in-law. On retiring for the night, it transpired that, because the senior *olmurrani* had come home, he, I, and one of the younger sons who is still an *olayioni* (uncircumcised youth) would occupy one of the beds in our "younger mother's" house (*enkaji*), the house of our mother's younger sister; the two junior *ilmurran*, including my brother, would occupy another room. By this chance arrangement, the senior *olmurrani* and I lay awake, talking half the night. I probably learned more about the "Ilparakuyo predicament" in that intimate conversation than months of formal questioning could have taught me (cf. Parkipuny 1975: *passim*). He told me about the cattle that had died, and his attempts to help his father, first concentrating on the manipulation of the livestock trade, then in attempts at other "self-employed" money-making activities which had brought other Ilparakuyo some measure of success; all had so far failed. He told me about his plans for the future, about his vision of what the future could and should be; and so we moved on to a general discussion of what "success" in life could mean for him at the present, and what it meant for me. We discussed the role of "medicines" in success, and the abilities and inabilities of the *iloibonok*, both those minor ones who act as diviners, and the greater ones whose prophecies and medicines should help the whole community.

The relations between his family, his *enkang'*, and others in the community, both far and near, became clearer as our conversation proceeded, illuminating in turn the interrelationships amongst those other *inkang'itie*. The significance of kinship and affinity in terms of property began to emerge, and the way in which we had a very clear and precise cognitive "map" of the significant ties binding this widely-dispersed community, which to superficial observation looks so fragmented, into one with a deep sense of identity and a dynamism which is in part a will to survive as Ilparakuyo, not as something else, I learned, quite incidentally, of the relationships between a set of three brothers, all prominent men and heads of their own *enkang'*, one of the Ilkidotu age-set, two of mine, Ilmedoti. This information was later to be of major importance to me in understanding certain political relationships in the community at large; but this must also await an analysis elsewhere.

The following morning we walked in the rain to visit our future in-laws. On the way, I heard something of the history of some of the 15 or 20 *inkang'itie* in the area: where they come from, whom they come with, and why the Wakwere had been moved out of the area in the early 1960s. This information was confirmed by reference to the only map available of this area: it was to be an uninhabited "forest reserve" in a plan devised during the late colonial period; it is now, at least in part, an Ilparakuyo settlement. Throughout this period I had not asked one single, pointed, "closed" question, to which I required one among a limited range of "reponses"; the "interpretations of the situation" which were given to me were meant to teach me at least the basic minimum I should know in order to behave as a reasonable human being in the given situation. Later, I did extend my inquiries, but along the lines that had already arisen out of the situation. I was not there to conduct "interviews" or fill out questionnaires; in fact, it is highly unlikely that I could have even lived for this short period at this *enkang'* if those had been my intentions, or gained the insights I did into the community and its values in the brief 24 hours I lived with this hospitable family. Our relationship continues, both there at the *enkang'* and when the two brothers visit Dar es Salaam.

VI

These brief sketches of Ilparakuyo relationships among themselves, with me, with others, and with government, should have corrected an impression that might have arisen in the previous sections of this Chapter. The realization of the intersubjective origin of sociological data does not mean that "scientific objectivity" is thrown overboard; I do not advocate, to paraphrase the adage, the expulsion of the baby with the bathwater. The things that I have written down, that fill my notebooks, of my intersubjective experiences with Ilparakuyo, and the interpretations that I have so far given them, have also at least partially been the result of my sociological training, my teaching the subject, and more than 15 years of sporadic research. Every one of the interpretations I have made above, either in the very process of writing down my fields notes, or in later reflection, is "informed" (or, alternatively, "misinformed": that question remains open) by some theoretical and methodological considerations, some of which I trust are by now evident. Recognition of the intersubjective origin of social data must be accompanied by what may be called "theoretical reflexivity" on the part of the scientist as individual, if it is to lead to a critical science of society. It does *not* mean that the data of sociological knowledge are haphazard, randomly experienced subjective impressions. I say more on this later; here I turn briefly to an examination of how hypotheses can, or should, guide the selection of relevant data to be recorded, although they should not exclude other data which may be more relevant than those sought, both for the problem in focus and for others not yet formulated; in other words, the principle of serendipity should always be allowed for.

Hypotheses which guide the selection of data may be constructed a priori to any given situation in that they may be derived from comparative evidence and data relating to societies or situations other than those under consideration; or, of course, they may originate in mere deduction. Such hypotheses are the most prone to refutation since they may not only (like any hypothesis) be shown to be false, they may also be irrelevant from the beginning. In the social sciences, the "strongest" hypotheses, and therefore those most worth concerning oneself with, arise out of the very process of interaction, the intersubjective context in which the sociologist utilizes his theoretical equipment, his interest, and more often than not his "intuition", in his interaction with others who, of course, are also bringing to bear on the situation their cognitive notions, interpretation, and interest.

This applies *a fortiori* to the identification and selection of "problems" to be investigated in the first place, even before any hypotheses are constructed. The "problems" of a given society or community may often be stated by the members of that community or society in "down to earth" or "commonsense" terms: we don't have enough cattle to feed ourselves; we don't have enough water and grazing for our cattle; our children don't obey us any longer; our wives are going astray. It is not enough for the social scientist to sort out these problems into categories, some of which, say, he may relegate to the hydrologist and say, "that is not my problem". It *is* his problem, for each of these has a sociological dimension, if not a social origin. As these problems arise in the intersubjective context, it is the sociologist's task to "translate" them into sociological terms, and then devise means of going about investigating them; *but* this *translation must be meaningful to all parties concerned,* not only to some esoteric coterie of inspired individuals.

The methodological implications of this interpretation and translation have already been discussed, as have the sociologist's unique contributions to the exercise. I now turn to a couple of examples of how a whole line of inquiry and thought, resulting in the construction of hypotheses, can arise out of the intersubjective context of critical participation.

In my discussions and wanderings with Ilparakuyo *ilmurran* and elders, it soon became evident that *olpul*, the meat feast (the term also refers to the place at which the feast occurs), was a critical institution for society, not only in symbolic and ritual terms, but for economic and political reasons as well. This realization came first as a kind of intuitive "feeling", while I was still groping with even basic linguistic understanding. As first, *olpul* (pl. *ilpuli*) seemed to be the result of a purely negative and "irrational" set of prohibitions: *ilmurran* are not allowed to eat meat at the *enkang'*, or even in the periodic young people's villages (*imanyat*, sing. *emanyata*).[8] There seemed to be a contradiction here: why should an institution of such apparent importance to Ilparakuyo and other Maasai (cf. Hollis 1905: 292, Spencer 1973: 23; Jacobs 1965.), over which a great deal of thought, planning and expense is involved, be merely the result of negative irrationality? That *ilpuli* have been a feature of the cultures of all Maa-speaking people over a very long period, and the sites can be used as indicators of their historical movements and presence in eastern Africa, has recently been fully demonstrated (Gramly 1975).

This, then, was the situation: the prominence of *olpul* in the minds, plans, and actions of Ilparakuyo indicated its importance, it was a "problem". Available evidence indicated a purely negative and irrational basis for the institution. It was hypothesized that there must be some more "positive", "rational" basis for its apparent importance. Eventually, it was discovered, in a manner described below, that the "answer" lay in the concept of *entoroj*. This is simultaneously a concept, an institution, and a "state of being" which is critical to the entire age-set structure of Ilparakuyo, to their economic values, and ultimately to their political structure. It is therefore also crucial to an understanding of their relations with non-Maasai, and hence may be of enormous importance for the process of development and the future of their society. And *entoroj* can only be attained, and therefore maintained, through the institution of *olpul*, for it is only by giving a beast at *olpul* that a youth can attain *entoroj*.

The evidence for this rather sweeping assertion is presented in Chapter 3. The point I am trying to make here is that the significance of *olpul* as the "womb" of *entoroj* struck me only through my everyday interaction with Ilparakuyo *ilmurran*, both in the community and in Dar es Salaam. I followed it up as a "hunch", an intuitive guess, and its connections with *entoroj* and the vast implications of the latter were "opened up" for my understanding. In fact, two chance remarks in entirely different situations led me to it. The first was at my house in Dar es Salaam. At supper at which two *ilmurran* were present, I asked them why they could eat meat at our *enkang'* in Dar es Salaam, and not at our *enkang'* there, in the village. The response was straightforward: there is no *entoroj*, I have no *entoroj*, since I have never given a beast at *olpul*. If I had done so, then as *ilmurran* they could no longer eat meat here at this *enkang'*; the whole *enkang'* would be imbued, as it were, with *entoroj*.

The second was a remark jokingly made by an age-mate of mine (*olaji*) who, observing me drinking milk with some *ilmurran* at our Ilparakuyo *enkang'*, said, "Peter, why do you drink milk with these youths when you have not given a beast at *olpul*?" Suddenly I saw the whole interrelationship between the limited nature of the domestic mode of production, sharing, relations amongst age-mates, between age-sets and the homesteads (*inkang'itie*) and the fundamental logic behind them with the interlinking institution of *olpul*: all from the juxtaposition of two chance remarks from the everyday context and logic of the intersubjective context of communication. Hypotheses that may guide the direction of inquiry and data collection, therefore, arise directly out of the combination of two elements: an *awareness* of the intersubjective origin of "social facts", and what C. Wright Mills called the sociological imagination.

Olpul, however, led me to ponder upon something else: the dramatic phenomenon of "shivering" (*olokirki* from *akirkira* "to shake" or "rock") and "shaking" (*enkigoroto*, from *agor*, "to strangle" cf. Kisongo Maasai *apush*), which, after dancing, and drinking medicines at *ilpuli*, *ilmurran* induce as something fitting and desirable (cf. Spencer 1965: 263-70, and *passim*). Spencer's excellent analysis provides many insights to the Ilparakuyo phenomenon, and lead to the general hypothesis that the "trance" induced during shaking has little to do with the medicines drunk by *ilmurran* (which in any case are said by Ilparakuyo to be purely for providing greater physical strength and health) but provides instead an institutionalized method of controlling their emotions and submitting to the strains in the authority structure of the age-grade system. One may further hypothesize that it also provides a "training" for elderhood, where dignified behaviour demands control of the emotions, and rational, even if forceful, argument. Ilparakuyo say *"Megel nkishu 'pere"*, "do not separate cattle with a spear" (you may destroy many): i.e., if you settle problems in anger you will hurt many people; always use moderation (cf. Massek and Sidai 1974: 36).

This is not the place to expand upon this analysis for Ilparakuyo; the point I wish to establish is that, through the age-set system, its checks and balances, and such "control" mechanisms as shaking, Ilparakuyo (and other Maasai) men have a "built-in" method of emotional self-control, so necessary for the functioning of the system. Women, however, do not.

VII

It might be argued that, in some senses, the phenomenological method advocated here has been forced upon me by the peculiar circumstances of a somewhat unique society. If that is so, then so much the better, since the methodology not only posits the origin of sociological knowledge in inter-subjectivity, but also arises directly from it. But I think I have also made it clear that it would be applicable to the analysis of all social formations; and in particular where the dominant mode of production is predominantly pre-capitalist as would be the case for the most peasant communities in Tanzania.[9] I make this distinction in the levels of the postulate of adequacy because it enables us to relate the methodology advocated to Marx's concepts of the transition from "primitive" modes of production to later forms. This is to be found, for example, in the *Grundrisse* (Marx 1973: 472-88 and *passim*): where the individual relates as a "total being" to the means of production within the context, and only within the context, of the community as representing the relations of production. Pastoralism is postulated as "the first form of the mode of existence" based upon clan organization, and this "clan community, the natural community, appears not as a result of, but as a presupposition for, the appropriation (temporary) and utilization of land" (Marx 1973: 472). In social terms,

> The individual relates simply to the objective conditions of labour as being his; relates to them as the inorganic nature of his subjectivity, in which the latter realizes itself, the chief objective condition of labour does not itself appear as a *product* of labour, but is already there as its nature. (Marx 1973: 485)

There is no alienation of labour here, and any knowledge that objectifies the product of it rather than the process of it is itself alienated, and not knowledge of the "real world".

In similar vein is Schutz's critique of the utilitarian principle and the marginal principle in classical and modern bourgeois economic theory as they stand as guiding tenets of their epistemology, and hence their methodology. He notes:

> Our scientific activity and, particularly, that which deals with the social world, is also performed with a certain means-end relation (interest), namely, in order to acquire knowledge for mastering the world, the real world, not one created by the grace of the scientist. We want to find out what happens in the real world and not in the fantasies of a few sophisticated eccentrics. (1970: 113)

A Marxist phenomenology would thus contain the two procedural elements: 1) interpretation and translation of the "real world" of everyday life through the intersubjective situation in which the social scientist is involved, which illuminates the common and elemental link between knowledge and interest; and 2) the translation in turn of the knowledge produced into action by theoretical reflexivity: this is what I have called "critical participation". Knowledge obtained through processes of mere observation or data collected upon the unsound assumption of ontological "objectivity" is ultimately alienated knowledge. O'Neill sums this up well in answer to the question, "Can phenomenology be critical?"

> The ultimate feature of the phenomenological institution of reflexivity is that it grounds critique in membership and tradition. Thus the critic's auspices are the same as those of anyone working in a community of language, work and politics. In the critical act there is a simultaneity of authorship and authenticity which is the declaration of membership in a continuing philosophical, literary, or scientific community. The critic does not alienate himself from the community, which would be the consequence of an absolute knowledge and ultimate nihilism. This is not to say that the critic is not rebellious; it is to remark upon the consequences of solitude and solidarity as the starting points of criticism. (1972: 234)

This reflexivity is a particular aspect of the more general concept referred to by Piaget as "reflective abstraction" in his exposition of the theoretical convergence of structuralist analyses in mathematics and physics, Chomsky's generative grammar, and structural analyses in the social sciences (Piaget 1970: 139-40, and *passim*). A Marxist phenomenology would be truly scientific throughout its methodology, from the collection of data to its final interpretation and translation into praxis.

Notes

1. Written in July 1976.
2. Ilparakuyo have a proverb, *"Meya esile nkare"* – "a debt is not borne away by water": debts are passed on from one generation to the next and are not extinguished by death (cf. Massek and Sidai 1974: 24).
3. I do not here enter into the controversy between ethnomethodologists and statisticians, Marxist or bourgeois, about the uses and abuses of statistical data. For a partisan statement of this controversy, see Hindess 1973.
4. As recently as 1970, two Sussex University psychologists, both educated at Cambridge, concluded an article on the Skinnerean analysis of behaviour with the words:

    > although we have been somewhat eclectic, we believe the line we have taken is essentially Skinnerean and that it includes all the really crucial features of Skinner's position . . . This type of analysis has been remarkably successful and offers, we believe, by far the most promising approach to the understanding of behaviour. (Boakes and Halliday 1970: 372-3)

5. The rectification of this state of affairs is stated as one of the central concerns of phenomenology:

    > To distinguish the different meanings which externally resemble each other. For example, obedience may be expressed in the same gestures [observable behaviour in a Skinnerean sense], whether it is the result of love, of self-interest, or of fear. (Aron 1957: 26)

6. While there are considerable differences between the position taken here and Colin Turnbull's consistent emphasis for a shift in social anthropology to some middle position between "subjectivity" and "objectivity", as well as in our conceptions of what subjectivity means for the social sciences, my debt to his work will be obvious to anyone familiar with it (e.g. Turnbull 1961, 1965, 1972).
7. There are many Ilparakuyo songs (*isinkolioitin*) and recitations (*eoko*) that tell of the exploits of Ilparakuyo *ilmurran* against the iniquities of some venal Wakwere, and in which a good deal of hostility is expressed.
8. Ilparakuyo no longer have *imanyat*, and many of the functions of these "warrior camps" are carried out at *ilpuli*: see Chapter 3.
9. All social formations contain more than one mode of production, of which one is "dominant". The passage above should not be construed as implying that the Ilparakuyo economy is immune from the inroads of peripheral capitalism and petty commodity relations; see Chapters 1, 5, 6, and 7.

3. Olpul and Entoroj: the Economy of Sharing

"Mipej olpul litadaare."
"Don't burn the meat-feasting site you have once used" – never leave ill-feeling behind when you leave a place where you have lived in harmony; you may return.

For several reasons, the analysis presented here is both empirically and theoretically tentative and preliminary.[1] The data upon which it is based were collected during brief and sporadic periods of fieldwork, but mitigating circumstances which possibly enhance the quality of the material thus obtained have already been discussed (Chapter 2). Even the data available, however, have not been fully analysed, since fieldwork is still in progress. My justifications for venturing this early essay include the following: a) Ilparakuyo are a Maasai-speaking pastoral people who are historically, linguistically, and culturally very closely related to the pastoral Maasai, particularly the southern sections of the latter such as the Ilkisonko, while differing radically from them in their politico-economic circumstances as well as in many features of social organization; b) there is very little published material on Ilparakuyo society, Beidelman's pioneering work being the most valuable (1960, 1961a, 1961b, 1962, 1965a, 1968); c) Ilparakuyo present a unique case in eastern Africa of a pastoral people who has existed since far earlier than the colonial period in relations of inter-dependence (one might even say "symbiosis", alternatively peaceful and hostile) with culturally distinct Bantu-speaking cultivators or semi-pastoralists (cf. Jacobs 1975: 406-7, Beidelman 1960 and *passim*, Ndagala 1974); d) they therefore provide a critical case study for any discussion of development strategy in the context of Tanzania's policies of rural transformation on socialist principals, where relations of interdependence between pastoralism and cultivation are important.[2]

Some preliminary remarks must also be made upon the theoretical and methodological foundations of the present discussion. My attempt in what follows, to explain sociologically two unique (but crucial) aspects of comtemporary Ilparakuyo social structure and culture, begins from my interpretation of Ilparakuyo conceptions and interpretations of them; but this is only a beginning. My fieldwork is grounded in a conception of the intersubjective reflexivity of sociological knowledge and the data upon which it is based, and a consequent denial of the essentially alienating dichotomy between subjectivity and objectivity. The reasons for this are elaborated above (Chapter 2; cf. O'Neill 1972: 221-36), but their implications reappear in what follows.

The analysis I present, however, will undoubtedly be labelled "structuralist", and to a certain extent this label would be valid. All labels are crude, but owing to the ubiquitious propensity of the human mind to apply them, I must dwell briefly upon these issues here.

Although the Ilparakuyo institutions examined here are essentially politico-economic, they are embedded in an ideological complex with strong symbolic, and therefore ritual and religious, implications. In fact, because they exhibit what could be labelled by the ignorant as arational (or even "irrational") taboos, prohibitions, and injuctions, they may mistakenly be thought to lie purely at the ideological level, and therefore be dismissed as irrelevant to current concerns. Part of the purpose of this chapter is to demonstrate the egregious fallacy in any such interpretation. In order to do so, a structuralist methodology becomes indispensable.

The overall framework that I attempt to employ derives also from a Marxist epistemology. Structuralist and Marxist *methodologies* (whatever they may be as "philosophical movements") are essentially complementary, since both postulate that the "reality" of social processes (structures and their transformations) is not manifestly accessible to the senses; rather, it is composed of a finite number of systematic, dialectical interrelationships which can only be arrived at by an analysis that "gets behind" the manifestations of social relations in any society (or social formation) at particular historical conjunctures, and also reveals the generation of new structural relations over time.

In fact, anyone who has seriously attempted to understand structuralism as a method of analysis will at once see that it is both admirably in accord with current developments in general scientific thought (cf. Piaget 1971, Monod 1972, Garaudy 1970: 66, 71.) as well as capable of enriching Marxist methodology in a complementary fashion (cf. Mustafa 1977). As Garaudy notes:

> The present success of "structuralism" may be explained both by the fact that it is a *philosophy* which corresponds to the concept of the world emerging, in the middle of the twentieth century, from the development of the whole body of natural and human sciences; and by the fact that there is derived from this concept of the world a *method* of investigation whose applications to the most diverse disciplines have proved to be extremely fruitful – as, for example, cybernetics. Moreover, the fruitfulness of the method is even greater when structuralism and cybernetics effect their conjuction in a dialectical perspective. (Garaudy 1970: 66, original emphasis.)

Furthermore, structuralist methodology, particularly when applied to the study of human societies, eliminates the false opposition between the ontological status of "social facts", and the epistemological foundations of any sociological theory dealing with them. Structuralism is the methodological antithesis of logical atomism and its intrinsic positivism (cf. Russell 1972), since it is not concerned with the problem of *being*, but with *relations*. I have already argued that the application of phenomenological methodology in sociological and anthropological research can yield data which are essentially amendable to both structuralist and Marxist analysis. When Diamond (1974: 95 and *passim*) in an interesting but in many ways misguided critique of Lévi-Strauss, says that the latter "had substantially dismissed phenomenology in *Tristes tropisques*", he is seriously in error. The critical interconnection between structuralist analysis and phenomenology has been admirably demonstrated by Boon (1972) and Lewis (1966), among others. We may also note in passing that Lévi-Strauss dedicated his book, *La pensée sauvage* (1962), to Maurice Merleau-Ponty, and the common ground between structuralism and phenomenology in their mutual relationship to *Gestalt* psychology has frequently been indicated (eg. Hughes 1968: 265, Boon 1972).

This is neither the place nor the time to explore the theoretical complexities between Marxism and structuralism: most of the issues have been raised, if not solved, by Lucien Sebag in his *Marxisme et structuralisme* (1964). Suffice to say here that, despite the hostility of Marxists such as Lefebvre towards Lévi-Strauss' alleged and widely-publicized "anti-historicism", Garaudy's succinct statement upon the issue is the most accurate:

> The prospects opened up to Marxist research by structuralism and cybernetics rule out dogmatic, mechanistic, reifying (*chosistes*) interpretations of materialism, and the equally dogmatic, speculative, theological interpretations of dialectic.
>
> . . . By bringing out valid laws of correlation or development at different levels of the real, from physics to sociology, from biology to aesthetics, the methods of structuralism and cybernetics have given the notion of the "dialectic of nature" put forward by Engels both its most striking confirmation and immense possibilities for research and development. (Garaudy 1970: 71, 73)

Although Lévi-Strauss is perhaps the most famous and controversial proponent of modern structuralism – and the present analysis is largely indebted to his work – he is not the only structuralist theoretician. Althusser's "re-readings" of Marx (Althusser 1969, Althusser and Balibar 1970) owe a great deal to structuralist methodology, as does Lucien Goldmann's penetrating Marxist critique of Racine and Pascal (1964). Peter Caws is correct when he states:

> The founding father [of structuralism] is generally agreed to be Lévi-Strauss, but there are at least four other people who occupy essentially independent positions, namely, Jacques Lacan, Louis Althusser, Barthes, and Michel Foucault (1968: 76)

Although Lévi-Strauss firmly denies any connection between his own work and that of , say, Foucault.[3]

The "debate" between Lévi-Strauss' "dialectical anthropology" and Jean-Paul Sartre's historical materialism is *not* representative of either structuralist views on history or Marxist views on structuralism (Sartre 1960, Lévi-Strauss 1966: 245-69 and *passim*). Much of what antagonizes some Marxists in structuralism has been shown by Garaudy (1970: 73-5) to be somewhat idiosyncratic in the work of Lévi-Strauss, rather than an integral element in structuralist methodology itself, although Garaudy may over-simplify to some extent. Lévi-Strauss (e.g. 1963: 324-45, 367 and *passim*) himself has certainly gone far in reconciling his views with Marxist criticisms, in that he considers structuralist and Marxist methodologies as complementary.

Perhaps the clinching argument in all this debate, in support of the essential complementarity and compatability of Marxism and structuralism, is provided by Maurice Godelier's brilliant article, "Système, structure, et contradiction dans *Le capital*" (1966/1972). Having noted that, "When Marx assumes that structure is not to be confused with visible relations and explains their hidden logic, he inaugurates the modern structuralist tradition". Godelier (1972: 338) goes on to demonstrate in a most convincing way how Lévi-Strauss' analysis of the Murngin kinship system (1949: 216-46 [1969: 168-96]) and his overall concept of social structure (Lévi Strauss 1963: 277-323) are essentially comparable methodologically with historical materialism. Furthermore, Godelier demolishes the accusation of anti-historicism levelled against Lévi-Strauss:

> This brief comparison between Marx and modern structuralism . . . has allowed me to isolate in Lévi-Strauss' practice two principles of structural analysis: the first, that structure is a part of reality, but not of visible relations; the second, that the study of the internal functioning of a structure must precede and illuminate the study of its genesis and evolution. I have already shown that the first principle can be found in Marx. I shall now go on to show that the architecture of *Capital* cannot be understood without the second. (Godelier 1972d: 342-3)

But perhaps the part of Godelier's argument that is the most strikingly relevant to the present analysis is his concluding discussion of the nature and role of kinship relationships in societies with a relatively low level in the development of productive forces. The problem is, "How, within Marx's perspectives, can we understand both the *dominant role* of kinship and the *determinant* role of the economy in the last instance?"[4] Godelier concludes that a solution to this problem is impossible "if economy and kinship are treated as base and superstructure". He concludes:

> In an archaic society kinship relations *function* as relations of production, just as they function as political relations. To use Marx's vocabulary, kinship relations are here *both* infrastructure and superstructure and it would be a fair guess that the complexity of kinship relations in archaic societies relates to the multiple functions they take on in such societies. It could also be suggested that the dominant role and complex structure of kinship relations in archaic societies are related to the general structure of productive forces and their low level of development, which impose the co-operation of individuals and therefore group life for subsistence and reproduction. (Godelier 1972: 364-5, original emphasis)

Lévi-Strauss (1949: 48 [1969:38]) makes precisely the same point in *Les structures élémentaires*.

It will be seen that, in Ilparakuyo society, not only do *kinship* relations "function" as relations of production, but also *age-set* (and associated ritual and symbolic) relations do so too. If it can be argued that this is an unwarrantable transformation of an argument about kinship relations to other kinds of relations (namely, age-sets), I must counter in turn with an essentially Lévi-Straussian argument. Ilparakuyo belong historically and culturally to the eastern (or southern) Nilotic peoples of eastern Africa, as do, of course, the pastoral Maasai. In a critical comparative study of social structure and stratification amongst some Nilotic peoples, Southall states that

> Eastern Nilotic age organization is particularly compatible with elaborate complementary symbolic identifications, usually dichotomous, which do not appear with the same elaboration among most of the western Nilotes . . . It would seem that there is a fundamental structural explanation. Where segmentary lineage organization is the major organizational principle [western Nilotes], there is no need for an elaborate structure of cross-cutting symbolic oppositions and identifications. Not only is there no need, but there is *nothing in the system likely to give rise to them*. (Southall 1970: 32, my emphasis)

Hence, at similar levels of the forces of production, where kinship relations, for various ecological, demographic, and technological reasons, do not "function as relations of production", age organization and symbolic dual organization do. Southall concludes, "We do not therefore argue that age organization and segmentary lineage structure are incompatible, but the full and *dominant* development of the one is incompatible with the other" (Southall 1970: 34, my emphasis)

This preliminary excursion into structuralist and Marxist "anthropologies" and their interconnections in what follows has been necessary because developments in the latter as seen, for example, in the work of Meillassoux, Godelier, Terray, and Bonte, demand a statement of the assumptions upon which any contemporary anthropological and sociological analyses are based. With these issues in mind, I now turn to my analysis of the structure of *olpul* and *entoroj* among Ilparakuyo.

II

Ilparakuyo today live in a series of relatively small communities, or "concentrations" of large homestead groups (*inkang'itie*), scattered amongst the various Bantu-speaking (and other) cultivators and semi-pastoralists (Beidelman 1960: 270ff). Their "diaspora" stretches from Upare in the north and east, down through Handeni, Morogoro, west Bagamoyo, Dodoma, Iringa, and into Mbeya Region in the south and west, to which they have been moving in considerable numbers in the past few years. They consider themselves as a rather loosely-organized "section" (*oloho*) of the pastoral Maasai; but they do not identify themselves as Ilmaasai "proper", except in relation to "outsiders (*ilmeek*, sing. *olmegi*).

They are subdivided internally into a number of named territorial sections (also *ilohon*, sing. *oloho*),[5] amongst which there is a great deal of individual movement back and forth, and, to a lesser extent and over larger periods of time, residential mobility. In the latter case, fairly large groups of related homesteads tend to move from and to the same areas, although not necessarily at exactly the same time.

The most relevant internal divisions for our present purposes are: *oloho o'nyokie*, "the red earth" (Lugoba, west Bagamoyo); *oloho o'sinyai*, "sandy area" (Chamakweza, cf. Ndagala 1974: 11 and *passim*); *oloho le sekenkei*, "the iron section" (area along the Dar es Saalam – Morogoro railway line); *oloho lo'ladoe*, "the place of the Wadoe people" (to the north of Bagamoyo District); *oloho le'kapirore* (the Handeni area); and *oloho le'muasuni* (the section of Tanga Region). All these divisions are relative. For example, Ilparakuyo of Kibirashe (between Handeni and Kibaya) call all Ilparakuyo living in Bagamoyo "The Doe section" (*oloho lo'ladoe*), while we call them indiscriminately *oloho le'kapirore*, when they make internal distinctions among themselves.

The separation of Ilparakuyo from the other Maasai sections seems to date from mutually hostile relations in the late 18th and early 19th Centuries; other evidence points to their earlier intrusions into many of the areas now occupied by them (see Chapter 4). Thomson notes, "The original home of the Wakwafi [i.e. Ilparakuyo] was the large district lying between Kilimanjaro (Ugono, and the Pare in the west, and Teita and U-sambara in the east." (1885: 240)

Hence, although Ndagala (1974: 32-3) interprets certain district records as implying that Ilparakuyo of west Bagamoyo entered the district for the first time in about 1936, there is evidence that they were there, perhaps in smaller numbers than at present, much more than a century ago. Given my own evidence from Ugogo (as yet unpublished) and other data, Beidelman's statement appears to me the most accurate:

> Baraguyu have resided in parts of Gogo, Sagara, Kagaru, and Nguu for over half a century. They also occupied areas to the east in relatively early times. In 1837 they were reported to be at Lugoha [Lugoba?] in Bagamoyo District However, mission informants from there insist that no Baraguyu were present in 1917, so we may assume these Baraguyu were driven out during the intervening years. Baraguyu began attempting to re-enter Bagamoyo District at Sadani in the 1930s but were ordered back by the local District Commissioner. They were able to filter in despite this, and at present there is a fairly large Baraguyu population in Bagamoyo District. (Beidelman 1960: 250-1)

I labour this point somewhat for two reasons: a) that a major part of Ndagala's analysis (1974: 32-5) of the relations between Ilparakuyo and the cultivators (Wakwere) in west Bagamoyo is based upon what he considers an evident hostility over the relatively recent intrusion of the successfully pastoralist Ilparakuyo into an area that previously had a relatively flourishing system of cattle ownership and mixed farming, decimated by tsetse fly in 1926; and b) that, rather, the structure of Ilparakuyo pastoralist – Bantu cultivator relations in this area (as one aspect of the following analysis) seems to imply the opposite: an integration of both categories of people in a mode of production in which two *superficially* antagonistic structures in the relations of production are in fact grounded in a complementarity of considerable historical depth. Furthermore, this complementarity is not the same as the relation between "kulaks" and/or "capitalists" and poor peasants, or workers, in a capitalist mode of production, and is therefore not intrinsically exploitative in any sense. If exploitative relations be found, then they originate in the colonial and post-colonial mode of production and the intrusion of peripheral capitalism, not in the "cultivator-host/pastoral-guest" dichotomy used by Ndagala (1974: 32, and *passim*).

In the light of this latter point, Ndagala's statements that "Both peoples have maintained their economic statuses, that is, relative poverty of the Wakwere and relative wealth of the Wakwavi,"[6] and that "Being a minority group in the country with large concentrations of wealth in their hands, the Wakwavi are not only a tribal or an occupational group, but also *a class* of their own". (Ndagala 1974: 20, 21), fall into *historical* perspective. This is because he places the origin of Ilparakuyo – Kwere relations in a much too recent historical period: the colonial epoch; thus he fails to account for the essentially interdependent nature of pastoralist – cultivator relations in such a situation prior to colonial intrusion.[7]

The present analysis is therefore based upon the assumption that the elements of Ilparakuyo – cultivator relations so analysed are a crucial component of both types of society and cannot be understood in their contemporary manifestations unless their interrelationship and historical development, which antedate the colonial political economy, are taken into account (cf. also Monod 1975: 102, 130).

This historical interpretation, as I have noted, places Ilparakuyo in a unique position in terms of their development potential in the context of the overall socialist transformation of agriculture in Tanzania; a position which may be summarized as follows:

a) Ilparakuyo, contrary to Jacobs' view (1965a, 1968: 24-8, and *passim*) are not necessarily and have not been historically the "aggressors" in their relations with cultivators and colonial intruders, and other pastoralists.

b) Their position at present is that of a highly viable, specialized economy *in relation to* their cultivating neighbours, with whom they have (relatively peaceably) coexisted for 150-200 years.

c) They therefore do not suffer from the ultimate "Maasai predicament" (Parkipuny 1975) to the same extent as the pastoral Maasai, of becoming "either/or" something else; they *choose* to be pastoralists in an area quite amenable to, and actually being exploited as, an agricultural regime.

d) Any analysis of their present institutions and social structures must take all of these factors into account. Among their key institutions and structures involved are *olpul* and *entoroj*, not only in terms of Ilparakuyo social structures themselves, but also their interconnections with the other structures in their overall contemporary situation, as it has developed historically.

III

I am not directly concerned here with the ritual and symbolic aspects of *olpul* (pl. *ilpuli*), in the sense of a full-scale analysis; but some of these aspects must appear as an integral part and critically important element in the ensuing analysis. My strategy is first to describe rather crudely the salient points of *olpul*, since little is known about it even upon the descriptive level, from the available literature (but see Jacobs 1958: 7, 9, 1965 *passim*; cf. Gramly 1975: 110; Hollis 1905: 292). Almost all the material available on *olpul*, moreover, relates to pastoral Maasai;[8] *olpul* among Ilparakuyo, while sharing many of the overall characteristics of Maasai *ilpuli*, has some quite distinctive features, especially in relation to associated structures. Nevertheless, its basic functional importance *vis-à-vis* the age organization is essentially the same as for the Maasai, and comparative material from the latter will be used throughout. On the symbolic level, material from other Maasai-speaking groups such as the Isampurr (Samburu) is also relevant.

The term *olpul* means both "a meat feast" and the *place* at which it occurs – as indicated in the proverb quoted at the beginning of this chapter. This identity of place and action is not merely fortuitous: the idea of "place" is quite critical in an interpretation and understanding of the institution in structural terms. Furthermore, the word may be applied to the slaughter of an animal at any time for any purpose, ranging from sacrifice and medicinal slaughter for minor ailments, to meat provided for a woman to "strengthen her" after childbirth, to welcoming certain categories of kin and affines, to major feasts. But the "proper" *olpul* is initiated primarily by the *ilmurran* (young circumcised men) for their own purposes and age set activities, and this is what I shall concentrate upon here.

Contrary to the more bizarre versions of the "cattle complex", the Ilparakuyo attitude to the slaughter of livestock is basically mundane, although it is never done (normatively) for purely subsistence purposes. If it were, the inescapable ritual injunctions surrounding the consumption of meat, in any context, would be inexplicable; it is always "ritual" in one way or another. The core of these injunctions is as follows. No beast may be slaughtered inside the homestead (*enkang'*), or anywhere within eye-range of it (except for a minimal number of circumstances which do not concern us here). No men of the *ilmurran* age-grade ("warriors"), particularly junior *ilmurran*, may eat meat which has even been looked upon by a mature, married women; therefore, no *ilmurran* may eat meat within the homestead. Hollis (1950: 292) states that in "proper" (i.e. full-scale) *ilpuli, ilmurran*, unmarried girls (*intoyie*, sing. *entito*) and lovers (*sanjan*, sing. *esanja*), as well as some unitiated youths (*ilayiok*) and servants (*isingan*, sing. *osinga*) may attend. They are often accompanied by senior elders who act as ritual advisors and tutors during the sometimes extended stay (two or three months) at *ilpuli*.[9] Again, in "proper" *ilpuli*, the "fathers" (*iloomenye*) of the *ilmurran* are not allowed to be present, although on many occasions now they do attend. This is largely because they realize that in effect, they are the ones providing the beasts for slaughter.

However, I have evidence of two kinds, both from experience and normative statements, that "fathers" are still usually not allowed at *ilpuli* of the *ilmurran*. The first is that in a description of one such "proper" *olpul*, an *olmurrani* told me, "On the second day of our *olpul*, we ate a good deal of meat boiled with medicines, which those who do not have *olpul* [*iltung'anak le'metii olpul*] such as fathers [*iloomenye*], who do not eat *olpul* meat, cannot." The second is that, when we were approaching the place of one proper *olpul* one day, in fact upon its final night, and at which *ilmurran* and *intoyie* from miles around had participated, the father of the *olmurrani* I was with was told to go home, while we went on. At this *olpul*, a retired elder was present in a ritual and tutorship capacity, and I (whose age-grade was "senior warrior") was allowed to attend.

The importance of these two injunctions is mentioned here, although their full implications will be seen later. The *ilmurran* holding the *olpul* were "junior warriors," their fathers (by integration of alternate age-sets into adjacent generations) would be junior elders or senior elders, and hence their *olpiron* ("fire-stick") elders. Thus, fathers and sons are on *one side* of the dual arrangement of alternative generations: they "belong together" (cf. Beidelman 1968: 81). Yet, paradoxically, they *cannot* attend "proper" *ilpuli* together.

Great quantities of meat, fat, soups, and medicines are consumed at *ilpuli*, which are carried out in remote, thickly forested areas where strangers, or persons in the categories not allowed to attend, are unlikely to stumble upon the feast. Shelters are constructed, both for the meat and the participants, by the *ilmurran* and the young girls, and the order of slaughter of the beasts is decided upon. This order is important, although the details of it do not concern us here. The *ilmurran* who have "provided" the beasts, which ideally should be cattle but may be goats or sheep, have a special place in the proceedings. The *olmurrani* who supplies an ox, rather than small stock, at *olpul* certainly enhances his own status, as well as that of his father, his homestead, and other close agnatic and matrilateral relatives.[10]

As the meat is consumed in greater quantities, mixed with a wide range of medicines, the *ilmurran* begin to sing "songs of *olpul*", especially the *enkipolosa* (. . . *netii osinkolio le'nkiri oji enkipolosa*), which induce trance and shaking (*enkigoroto*, from *agor*, "to strangle", or *aigor*, "to groan"; cf. *apush*: "to shake") and "violent" behaviour, a desirable state to be in before battle. (Cf. Mpaayei 1954: 53; Spencer 1965: 263-70; above, Chapter 2.) *Enkipolosa* may not be sung in or near the homesteads. The behaviour of *ilmurran* at an *olpul* was well described to me by one *olmurrani*:

> At *olpul*, when some *ilmurran* have eaten much meat and drunk much medicine [*ilkeek*, sing. *olcani*: lit. "shrubs", "trees", "wood"] they may sing *enkipolosa* . . . At any rate, each morning of *olpul*, about dawn, two *ilmurran* leave the *olpul*, go into the bush, and begin to sing the loud, sometimes plaintive, but violent, *enkipolosa*. Sometimes, an *olmurrani* who has eaten a lot of meat and medicine becomes "anti-social". He no longer wants to talk with people; he may take his sticks and knife, go off into the bush, and sleep alone and in silence. He does not like to hear noise, like laughter; he just wants silence and to be alone.

In the past, the *olpul* was associated with the warrior camps (*imanyat*, sing. *emanyata*) where *ilmurran* trained and prepared for war and raiding. Ilparakuyo no longer hold *imanyat*, and the *ilpuli* have taken over many of the functions of them. One retired elder told me, "the things to do with our religious customs which used to come at *emanyata* have now come to *ilpuli*". Thus, apart from eating, singing, and making love, *ilpuli* are used for building up the physical and emotional "strength" of the *ilmurran*, in practise in wrestling, discourse, and argument. Retired elders often attend and impart esoteric knowledge to the *ilmurran* concerning the law, medicines for various purposes, and so on. Gramly concludes from his investigations of 19th Century Kenya Maasai *ilpuli* sites that "warriors might take the opportunity to renew pigment dressings on their bodies and weapons, and excess pigment would be wiped in linear designs on the walls and ceilings of rock-shelters. Ornaments may be repaired and redesigned."

(Gramly 1975). There is also considerable evidence that bone and wood artefacts and ornaments were fashioned at *ilpuli* by pastoral Maasai.

But *ilpuli* in themselves are, and have always been, essential for the following reasons: before a circumcised youth becomes a "full warrior" (*olmurrani*), he must contribute a "first" beast at *olpul*, "which gives him *entoroj*" (. . . *enkiteng' neterie entoroj*, lit – " . . . it is the cow that 'begins' *entoroj*"). Until he does so, he cannot attain *entoroj*, and therefore cannot transfer fully from the status of circumcised initiate (*osipolioi*, pl. *isipolio*) who is, in Jacobs' words, "95% a full warrior", to that of *olmurrani*.[11] Even now, as a new but fully-fledged *olmurrani*, he should correctly be referred to as *olkiliai* pl. *ilkiliani*) (cf. Kulet 1972: 138 and *passim*). Within each age-set, and particularly apparent during the period of junior warriorhood, there arise three subsets: *ilcang'enopir* (sing. *olcang'enopiro*), "seniors"; *ilparing'otua* (sing. *olparing'otuani*), "middles"; and *ilkerimbuot* (sing. *olkerimbuoti*), "juniors". The fourth subset mentioned by Fosbrooke (1948) and Huntingford (1953: 119) does not occur among Ilparakuyo. The significance of these subsets is not quite clear as yet, but I have on occasion observed considerable tensions amongst their various members within one age-set, occasionally resulting in violence.

Once a youth has qualified by contributing to an *olpul*, the full force of sanctions concerning meat-eating apply to him: he now has achieved *entoroj*. This means that he may never eat alone, or drink milk alone – he must be with at least one other age-mate. He cannot eat meat anywhere near or in the homestead; and he is free to claim full rights of hospitality from every member of his age-set. He must share everything, including his most prized possesions including watches, radios, bicycles, etc.), with his age-mates, and never deny them anything within the normal bounds of reason, no matter where they come from. Most of the positive injunctions of *entoroj* last a lifetime, even when the individual reaches senior elderhood; but the negative prohibitions tend to fall away gradually. Elders can eat meat freely in all homesteads, but do not usually eat alone; they may, however, eat without the presence of an age-mate.

During *olpul*, youths and other participants do not eat or drink anything except meat, fat, soups, medicines, and blood. For the preparation of these items, pots or other cooking utensils are brought to the *olpul* site by those helping, and considerable quantities of firewood and water are also required each day. At some Ilparakuyo *ilpuli*, these tasks may be performed by neighbours who are Bantu cultivators, and who expect a gift of "meat which is not *olpul* meat", known as *enkelehe*; they usually received these in quite considerable quantities. Meat is also sometimes sent back to the homesteads (*inkang'itie*) for the women, children, and other elders, although this is not usual at "proper" *ilpuli* in remote forest areas.

Thus, throughout the sometimes extended periods of *olpul*, the theme is the *separation* from the community of the main participants. They are, in a sense "wild", associated with "nature", danger, bravery, and death. The theme of separation is strongly underlined at the end of a "proper" *olpul*, when the participants return to the community.

Before *olpul* is closed, word is sent to the homesteads of all those concerned to prepare the *mutai* feasts with which they are welcomed back. A final broth is made with special medicines (*lowuni*) and special songs are sung (*oloipirri*).

The site is abandoned and the fire extinguished as the sun is setting; but the *olpul* site is never destroyed. The skin (*olconi*) of each beast precedes the party to each *enkang'* from whence it came, and the returning party sing the violent *enkipolosa* as close as they dare to the homesteads, it being desirable that the *ilmurran* should arrive nearby – at least – in a shaking trace. The *ilmurran* drink blood extracted from the neck of an animal to "purify" themselves before entering the *mutai* feast.

Mutai is composed of "normal" food, of milk, maize, *ugali*, and vegetables: all foods that the *ilmurran* can eat "normally" at home. The *mutai* feast reincorporates each *olmurrani* into his homestead, and *must* be prepared for each one since they all must return eventually to their own homesteads, without exception (*metii ole'melo inkang'itie*). The *olpul* is over, the participants reabsorbed, some of them in their full new status, into the community.

IV

Despite the apparent complexity that emerges from this description of *olpul*, much has been omitted. For example, no reference has been made to colour symbolism (particularly red and black, but also white), which plays such an enormous role in all Ilparakuyo (and pastoral Maasai) ritual action. There is neither space nor time to expand upon these matters in any detail here. But in order to begin to understand the complexity of issues involved in Ilparakuyo *ilpuli*, with the associated concepts of *entoroj*, *mutai* and others, I must note some basic features of Ilparakuyo symbolic categories.

I have already hinted at the prevalence of dual symbolic classification among the eastern and southern Nilotes (cf. Southall 1970: 31-6, Nagashima 1966: 60-2, and *passim*). This is certainly true of Ilparakuyo and all Maasai-speaking peoples. Hence, Beidelman notes, and I entirely agree with him:

> The most basic feature of Baraguyu society . . . is the profoundly dualistic nature of Baraguyu social organization and its related ideology. To some extent, such features characterize all societies and all processes by which idea systems are constructed, but this seems . . . particularly well-developed within this society. Here I refer to the distinctions between spheres of God and creation, between Baraguyu and outsiders, society (camp) and nature (bush), and men and women . . . More specifically, there are dual oppositions within the three major types of social units from which Baraguyu society is formed: clans, polygynous families, and age-sets. (Beidelman 1968: 80-1)

That such dualistic structures and categories are common to all Maasai groups can easily be ascertained (cf. Huntingford 1953: 120 and *passim*; for the Arusha [Ilarusa], Gulliver 1961, 1963: 110-40, but see note pp. 144-6; for Samburu, Fratkin 1974; etc.).

In order to reveal the "real structures" that underlie the apparently arbitrary injunctions and prohibitions of *olpul* and *entoroj*, and how these relate to the structure and co-operation and interdependence both amongst Ilparakuyo themselves, and between them and others, we must examine some of these dualistic categories and notions. (See Figure 1.)

The first and most obvious is that *olpul*, as a totality in itself, represents "bush", or "nature" in its quite explicit connotations of *a place*. *Mutai*, on the other hand, is "homestead", or "culture". Thus, *olpul:mutai* – nature:culture. Furthermore, *ilmurran* (warriors) are themselves also on the fringes of the structure of political relations: they are not really a part of that structure until *eunoto*, which makes them senior warriors, and not "in power" until *olng'eher*, which makes them junior elders (Jacobs, 1958, 1965a). But the *ilmurran* are in fact in the process of "creating" the ethos of "community", by establishing the principle of reciprocity amongst themselves (*entoroj*), which cuts across the lines of descent. This is symbolically and structurally true in a very literal sense: youths are not a part of society, have no rights in the political or symbolic domains, in what could be called the "public domain", until they are circumcised. This act, which is performed individually in each homestead, takes them 95% of the way, since they are for the period of curing *isipolio*, who wear women's clothes and possess blunted weapons. They still have no sense of community. It is *olpul* that gives them that sense of community by *creating* its principle of *entoroj*, of sharing everything as equals in a world of love and emotion. *Entoroj*, however, is only the beginnings of community, it is not yet "structure" – it is not authority in a system of "ordered relations between structures". This comes only after two steps: *eunoto* and *olng'eher*. Thus: warriors:elders – community:authority. The first linked series of oppositions may be expressed as follows: *olpul*: *mutai*;[12] roasting:boiling; *ilmurran* (warriors): *ilmoruak* (elders); *intoyie* (unmarried girls): *inkituaak* (married women); nature (bush):culture (homestead); community:hierarchical authority.

However, the age-set system is also divided into a dual system by the identification of alternate age-sets by the *olpiron* (fire-stick) link. When a youth is circumcised, a new fire is lighted with fire-sticks on the spot in the cattle-byre where the operation took place, by an elder in his father's age-set, and involves the use of particular medicine (*olokorr*) for the youth's recovery, success, and virility. Through this system, the age-grades of Ilparakuyo society are polarized into perpetual dual organization (cf. Beidelman 1968: 91), the vertical line being maintained by descent (father/son) and the ritual *olpiron* link ("fire-stick elder/fire-stick junior"), the horizontal line being based upon the distinctions between age-grades, elders/warriors, seniors/juniors.

Figure 1: Ilparakuyo Symbolic Categories

1)	warriors: elders – community	:	authority
2)	olpul	:	mutai
	roasting	:	boiling
	ilmurran	:	ilmoruak
	(warriors)		(elders)
	intoyie	:	Inkituaak
	(unmarried		(married
	girls)		women)
	nature	:	culture
	(bush)		(homestead)
	community	:	hierarchical authority
3)	junior elders		senior elders
	junior warriors		senior warriors
4)	olpul	:	mutai
	son	:	father
	olpiron junior	:	olpiron senior
	nature	:	culture
5)	mother	:	father
	matrilateral	:	agnatic
	and affinal kin		kin
	red	:	black
	women	:	men
	female	:	male
6)	juniors	:	elders
	community	:	authority
	non-Ilparakuyo	:	Ilparakuyo

The junior *ilmurran*, whose business is primarily *olpul* and who also have the greatest stake in it, cannot invite their "fathers" (*olpiron* elders), since it is the latter who represent the tenuous link the *ilmurran* have with the hierarchial authority of the political structure, and who will eventually sponsor their entry into it. If the *olpiron* elders/fathers come to the "same side" of the opposition as their sons/*olpiron* juniors, the link which transforms the status of the latter into full, authoritative membership of Ilparakuyo politico-economic structure is broken, and the system collapses ("symbolically"). Thus: *olpiron* elder:*olpiron* junior: –

authority: community – culture:nature. In other words: *olpul:mutai* – son:-father; *olpiron* (warrior):*olpiron* (elder) – nature:culture. Similarly, if a junior *olmurrani* eats meat in the homestead, he is "behaving like an elder", and also destroying the opposition between structural components in the complementarity between them; and so on.

It is here that the link between the age-set system and that of descent and kinship is also established, as well as the symbolic opposition between men and women. All Ilparakuyo (and pastoral Maasai) clans (*enkishomi*, pl. *inkishomitie*) are ultimately grouped into two major categories of "moeities":[13] *iloorokiteng'*, "those of the black ox", senior, "greater", right hand; and *iloodomong'i*, "those of the red oxen", junior, "lesser", left hand (cf. Beidelman 1960: 260; Sankan 1971: 1-7; Huntingford 1953: 120; Gulliver 1961, 1963).[14] This dichotomy is present at all levels of agnatic descent categories, each *enkishomi* (clan) being subdivided equally into two "subclans" (*ilgilat*, sing. *olgilata*, lit. "room"), one black and superior, the other red and inferior.

Finally, all these distinctions in agnatic descent categories are thought of as originating in the structure of the polygynous family. Every mature married man has at least one "gate" (*enkishomi*) into his cattle byre, whether he shares a homestead (*enkang'*) with another mature married man or not. Wives, in order of marriage (modified by their procreative history) are divided into "those of the right hand" (*olpahe le'tatene*) and "those of the left hand" (*olpahe le'kedyianye*), and normally reside upon the right (senior) or left (junior) side of the husband's gate, facing in. (The Maasai term for similar divisions is *entaloishi*, which has a somewhat similar connotation in Ilparakuyo, but not the same as suggested by Jacobs [1970: 28].) The agnatic group created by the marriage of one man is subdivided by the affiliation of each mother; and, as Jacobs points out for the pastoral Maasai, Ilparakuyo value more, *in actual practice*, their matrilateral and affinal relations than those created by agnatic descent, in terms of the community at large.

Thus, starting from the "top down", the symbolic duality between black and red coincides with the dualities between right and left, male and female, patrifiliation and matrifiliation, from the "bottom up". A further series of oppositions may thus be added: mother:father; matrilateral kin and affinal kin:agnatic kin; red:black; left hand: right hand; women:men; female: male.

The interconnections amongst these sub-sets of symbolic and structural oppositions must by now be apparent, for one or more are replicated in each series, linking them together in an overall series of dual classifications. I may add one final subset for the purposes of summarizing the present discussion: juniors:elders; community: authority; non-Ilparakuyo:Ilparakuyo.

There is one final link in the present chain; how do we connect the idea of Ilparakuyo relations with non-Ilparakuyo to the initial opposition between *olpul* and "*non-olpul*"? To establish this link, one further question must be asked: what are the "mediators" in each of these sets of oppositions? What are the elements that *do* bridge the otherwise symbolically "impossible" contradiction? There are several of these mediating elements, the most important of which are, for present purposes: cattle, fire, cooking itself, and, therefore, *olpul*.

Cattle (and by extension, other domestic livestock as well) are at the centre of *olpul*: their products are literally the "stuff" of the "means" of communication in the creation of *entoroj*, and hence the Ilparakuyo community based upon descent relations and age organization. Ilparakuyo and other pastoral Maasai myths and legends tell of the origin of the earth, men, cattle, and grass (cf. Hollis 1905: 266-9; 270-1; Beidelman 1968: 86-8). Cattle originate "in the bush", but become the symbol of community: they provide a mythical mediator between nature and culture, by providing the context of the creation of the latter from certain elements of the former, with the help of the activities of a creator-god. But the *Iltorrobo* (sing. *Oltorroboni,* "the Dorobo") are also instrumental in the transition, for they are the first to "discover" cattle but lose them through their ineptitude in such matters. Morever, the "Bantu" cultivators are also related to Ilparakuyo (and Maasai) by myth, again losing their real wealth in cattle through their greed (Hollis 1905: 272-3). And, indeed, the Bantu are the descendents (called *Ilmeek*) of the "elder brother" (*olayioni lenye botor*) of the "original family". Thus Ilparakuyo (Maasai) not only become the *owners* of cattle as descendents of the younger brother (*oloti*), they also became the *providers* of pastoral products, without which neither community could survive satisfactorily. And these pastoral products became the means of "communicating", of mediating, between the Ilparakuyo and the non-pastoralists, the Maasai and the non-Maasai communities.

The Iltorrobo are still considered essential by Ilparakuyo for the continued existence of their community, primarily for the critical ritual services they provide in such ceremonies as circumcision, but also for information about the "bush" – good grazing, water resources during times of drought and trouble, as well as for honey for beer-making (*enaiho*, essential for all rituals) and the material goods such as pottery, metal implements, and medicines (cf. Jacobs 1975: 407). Thus, the "creation of community" through mediating nature/culture is a two-way process, continuous in nature, and non-Ilparakuyo (non-Maasai) are essential to this process.

Finally, Iltorrobo are mythically associated with the origin of fire through the use of fire-sticks (*olpiron*), one of which is male, the other female, as well as for cooking (Beidelman 1968: 888). Thus, "affinity" and the organization of the age-set system into dual categories of "fire-stick seniors/juniors" is encapsulated in Ilparakuyo symbolism and mythology, and is also connected thereby to Ilparakuyo/non-Ilparakuyo relations.[15]

V

I have tried to demonstrate the *olpul/mutai* complex, and the condition and status of *entoroj*, lie not only at the heart of social structures, but also symbolically represent for Ilparakuyo the context of their historical inter-dependence of relations with non-Ilparakuyo (non-Maasai) in a broader, total social formation. For Ilparakuyo, they certainly do not mean or repre-sent exploitative relations of any kind; rather, they creatively represent rela-tions of interdependence. My argument no doubt needs further substantiation than is possible here. But the crux of my argument is that it is *through* these institutions that relations between what could otherwise be considered essentially hostile and antagonistic structures are mediated. If these rela-tions are exploitative in the current political economy of Ilparakuyo and the religious and symbolic structures involved have been transformed into such exploitative relations both within and without the community (cf. Bonte 1975), they are the result of the colonial political economy, and do not have roots in an aggressive and exploitative pre-colonial, pre-capitalist situation.

That this transformation into exploitative relations has actually occurred is still a matter of research and has not yet been demonstrated, although it is suggested as the essential element by Ndagala (1974). But even if it is so established, without the historical generation and transforma-tion of structural relations which I have suggested here, any remedial action which may be taken for the benefit of the whole social formation of these areas, in particular west Bagamoyo, in which pastoralists coexist with cultivators, will be doomed to failure. The understanding and meaning of *olpul* and *entoroj* among Ilparakuyo, and the relations between these struc-tures and others within the Ilparakuyo community and between Ilparakuyo and non-Ilparakuyo, appear to me to be central to any such exercise. From the evidence presented here, it may well be argued that, even from the cultivators' (Wakwere) point of view, as they have so little interest in the acquisition and control of livestock, they accept the "division of labour" and the accompanying dualities and reciprocities which have such deep his-torical roots, in their relations with Ilparakuyo. But this has to be argued by someone else in another context. At any rate, I think the evidence supports the idea that this "division of labour" within an overall mode of production has very deep historical roots which pre-date considerably the advent of a colonial exploitative system, which demanded different forms of commit-ment to petty commodity relations from the two communities.

Notes

1. The Maasai word *entoroj* should correctly be spelled *enturuj*, where *u* repre-sents an open vowel (Tucker & Mpaayei 1955; xiv), very far from a high fron-tal *u*, which also exists in the language. I have therefore written *o* throughout. (This analysis was written in 1976.)
2. Ndagala's study (1974), as yet unpublished, deals with the several aspects of the political economy of the Ilparakuyo (for whom he uses the coastal Bantu term *Wakwavi*) during the late colonial period and the post-colonial situation up to 1973.

3. Caws 1968: 76. It is interesting to note that both structuralist and Marxist anthropologies, including Marx and Engels themselves, claim inspiration from the work of L.H. Morgan, structuralism largely from Morgan's *Systems of Consanguinity and Affinity* (1870; cf. Lévi-Strauss 1949), Marxism from his *Ancient Society* (1877, see e.g. Engels 1884, in Marx and Engels, 1970: 191-334; cf. Krader 1972). Terray (1972: 89 and *passim*) attempts to demonstrate that a Marxist reading of Morgan is "more profound" than a structuralist one; but he does not address himself to the question as to why both readings are possible, and (more importantly) *not incompatible*.

4. This is somewhat similar to Terray's development of an Althusscrian position in his exegesis of Meillassoux's work (Terray 1972). However, Godelier's reading of Lévi-Strauss is far deeper than Terray's, and it is significant that the latter makes no mention of Godelier's article.

5. This word would be pronounced *olosho* in more northern sections of Kenya Maasai and northern Tanzania. However, the Ilparakuyo pronunciation is very similar to that of the southern Ilkisonko with whom they intermarry and intermingle a great deal.

6. He adds, significantly, "*Of late*, the Wakwere are being employed by the Wakwavi on various tasks" (my emphasis).

7. Beidelman amply demonstrates the complementarity rather than the exploitative nature of Ilparakuyo – Bantu relations. He may sound tentative when he says (1960: 255), "Whatever the case in the past, Baraguyo at present *cannot* live on the products of their stock alone" (cf. Beidelman 1961a, 1961b), but he is essentially accurate, in my opinion.

8. Except probably Hollis, cf. Beidelman 1968: 79.

9. I have never seen *intoyie* at meat feasts but they join the "warriors" for the *mutai* period after the feast; this is also true for the Ilpurko section of Kenya Maasai. Hollis mentions that "mothers" (*noong'otonye*) can attend; this is not possible for "proper" *olpul* among Ilparakuyo, and may be an error, unless they represent women beyond the menopause.

10. In his excavations of pastoral Maasai *olpul* sites, in caves and rock-shelters in Kenya, dating from the 19th Century, Gramly (1975: 117) notes that the bone remains indicate the predominant slaughter of cattle over that of goats and sheep. He adds, "This is exactly the reverse of what one might expect to see in the midden of a modern, open air pastoral Maasai settlement where ovicaprid bones are in the greatest number."

11. Female initiates are also called *isipolio* (sing. *esipolioi*) during their period of "curing". Jacobs notes that for the Maasai youth

    > wanderings of *isipolio*-hood are shortlived; with the new restrictions on eating, he is commonly invited [to] and eager to participate in the private meat-feasts (*olpul*) of his junior warrior age mates which are held secretly in isolated bush. He is usually invited to his first *olpul* by his age-mates of the preceding circumcision seasons, while his second *olpul* is occasioned by his sharing meat with them. He brings a goat which is slaughtered and eaten by all, but not before he is washed in the blood of the goat by the entire gathering. He is now considered 100% warrior and proceeds to act the part." (Jacobs 1958: 7)

12. Although some meat, fats, and soups are boiled at *olpul*, this basic opposition

is still present, as women cook in the homesteads (normally) by boiling; men cook in the bush (normally) by roasting. *Olpul* itself, therefore, is in a sense a "mediator" between the two modes of preparation (see below).

13. I put the term "moieties" in quotation marks, because they are not strictly exogamous categories at this level, although the *principle* as operating at lower levels of descent influences the rules of exogamy. (See Jacobs 1970, for Maasai, who use a somewhat different terminology).

14. By perhaps what is a typographical error, Beidelman (1960: 260) reverses the terms, calling *iloodomong'i* "black" and *iloorokiteng'* "red". The Samburu categories are "those of the black cattle" (*ilorrokishu*) and "those of the white cattle" (*ilooiborkishu*): cf. Huntingford 1953: 120.

15. Gramly's investigations of 19th Century Kenya pastoral Maasai *olpul* sites shows that *ilpuli* took place in "boundary" or "marginal" areas, *between* Maasai country proper and the areas of non-Maasai, such as Kamba and Kikuyu. This added dimension of the intermediacy of "place" in *ilpuli* in Maasai – Bantu relations strengthens my overall analysis, although since Ilparakuyo have lived in interstitial "pockets" with the Bantu, any such clear-cut spatial symbolism cannot be established further for them.

4. History and Time

> "*Iyiolo ening'uaa, kake miyiolo enilo.*"
> "You know from whence you come, but not where you are going."
> "*Meisho ilimot; inkulie ebaya*"
> "When events occur, only part of the truth is made known" – lit. "All the news is not told; others merely arrive there."

In a manner somewhat unusual in anthropological discourse, most writers on the Maa-speaking peoples of Tanzania and Kenya include in their works an early section or chapter on what is often called "Maasai traditional history". For example, in his pioneering work on "An Administrative Survey of the Maasai Social System", Fosbrooke (1948) devotes a leading and major section to Maasai history and, in a later publication, he deals explicitly with what he calls a "tribal chronology" of the pastoral Maasai (Fosbrooke 1956). Similarly, Beidelman pays considerable attention to the historical connections of the Ilparakuyo (Baraguyu) section of the Maasai peoples of Tanzania in his equally pioneering article, also published in *Tanganyika Notes and Records* (1960).

There is an "ethnographic" reason for this relatively atypical anthropological obsession with Maasai history, and it arises from the dominance of age-set organization amongst most of the Maa-speaking peoples. Al Jacobs, who has done extensive fieldwork among the Maasai over a considerable period of time, has noted that:

> Although the Maasai plan future ceremonial and economic events according to a lunar calendar of thirty days to the month (*olapa*) and twelve months to the year (*olari*), historical events are always reckoned in relation to the age-set (or sets) who were warriors at the time. (1965a: 48)

Fosbrooke also makes his position clear:

> We are fortunate with the Maasai, in having a tribe with an age-group system of regular periodicity, so that it should be possible to get a reasonably

accurate dating of an event if it were only known who were the warriors at the time of its occurence: (1956a: 48)

Other elements also account for this historical focus in Maasai studies, such as the relative importance of the pastoral Maasai and Ilparakuyo in the historiography of East Africa over the past 150 to 200 years; but the dominance of the ethnographic fact has also recently attracted a significant number of historians of various persuasions to do research among the Maa-speaking peoples (eg. Bernsten 1979a, 1979b, forthcoming; Lawren 1968; Waller 1976, 1978; Vossen 1977a, 1977b).

It is evident that there are fairly sound ethnographic reasons for combining a discussion of Maasai notions and concepts of "time", which should ultimately encompass the entire "culture area" of the Maa-speaking peoples, with a consideration of some elements of the history of a specific social function within the wider field, i.e. the Ilparakuyo. But I have selected a historical approach to the problem of "time" among Ilparakuyo and Maasai for other than merely ethnographic considerations; given the theoretical position I adopt, it could scarcely have been any other. It will become clear as we proceed that the theoretical problematic I propose has not been employed at the expense of ethnographic detail and historical investigation, but arises out of a perception of the latter as being ultimately the same thing.

In order to arrive at a satisfactory theoretical starting-point, I first outline briefly what may be called some of the "classical" forms of anthropological investigation into the time reckoning concepts and procedures of what are usually referred to as "other cultures" but I prefer to call pre-capitalist or non-capitalist social formations.

II

The various forms of time reckoning manifested in different cultures and through history, and the relationship between conceptualizations of time and space, have been the subject of an enormous amount of inquiry and speculation (see for example, Thompson 1967; Hall 1959; Alexander 1945). But anthropological studies of the topic may be grouped in four basic (but not exclusive) categories as follows:
a) the approach of "abstract mentalism", which must not be confused with psychological or psychologistic paradigms;
b) the "abstract empiricist" approach, characteristic of functional analysis;
c) overlapping closely with b), but distinct from it, the approach of "structuralist totality";
d) what may be called the "philosophical-theological" approach, characteristic of some recent writings on African (and other "non-western") philosophy.

The first, which I have termed "abstract mentalism" in the strict sense of "pertaining to the effects of mental activity", is most clearly foreshadowed in the work of Lucien Lévy-Bruhl, with his literally voluminous exposition of what he called "primitive mentality" or the "mental functions of inferior societies" (1910, 1923, 1938). The objection may be made that his work is discredited and is no longer a force in anthropological thinking and interpretation; but Lévy-Bruhl has been restored to an albeit shadowy place in the pantheon of anthropological ancestors by sympathetic and extensive attention in (amongst others) Evans-Pritchard's *Theories of Primitive Religion* (1965) and, perhaps more significantly, in Rodney Needham's *Belief, Language, and Experience* (1972).[1]

In fact, Lévy-Bruhl's thesis, often unrecognized and unbidden, lurks in many anthropological discussions of concepts of time and other "cosmological" notions in "non-Western" cultures. Although Evans-Pritchard attempts to clear Lévy-Bruhl of both psychologism and racism, successfully in the former, he notes (1965: 88) that "there is no reputable anthropologist who today accepts [the theory] of two distinct types of mentality " – the "civilized" and the "primitive". But despite this, other aspects of Lévy-Bruhl's work apparently still excite the anthropological imagination. As Needham notes:

> there has . . . persisted in the received ideas of social anthropology what can only be regarded as a travesty of Lévy-Bruhl's theory which seems likely to induce others to continue to ignore or belittle him.
> . . . Yet one need do no more than read carefully what he actually wrote in order to see the degree of justice in Mary Douglas's judgement [in *Purity and Danger*, 1966] that "it was he who first posed all the important questions about primitive cultures and their distinctiveness as a class," and to agree with her expostulation that "he has not deserved such neglect". (1972: 161)

What *did* Lévy-Bruhl say about concepts of time, and how are they still lurking about, albeit in ghostly and unjustly maligned form? At the end of his book on "primitive mentality", he sums up his findings as follows:

> The primitives' idea of time, which above all is *qualitative*, remains vague; and nearly all primitive languages are as deficient in methods of rendering the relations of time as they are copious in expressing spatial relations. Frequently a future event, if considered certain to happen, and if provocative of great emotion, is felt to be already present. (1923: 445-6)

Although Lévy-Bruhl is clearly trying here to establish an important, socially determined, distinction between "his own" conception of time and that of "primitives", he cannot possibly account for the causes of it because he a) adheres to the "classical" but idealistically erroneous notion that "behaviour is a product of thought" (cf. Evans-Pritchard 1965: 98); and b) is unaware that he is making an implicit comparison with another historically and socially determined notion of time: his own. The final part of his statement concerning the conceptualization of future events has, unfortunately, entered into anthropological and philosophical discourse on concepts of time, causing serious errors.

Quite clearly, Lévy-Bruhl's conclusion about "primitive time" involves an unstated epistemological assumption about something else, which we assume is some form of "civilized time". And sure enough, here it is:

> Primitives do not see, extending indefinitely in imagination, something like a straight line, always homogeneous by nature, upon which events fall into position, a line on which foresight can arrange them in a unilinear and irreversible series, and on which they must of necessity occur one after the other. To the primitive time is not, as it is to us, a kind of intellectualized intuition, an 'order of succession.' Still less is it a homogeneous quality. It is felt as a quality, rather than represented. (1923: 123-4)

It is the latter point that is taken up so strongly by Needham. He writes (1972: 8) that Lévy-Bruhl was the first in the "anthropological tradition" to inspire in him "as a comparative problem, though with another intent, the question of the line of demarcation between belief and experience". Elsewhere, Needham concludes – and this is important – that Lévy-Bruhl's "crucial advance consisted in concentrating analysis on the most general logical articulations of alien ideologies, rather than their component meanings and their social contexts". It is precisely from this point, Lévy Bruhl's separation of his so-called "alien ideologies" from their social contexts, that my critique proceeds; but *not* in the usual "structural-functional" manner, as I take pains to point out.

In his endeavours to disentangle belief and experience, Needham not only acknowledges the inspiration of Lucien Lévy-Bruhl (among others), but correctly places him in the context of the classical philosophical tradition of the bourgeois enlightenment. His particular exemplars are Hume and Wittgenstein; Hume for his repeated

> attentions to the notion of belief, which he could not account for and could not leave alone, [and which] brought out the capacity and the problematical nature of this commonplace category of everyday discourse and psychological report. (Needham 1972: 8)

Needham explicitly derives his inspiration from Lévy-Bruhl and Wittgenstein precisely because he sees them addressing critical issues in the mainstream of bourgeois philosophy (Needham 1972: 161-76), but Lévy-Bruhl also because he was "a founder, together with Durkheim and Mauss, of the comparative and sociological study of forms of classification and modes of ratiocination . . . [and] . . . he effectively inaugurated a comparative epistemology". That Lévy-Bruhl was concerned with some form of a comparative epistemology cannot be countered; that he was the "founder" of a comparative epistemology, effectively inaugurated by Marx half a century before, must be denied.

There is a reason for this apparent oversight on Needham's part, and it is important for the present discussion to pursue it a little further. Needham himself admits (1972: 183) that it was "questionable" for Lévy-Bruhl to lump the "collective representations of non-western societies" into one simple type, even if the ethnographic record was at that time weak, as Mauss had already pointed out (Mauss 1923). Needham also notes that Lévy-Bruhl "recognized" the implication that, by juxtaposing "primitive mentality" and "western thought" he was making assumptions about "his own" concepts of experience and belief (including, of course, time), but he fails to see that this very fact destroys his claims for a Lévy-Bruhlian "comparative theory of knowledge" or epistemology (Needham 1972: 184). Despite moments of insight – relegated to footnotes – Lévy-Bruhl obviously assumes, in typical late 19th and early 20th Century fashion, that his own conceptualizations of the nature of time, space, experience, and belief were self-evidently "rational" and "scientific", representing the "logical unity of the thinking subject".[2] Both Lévy-Bruhl and Needham, following in the footsteps of the same philosophical tradition, fail to apprehend the fundamental epistemological break represented by Marx's much earlier critique of Hegel and Feuerbach, as it uncomfortably involves a self-critique of the historical and sociological grounds for their own ratiocination about time and other "things", a point to which I return.[3]

In other words, by recognizing "differences", the "abstract mentalist" approach (a form of philosophical idealism) does not positively impose the constructs of one culture upon another, but "negatively" destroys the basis for understanding by an idealistic "comparison" which ignores the social and historical origins and social production of *both* sets of concepts.

I have characterized the second approach to the anthropological study of time as both "abstract" and "empiricist". Most studies of African time concepts (with the notable exception of Thornton's book on the Iraqw of Tanzania, 1980) combine elements of this approach with some strands of the former Lévy-Bruhlian one. Such a combination leads to the inclusion of a discussion of "concepts" in the context of linguistic analysis on the one hand, and "structural time" in the particular sense of "genealogical time" on the other. A number of these studies reflect with apparent perplexity upon the "dissociation" or contradictions that occur between these two "levels" of time in the same cultures.

Whatever the theoretical drawbacks of such studies – critiques of functionalism abound, and I mention some of them later – they had the value of focusing attention upon the detailed elements that go to make up a people's "cosmological" notions of time, from everyday routine to notions of historical process, if not history. Evans-Pritchard's seminal article on "Nuer Time Reckoning" (1939) set a pattern, and two other excellent examples are Beidelman's "Kaguru Time Reckoning" (1963) and Bohannan's

"Concepts of Time among the Tiv of Nigeria" (1953).[4]

Commencing with a distinction between "structural time", which is "entirely progressive", and "ecological time", which is "only progressive within an annual cycle", Evans-Pritchard discusses Nuer notions of days, months, seasonal cycles, years, genealogical history, and mythology. Despite the promising start of "placing" Nuer time concepts in their structural context, Evans-Pritchard strays, perhaps unconsciously, into Lévy-Bruhlian territory. In the middle of an incredibly rich ethnographic description, he suddenly states:

> Though I have spoken of time and units of time, it must be pointed out that, strictly speaking, the Nuer have no concept of time and, consequently, no developed abstract system of time reckoning. (1939: 208)

Genealogical time is "structural time", not historical time (p. 213), and beyond the constricted limits of genealogical time we arrive at tradition and myth:

> Valid history ends a century ago . . . though it astounded me, it is no way remarkable to the Nuer, that the tree under which mankind came into being was still standing in western Nuerland a few years ago and would still be standing had it not recently been burnt down. (Evans-Pritchard 1939: 215-16).

During the course of his excellent descriptive study, however, Evans-Pritchard makes two points of considerable theoretical significance to us. First, he writes that "time is not always the same to Nuer at different seasons" – the dry season appearing to represent "slow" time, the wet season "fast" time; and second, there appear to be different "levels" of time reckoning among the Nuer – physical, ecological, and social – each of which has its own "rhythm". He notes (1939: 192) that there are "three planes of rhythm: physical rhythm, ecological rhythm based on physical changes; and social rhythm based on ecological changes. Nuer concepts of time are based primarily on the social rhythm", although they obviously "recognize" the others. Although the theoretical integration of these different (and frequently contradictory) "planes of time" is not relevant to the everyday existence of Nuer (or the members of any other culture or social formation, for that matter), the general import of Evans-Pritchard's article (one might say its very *raison d'être*) is that such an integration is possible in certain circumstances relatively unique to the Nuer social formation; but he does not specify what these are. I suspect these circumstances would be manifested in Nuer consciousness of the historical development of the material practice necessary for the reproduction and continual adaptation of their social formation; in other words, their political economy, as I try to demonstrate for Ilparakuyo.

Beidelman's discussion of Kaguru time reckoning differs from Evans-

Pritchard's in two important respects, first in suggesting that "a study of Kaguru time reckoning does not show a dramatic relationship between these concepts and Kaguru social structure and economy", and second in establishing that Kaguru have not only one but two terms for the abstract notion of time (Beidelman 1963: 10-11). Consequently, his analysis virtually ignores "genealogical" time and focuses almost exclusively upon conceptual and categorical notions. It would seem to me that these are crucial differences. But while Beidelman notes that if Kaguru (as for the Nuer) do not have "chronology as we know it", and although" . . . this is hardly surprising in view of the very different preoccupations of such peoples and the absence of written means to record history", he does not question *why* differences exist between, say, Kaguru and Nuer; *why* "chronology" became important to "western" bourgeois historiography; and why this importance is decreasing. These are all questions of both theoretical and practical relevance. The lead suggested by the linking of time concepts with "the very different preoccupations" of the Kaguru is not taken up; but Beidelman does make the crucial point that Kaguru notions of time have been *radically* changed by the impact of both Arabization and European colonialism. In other words, the penetration of mercantile and peripheral capitalist relations of production and their vehicles of expression.

In sum, Beidelman and Evans-Pritchard, while not explicitly postulating a notion of "primitive mentality" in the Lévy-Bruhlian sense, and differing in their notions of "structural time", both present us with an analysis of temporal concepts in which comparisons are made with a given notion of "our" time, i.e., the time concepts of "western" philosophical and "scientific" investigation; but the implications of this comparison are not explored.

Bohannan's study of Tiv time concepts is along much the same lines, except that he does make some interesting additional points. He states, for example, that Tiv place incidents in time, both future and past, by "a direct association of two events", or a "conjuncture" (Bohannan 1967 [1953]: 316). Furthermore, Tiv indicate periods of *future time* which exceed four or five years, either by specific seasonal or cyclical events, or by life-expectancy events of a particular person (1967: 324). Finally, although Tiv do not associate their fairly deep genealogical reckoning with "myths and legends" (why should they?), they *do* associate genealogoical progression with population trends and territorial expansion (Bohannan 1967: 326). Hence there is quite clearly among the Tiv a notion of constant historical change, linking together ecological, demographic, and social factors, despite their different temporal "rhythms", into one coherent process.

Before I turn to a discussion of the third approach, it should be noted that these emphases in Bohannan's analysis are consistent with the more strictly structural-functional approach to genealogical time reckoning embodied in the more dynamic studies of descent and kinship, such as in Fortes' work on Tallensi and Ashanti (Fortes 1945, 1949a, 1949b).

The approach I have characterized as "structural totalization" is ③ manifested in a number of recent studies which emphasize on the one hand the symbolic nature of time concepts, and on the other the use of analogies derived from linguistic analysis – such as the abstract notions of synchrony and diachrony (e.g. Lévi-Strauss 1966, and *passim*; Zein 1974; Leach 1961; Rigby 1968a). The intellectual debt these studies owe to the second type already discussed is obvious; but some of the latter have gone much further in questioning the epistemological issues involved in discourse about time concepts, not only in pre-capitalist social formations but also in western bourgeois theory and practice. To some extent, then, this approach has shaken the false epistemological certainty of the implicit comparison made in studies of the previous type; and in part this is due to the attempted (if not entirely successful) *rapprochement* between structuralism and the Marxist problematic in French anthropology and philosophy. If some of these studies ultimately end up as further examples of "abstract empiricism", it is not for want of trying to penetrate some of the categories of bourgeois thought.

I begin with the example of Leach's brief but penetrating (as well as entertaining) studies, "Cronus and Chronos" and "Time and False Noses" (1961: 124-36).[5] Leach correctly states that "there is nothing intrinsically geometrical [i.e., linear, cyclical, circular] about time as we actually experience it", and he goes on to demonstrate that the "notion that time as a 'discontinuity of repeated contrasts' is probably the most elementary and primitive of all ways of regarding time" (1961: 126, 134; cf. Rigby 1968a). But he rests his case upon the epistemological "given" of *experience*, and one cannot help but wonder if we are not back with Needham's problems with belief and experience, and the shades of Lévy-Bruhl. Leach notes some difficulties here when he comments (1961: 132) that "we experience time, but not with our senses. We don't see it, or smell it, or taste, or hear it." How then do we "experience" it? This dilemma is reminiscent of Lenin's remark, following Marx and Engels, that bourgeois philosophers, having set up the abstract notion of reified "objective" time, then want to "feel", "taste", "see", it; that is, *actually* experience it. (Lenin 1962: 177ff; Engels, 1940: 327, 1975). Leach also states that even historical time is a "fairly simple derivative" of experience (1961: 125); but if the experience itself is suspect, where are we?

The problem is that whereas in the Kachin case, Leach emphasizes the time dimension as a product of the history of changing social relations, in the more "structuralist" analyses under review this historicity is lost. This is at least in part due to his over-commitment to the structuralist dichotomy between synchrony and diachrony, and the focus on "mythical time"; "my own explanation", says Leach of the diversity of temporal concepts, "is of a more structural kind" (1961: 129).

The Marxist critique of these structuralist tenets is a bridge to the approach I attempt to develop here. But first a brief word on the fourth approach which I have characterized as the "philosophical-theological". This is the most eclectic of all the theoretical positions discussed. John Mbiti, for example, inexcusably (though understandably in view of his terms of reference) generalizing about "African" concepts of time (1969: 17), maintains that "according to traditional concepts, time is a two-dimensional phenomenon, with a long *past*, a *present*, and vitually *no future*" (his emphasis).[6] His generalization turns out to be based upon his understanding of the tense structures of two Bantu languages, Kikamba and Gikuyu,[7] which in turn is further linguistically expanded into the Kiswahili concepts of *sasa* ("the now period") and *zamani* ("the long past"). The latter period has its own "past", "present", and "future". Mbiti's contention that "African" concepts of time encompass no *definite* future beyond six months to two years, and no *indefinite* future at all, is strongly suggestive of Lévy-Bruhlian influence. It has already been refuted for the Tiv by Bohannan (above), and it is unsupportable in numerous other cases. Despite the interesting and informative complexity of Mbiti's overall analysis, there is a total lack of historical context in his discussion; and explanatory comparison is further confounded by references to the lack in "African traditional thought" of concepts of history moving "towards a future climax, or towards an end of the world". *Why* anyone should wish to postulate history as moving towards an end of the world as a condition for a historical concept of the past and the future is a question not examined by Mbiti.

The influence of this approach, proposed as it is by such sympathetic observers as Mbiti, can also be seen in the work of others attempting a more rigorous comparative analysis. In his otherwise excellent study of African religions, for example, Ray (1976: 40-1) assumes that African concepts of time are relatively "ahistorical", while of course denying that Africa lacks "a sense of history". Ray, like Mbiti, is also led to the implicit epistemological comparisons of bourgeois futurology when he states that, "What African thought did not conceive was an indefinite future, stretching beyond the immediate future of the next two or three years". (1976: 41) I show later that Ilparakuyo and Maasai, for example, do have such a concept; but it exhibits a specific form commensurate with the nature of their social formations, and is not a mere replication of the (also specific) notions of the future embodied in capitalist ideology, bolstered by Christian dogma and eschatology.

It can be stated without too much distortion that all of these anthropological and philosophical approaches to the understanding of time and temporal concepts, even when they do make reference to "historical" time and the nature of historical reality, treat the latter as a separate dimension of time; a separate "entity" which may, or more often may not, be like "our" conception of history, which is taken as a self-evident truth. History is thus treated as either non-existent in African (and other so-called "primitive") societies, or as an analytically distinct conceptual element amongst other such elements in an "cosmology" of time. There is seldom any attempt to place all these elements or "levels" of time reckoning, even where their existence is noted, in a total and specific historicity arising from the nature of the specific social formation under consideration, which in turn is itself a product of that specific historical development.[8]

III

What, then, is an alternative problematic? I have already noted that the structuralist approach to concepts of time seemed to bring us closest to a comparative and critical epistemological investigation that does not assume the conceptual apparatus of bourgeois society. This achievement is due, at least in part, to structuralism's insistence upon a totalizing theory and upon treating so-called "primitive" systems of thought as "practico-theoretical logic" (Lévi-Strauss 1966: 75, and *passim*). But this theoretical gain seems to get bogged down in a) the abstract dichotomy between synchrony and diachrony, in which the latter becomes a contingent element in social reality and hence undermines the very historicity we are pursuing; and to a lesser extent, b) the intractable problems of the notion of "experience".[9]

In an illuminating little study, "Fulani Penetration into Nupe and Yoruba in the Nineteenth Century", Peter Morton-Williams notes that the

> property of structure permits social anthropologists to join forces with the historians. What separates them is an anthropological formulation of social structure and structural processes that is functionally independent of the dimension of time as the historian conceives it, structural theory employing a notion of generalized time that, like the scientist's time, has different properties. (1968: 4)

While taking issue with his assumptions about the "nature" of historical time (he inserts a disclaimer on epistemological debate), it is relevant to pursue his useful paper a little further. In criticizing the notion of functional stability stemming from a Radcliffe-Brownian position which postulates only "exogenous" sources of social change, Morton-Williams continues:

> The historian is concerned at least as much with the problem of changes originating in the society itself, for instance with acts of will intended to modify "the actually existing network of relations . . . " It is merely begging the question to propose a series of synchronic studies of a changing social structure at a succession of dates in the hope that the result will be a diachronic study illustrating laws of change. (1968: 4-5)

Here again we have a comment upon the unacceptable contingency of the diachronic. Although Morton-Williams achieves a penetrating analysis of a particular case, he does not pursue the matter to its logical conclusion: the further examination, and possible elimination, of the synchrony–diachrony opposition itself. Only then can some coherence be given to the different conceptual levels of time reckoning in the context of the specific historicity of a particular social formation and its development.

Brief mention must be made here of Thornton's important attempt to transcend this structuralist problem in his analysis of the Iraqw social formation (1980). I use the term "social formation" judiciously, for although Thornton does not, he is at pains to describe Iraqw society and culture not as constituting an ethnic isolate, but as the historical product of a complex regional formation involving Iraqw relations with their neighbours, Maasai, Barbaig, and so on. He also attempts to

> develop the argument that the cultural order of Iraqw as we observe it today . . . is the product of historical circumstances; but the structure so constituted is also, at any moment in the process, the producer of a continuing history. Structure and history account for each other. (Thornton 1980: 191)

Although this may appear to be little different from Morton-Williams position, Thornton goes further to argue that Iraqw society cannot be thought of as a given structure, "legitimated" by oral tradition and history, within which changes are generated; rather, "processes and means [praxis?] are legitimated by the oral tradition, *not* structures and ends" (1980: 184). Thornton arrives at this sophisticated position partly through his familiarity with Bourdieu's work (particularly Bourdieu 1977); but this in itself becomes a limitation upon his advance to an historical materialist problematic, as I show in my conclusion.

Marx's critique of Hegel is concerned basically with the nature of historicity and hence the conditions for the production of concepts of time. Kant was the precursor of the shift in science and philosophy towards a concern with the nature of time and time concepts; but a real critique of the whole idealist philosophical tradition's treatment of time awaited Marx's commentary on Hegel and Feuerbach. As Lefebvre notes:

> first to Hegel and then to Marx, the object of investigation and knowledge is time . . . With Hegel, extensibility in time ('becoming') comes firmly to the fore, takes on primordiality: mankind's life is now [perceived of] in time, is historical, its very consciousness a succession of changing stages and shifting moments. (1968: 27-8)

Marx's critique of Hegel's notion of time was at once an exposition of Hegel's betrayal of "his own finest insight when he gave to understand that his philosophy was the culmination of human thought and the contemporary nation state the end of history" (Lefebvre 1968: 28), as well as a critique of Hegel's notion of time and history as the apotheosis of ideological conceptualization.

Appropriately for his own mistaken logic (if somewhat ironically), Hegel declared that "What we understand by Africa, is the Unhistorical, Undeveloped spirit, still involved in the mere conditions of nature" (1900: 99; cf. Ray 1976: 42); while for Marx, "Change becomes truly universal, since both nature and history are now conceived historically. Man and all things human are from now on characterized in temporal terms" (Lefebvre 1968: 28). For Hegel, "historical time merely reflects the essence of the social totality of which it *is* the existence", which in turn is "the Spirit"; "Spirit is time", said Hegel in his Jena writings, an assertion later developed in the *Phenomenology*. It is "the essential character of historical time that will lead us, like so many indices, to the peculiar structure of [a] social totality" (Althusser 1970: 93). The distinction between synchrony and diachrony which so pervades contemporary anthropological problematics, structuralist or otherwise, is also based upon a Hegelian essentialist "conception of historical time as continuous and homogeneous and contemporaneous with itself", the idealist historian's "time present" (Althusser 1970: 96).[10] Althusser continues:

> The synchronic therefore presupposed the ideological conception of a continuous-homogeneous time. It follows that the sequence of a temporal continuity in which the "events" to which "history" in the *strict sense* can be reduced (cf. Lévi-Strauss) are merely successive contingent presents in the time continuum [cf. Morton-Williams' critique already mentioned]. Like the synchronic, which is the primary concept, the diachronic therefore presupposes both of the very two characteristics I have isolated in the Hegelian conception of time: an *ideological* conception of historical time.

Structuralism, therefore, far from having fulfilled its promise of liberating us from an ideological epistemology of all time concepts such as bedevil Lévy-Bruhl, his followers, and the other anthropological approaches I have described, perpetuates the very error we are trying to escape. And I can agree with Althusser when he concludes:

> If what I have said has any objective meaning, it is clear that the synchrony/diachrony opposition is the site for a misconception, since to take it for a knowledge would be to remain in an epistemological vacuum, i.e. – ideology abhorring a vacuum – in an ideological fullness, precisely in the fullness of the ideological conception of history whose time is continuous-homogeneous/self-contemporaneous. (1970: 107)

How, then, can we lay a foundation for the understanding of historical time, which is at once the source of all levels of the conceptions of time in a social formation, as well as their embodiment? In order to avoid an ideological conception of history, and hence the implicit ideological distortion of any discussion of time concepts,

> it needs to be said that, just as there is no production in general, there is no history in general, but only specific structures of historicity which, since they are merely the existence of determinate social formations (arising from specific *modes of production*), articulated as social wholes, have no meaning except as a function of the essence of these totalities, i.e., of the essence of their *peculiar complexity*. (Althusser 1970: 108-9, emphasis added)

This "essence", therefore, lies not in an abstract essence of conceptual time (Lévy-Bruhl's "scientific", "civilized" time) with which other concepts are compared, but in the temporal embodiment of social formations and their modes of production that give rise to those concepts themselves. The concept of historical time, together with the different conceptual levels and "rhythms" that make it up,

> can only be based on the complex and differentially articulated structure in dominance of the social totality that constitutes the social formation arising from a determinate mode of production, it can only be assigned a content as a function of the struture of that totality, considered either as wholes, or in its different levels. (Althusser 1970: 108)

I now turn to the Ilparakuyo and Maasai material, commencing with a selection of conceptual issues and various notions of temporal units – days, months, seasons, years etc. – looking finally at their specific embodiment in the historical social formation of the Ilparakuyo section of the Tanzania Maasai.

IV

There is a term in the Maasai language (Maa) that can generally be translated into the English word "time", as long as the latter is freed as much as possible from the epistemological assumptions we have already discussed. The Maasai word *enkata* has, as does its English counterpart, a plural form, *inkaitin* (*inkatitin* in some dialects). It may, for example, be used to refer to the two major seasonal units of the year, *enkata o'lari* (the rainy season) and *enkata o'lameyu* (the time of dryness, or the dry season). The word *erishata* (pl. *irishat*) can also be used to refer to varying units of time, but also to an area of space (from *arish*, "to separate", "divide").[11]

Enkata may also refer to specific points or periods in time as in *ti ai kata*, "at another time", *te ena kata*, "at this moment", or *nabo kata*, "one time" (cf. Mol 1978: 159-60). Similarly, one may say *te nkiti rishata*, "in a short time". Then again, *enkata* may refer to times with a particular *quality*, such as *enkata e'leng'on*, a time when everything is green, there is food for the herds, the cattle are healthy, and everything is healthy; a period which in other contexts may be referred to by other terms such as those for particular months.

Although it is not usually expressed by a verbal tense (most Maasai verbs combine present habitual and future in one form, except for a few which take an extra terminal vowel-*u*), Maasai do have a very definite concept of an "indefinite" future, expressed adverbially. For this the word *kenya*, or *akenya*, may be used, and refers to any time from the present to an unspecified future day, season, epoch, generation, or condition; or one may say *inkolong'i naapuonu*, "the days that will come".

Other fairly specific temporal concepts are *te ina kata*, "at that time", *taata*, "today", *oshi*, "usually", *oshi taata*, "nowadays", *oshi det*, "recently", *ade*, "later today", *taaisere*, "tomorrow", *metabaiki*, "tomorrow all being well" (the possibilities of tomorrow", lit. "may it be"), and so on. Referring to the past, there is *naaji*, "a little time ago", *duoo*, "a short while ago", "this morning", *ng'ole*, "yesterday", *naarri*, "sometime ago", longer than recently, *opa*, "formerly" (also *apa*, "long ago"). This latter concept, *apa*, may refer to any relatively remote time in the past up to "mythical time", the origins of man and the universe although, as we shall see, these are not topics of particular concern to Ilparakuyo and Maasai. It may be specified as "long ago" by the addition of *moitie*, and in this sense refers to the period of the origin of Maasai and, more specifically, the beginning of such sections as the Ilparakuyo. These are among the few true adverbs in the Maa language, functioning as demonstratives of time (others refer to manner).

Maasai divide the year (*olari*, pl. *ilarin*) into 12 months (*ilapaitin*, sing. *olapa*) of 30 days (*inkolong'i* sing. *enkolong'*). *Olari* also refers to the rainy season, *olapa* means "moon", and *enkolong'* the sun; although "day", "daylight time" can also be rendered by *endama* (pl. *indamaritin*), *dama* implying "during the day". These terms may, as we have seen, be used to refer to specific periods or times, as in *inkolong'i naapuonu*, "the days that will come" (i.e. "the future"), *ai olong'*, "another day", and so on.

The month is divided very specifically into 30 days according to the position of the moon, grouped into 15 "bright" days, *enkiborra* (from *aibor*, "to be white") and *enaimin*, 15 "dark" days (from *enaimin*, "darkness"). Daylight time and the night (*enkewarie*, pl. *inkewarietin*) are sub-divided into a number of periods, some relating to activities concerning the herd: "*eata Ilmaasai inkatitin enye enkolong' o enkewarie*", "the Maasai have various time divisions of day and night"; but the details need not concern us here (cf. Hollis 1905: 332; Mol 1978: 52, 112).

The complex progression of the 30 days of each month are described in great detail by Mol (1978: 105). It is sufficient here to make two points: a) as Mol states, "it is better to speak of nights or evenings of the lunar cycle than of days", and b) knowledge of this complex classificatory structure is now highly specialized, and Kiswahili concepts have practically taken over in everyday usage, except where elders, warriors, or women gather for ritual occasions. We may also note that in Maasai and Ilparakuyo folklore, there is a symbolic association between the night and men, and the daylight and women, the reason for this being, say Maasai, that "men, who are strong, go to fight [an enemy] at night, while women can work only during the day" (Hollis 1905: 279).

As the yearly cycle of 12 months is based upon seasonal activities, and the various Maasai sections inhabit a considerable area and variety of ecological and rainfall regimes, the exact relationship between particular months, seasonal divisions, and adjustments to discrepancies in the lunar year vary a great deal from one section to another. Hollis (1905: 333-4),

Merker (1910: 160), Sankan (1971: 65-6), Mol (1978: 105-6) all give various versions and, although the Hollis material is partially Ilparakuyo in origin (his main informant and assistant, Semeni ole Kivasis – or Justin Lemenye – was an Olparakuoni), the versions I have recorded differ slightly from all of these. That such variations are true for the Nuer as well (Evans-Pritchard 1939: 202-3) implies that they can be expected to occur in such widespread pastoral and semi-pastoral social formations.

V

Ilparakuyo and Maasai myths and legends are not generally concerned with the "ulimate" origins of mankind, and even those few that do make some reference to "beginnings" attempt to explain the differentiation of Maasai from others, such as the Iltorrobo hunters and gatherers or their Bantu-speaking neighbours (cf. Jacobs 1965a: 20-9; Hollis 1905: 264- 73; Galaty 1977, 1978a, 1978b, Beidelman 1960: 245-9; etc.) rather than any overall "human origin". In this, Ilparakuyo are similar to the Iraqw (Thornton 1980: 181, 183-4). But unlike the Iraqw, whose lack of myths of origin results in their also being without a "zero point against which to set a regularized chronology" and hence a history "with a backbone" (Thornton 1980: 186), Ilparakuyo and most other Maa-speaking peoples have a history with a sequence as well as a form of "chronology", the latter provided by the overriding succession of age-sets, generation-sets, and the culturally attributable uniqueness and peculiarity of each.[12] Of course, Ilparakuyo and Maasai do not postulate a fixed zero point such as the BC–AD distinction of the Gregorian calendar which, despite its relatively "scientific" adjustability to cosmic processes is, after all, tied to the prevailing religious beliefs as well as the non-religious ideology of "western" capitalist society (cf. Thornton 1980: 183). But the sequence of age-sets provides Ilparakuyo and Maasai with a conception of "time past" which can be translated into the system with which we are stuck, though not without some difficulty.

Ilparakuyo as well as other pastoral Maasai explicitly link the (albeit oral) historiography of age-sets to the genealogy of the most famous line of religious leaders and prophets (*iloibonok kituaak*, "the great diviners") who belong to a particular sub-clan of the Ilaiscr clan, the Inkidong'i, founded by Kidong'oi, the first (or in some versions, the second) "great diviner" (*oloiboni kitok*; cf. Hollis 1905: 324-30; Fosbrooke 1948: 13, and *passim*; Jacobs 1965a: 48-54, 1968a: 10-31; Berntsen 1979: 134-5; and *passim*; Huntingford 1953: 103, 121-2; Merker 1910: 18-22; etc.).[13] The main sections of the pastoral Maasai trace this genealogy of the *iloibonok* some nine to ten generations back from the present, taking us back to the middle or late 17th Century. Writing in the 1940s, Fosbrooke gives a date of 1640 for the "finding" of the first *oloiboni kitok* (1948: 3, 12; cf. Hollis 1905: 326) and notes that "this agrees with all my informants , who state that [it] took place before the earliest remembered age-grade [sic], i.e. before the beginning of the 18th century".[14]

The details of Fosbrooke's original correlation between age-sets and the genealogy of the great prophets, his own revisions, and Jacob's comments and revisions are set out in Fosbrooke 1948: 11-12, 1956: 193; Jacobs 1968a: 14-18, and need not be repeated. The progressive increase in the historical "accuracy" of these chronologies has certainly been established, and they provide a reasonable framework for the "translation" of the past two hundred years of Maasai history, although this could be extended by further analysis of the actual relationships of the *iloibonok* to Maasai society through a genealogy of some three hundred years (cf. Berntsen 1979).

My purpose at present, however, is not to unravel the details of Maasai historiography but to develop a notion of Ilparakuyo consciousness and apprehension of history and hence the theoretical context for the development of Ilparakuyo (and Maasai) notions of time. This may be achieved by limiting the discussion of two further aspects of the Ilparakuyo and Maasai social formations: a) the conceptual categories used in distinguishing between myths, legends, and stories about the past, and b) the tracing of an outline history of Ilparakuyo separation from the main body of pastoral Maasai, using a combination of age-set chronology and the genealogies of the major Ilparakuyo "great ritual leaders" since that separation, in conjunction with written sources.

Jacobs notes that Maasai make a clear distinction between what they call *enkatinyi*, "history and oral tradition" (from *enkata*, "time". pl. *inkatitin*; see above) on the one hand, and *enkiterunoto* "myths" (lit. "beginnings", from *aiteru*, "to start", "to begin") on the other (Jacobs 1968a: 14-15). Concepts which might include "history", "myth", and even "pedagogy" depending upon the context are *inkopa*, "things (matters, affairs) of long ago" and the word *inkoon*, "advice", "history", derived from *aikok*, "to instruct", "advise", "warn", the latter described by Mol as:

> such instructions e.g. as are given by the *olpiron* [fire-stick"] elders to the warriors on various occasions, [and] such instructions will also include bits and pieces of old customs, old happenings, etc. (1978: 82)

Although very similiar distinctions could apply, *mutatis mutandis*, to Ilparakuyo conceptualization of the past, the differences between the two main types of narrative are not always clear cut. Ilparakuyo, as with other pastoral Maasai, do recount historical events in relation to the succession of age-sets and the genealogy of the *iloibonok*; but the order is often confused beyond the third or fourth age-set prior to the present senior elders. This is due in part to the somewhat difficult categories of historical discourse available to the investigator. For example, "left hand" sets and "right hand" sets (*emurata e kedenye* and *emurata e tatene*) have different "nicknames" before the *eunoto* ceremony which promotes them to senior warriorhood; and different names may be used for the same age-set according to whether it is the *eunoto* name, or that given at *olng'eher*, the ceremony that confirms the status of elderhood. These problems in themselves are relatively amenable to a method of systematic cross-referencing; but the fact remains that elders give in different context varying versions of the names of earlier age-sets and the genealogy of the *iloibonok*. Furthermore, there is as yet no comprehensive published account of the actual operation of Ilparakuyo age-set organization, which differs in some important respects from that of pastoral Maasai.[15]

I describe in Chapters 3 and 6 certain aspects of Ilparakuyo age organization and age-sets, functioning as relations of production not only within the historical development of Ilparakuyo society itself, but also in the context of the wider social formations of neighbouring peoples and the modern state of Tanzania (cf. also Beidelman 1961a, 1968, 1960: 262-7). It is through the succession of age-sets, the attribution of particular qualities and practices to them as distinct historical units (remembered very often in songs and epic recitations), and their continuing role in the social (as well as symbolic) reproduction of the Ilparakuyo social formation, that the other elements of social structure such as descent, kinship, and generational relationships are articulated with wider historical developments.

With these points in mind, I present in Figure 2 a very tentative and diagrammatic sketch of historical developments since Ilparakuyo separation as a distinct social formation from other pastoral Maasai, concluding with a discussion of its implications for historical consciousness and time reckoning.[16] I have not distinguished in the age-set chronology between right hand and left hand groups, nor have I distinguished them from "generation-sets" (cf. Hollis 1905: 262-3; Fosbrooke 1956; Jacobs 1965a, 1968). The dates given in Figure 2 are very approximate times for the *opening* of new circumcision periods for what later became complete "age-sets" (*ilajijik*, sing. *olaji*) at *eunoto* ceremonies, including all sub-divisions and all three sub-sets (Ilcang'enopir, Ilparing'otua, and Ilkerimbuot; see Chapter 3) of each age-set. They were established upon the basis of oral evidence, textual corroboration, and the general principle that although "new age-sets among the Maasai [and Ilparakuyo] tend to be formed at regular intervals of about fifteen years, each age-set serves in the warrior grade for an average of twenty years", depending upon the political, ecological, and ritual conditions at the time. Similarly, the genealogy of the Ilparakuyo *iloibonok kituaak* rests on oral evidence, textual corroboration, and a generation span of about 30 years.

It seems fairly certain that Ilparakuyo finally established their political and ritual "independence" from Kisongo and other pastoral Maasai either just prior to, or during, the incumbency of Mtango as *Oloiboni kitok*, or great prophet, and many elders cite him as the first in the line of Ilparakuyo prophets. But there is evidence that there were moves to gain ritual control of the Ilparakuyo age-set system prior to this, as suggested in the "composite" genealogy represented in Figure 2. Two further points must be made: a) the genealogy given for the *Iloibonok kituaak* refers only to the

Figure 2
Diagrammatic Representation of Ilparakuyo Age-set Chronology and Genealogy of the "Great Diviners/Prophets" (*Iloibonok kituaak*)

Age-set[a] name	Approximate year opening circumcision + events	Genealogy of Iloibonok kituaak + events		Approximate year of succession
?	?	Teliang' (?)		?
Ilmeriho I	1795 (beginning of conflict with the other Massai sections)	Lengunat		1805
Ilkishomu	1815 1832 (final break with[b] Kisongo Massai and	Mtango		1835
Ilkenyeiyie/Ilisujita	1854 beginning of movement south into present Bagamoyo and Morogoro 1874[c] Districts)	Kirigo	Kirkong'	1855
Ilpariho/Isiyiapai (Iltapali)	1890 (movement westwards and south into Ugogo and Uhehe)[e]	Maitei (Resigned as "official" representative of Ilparakuyo to German administration 1918)[d]		1885
Ilkijaro/Ilmetimpot (?)	1907 (beginning of movement into Mbeya District)	Moreto		1920
Iseeta (*eunoto*)/Iltwati (*olng'eher*) (Ilkisalie)	1924 (current senior elders – 1980)			
Ilkidotu (*eunoto*) Ilmeriho II (*olng'eher*)	1942 (current junior elders – 1980)	Mutari	Senteu	1950
Ilmedoti (*eunoto*) "Ildobola"/ "Ilmesokile"	1957 (current senior warriors)			
Ilkipone (*eunoto*) Itareto "Ilmakaa"	1972 (*eunoto* ceremony 1980, but just moving out of junior warriorhood)			

Notes:

a.   Where available, I have given both names received at *eunoto* ceremonies (promoting junior warriors to senior warriors) and *olng'eher* rituals (promoting senior warriors to junior elderhood). "Nicknames" of age-sets given before *eunoto* (there are no "proper" names before this) are in quotation marks.

b.   See Lemenye 1956: 52, fn. 11 (by Fosbrooke), p.57; Thomson 1885: 240–2.

c.   In some versions of oral history, Ilparakuyo claim that the Ilkenyeiyie age-set fought the Germans at Handeni. If they were junior warriors (*ilmurran*) at the time, this would only have been possible if they had come into conflict with the forces deployed by the Society for German Colonization, which sent an expedition in 1884 to "sign treaties with native chiefs" in the Pangani River area and hinterland, or those of the German East Africa Company, incorporated in 1887–8. Or they may have fought the Germans as senior warriors, after *eunoto*, whose task it is to direct operations carried out by the junior age-set.

d.   See Chapter 5.

e.   Beidelman 1960: 248–53; 1962.

lineage of the Inkidong'i sub-clan of the Ilwarakishu (Ilaiser) clan which provides the ritual centre for northern and eastern Ilparakuyo, but their exact relationship with the Ilaiser Inkidong'i of the other pastoral Maasai is not known; and b) southern and south-western Ilparakuyo communities have another ritual centre with its own lineage of *iloibonok kituaak* (see p.10 above; Beidelman 1960: 264-5).

This is not the place to join the debate on the frequent identification of Ilparakuyo with "agricultural Maasai", also called "Wakwavi" and "Iloikop", and their presumed hostility and opposition to pastoral Maasai (e.g. Jacobs 1965a: 39-48, 1968: 21-8, 1972, 1979: 36, and *passim*; Krapf 1854, 1860: Galaty 1977, 1978b; cf. Berntsen 1979 and forthcoming). Certainly, Ilparakuyo have always, and still do, attempt to maintain as "pastoral"a system of production and reproduction of their social formation as they can, eschewing agriculture; although, as with most pastoralists, they frequently depend to a lesser or greater extent upon the agricultural produce of their cultivating neighbours, for which they trade. The arguments on this issue and the literature relating to this debate have been admirably surveyed by Berntsen (forthcoming).

Ilparakuyo historical traditions describe hostile relations with other Maasai sections, particularly during the period of some 40 years until about 1832, when they finally broke away and began moving into their present areas, dotted about among primarily Bantu-speaking cultivators; but their general "drift" south and west continues to the present time. It is also true that Bantu speakers on the coast currently refer to Ilparakuyo as "Wakwavi"; Gogo, Kaguru, Kimbu, and other Bantu-speaking peoples of central Tanzania, however, amongst whom large groups of Ilparakuyo live, refer to all Maa-speaking peoples (except the Ilarusa, "Arusha") as "Wahumha", or variations thereof (from "Humba", "Ilumbwa"). Several Ilparakuyo elders claim historical connections with "Ilumbwa", whom they currently identify as the Kalenjin-speaking Kipsikis who are frequently (but erroneously) known by that name, and who are also called Ilkakisang' (sing. Olkakisang'i) by pastoral Maasai (cf. Huntingford 1953: 10; Hollis 1905: 280-1); and some other pastoral Maasai sections call Ilparakuyo "Ilumbwa" (cf. Beckwith and Saitoti 1980: 18). That at least some elements of Ilparakuyo have had an identity distinct from contemporary pastoral Maasai sections dating from a period much earlier than outlined, including perhaps ritual independence, is suggested by evidence in various sources (e.g. Thomson 1885; Johnston 1886). And linguistic evidence linking the Ilparakuyo dialect of Maa with that of the Isampur (Samburu) at the extreme northern end of the Maa-speaking diaspora offers the possibility of close contact with Kalenjin speakers on their movement south (Vossen 1977: 10-13), as well as earlier separation. This does not, however, alter materially the connections and conflicts with Kisongo Maasai at the later period of the 18th and 19th Centuries as outlined.

The term "Iloikop" is even more ambiguous as an appellation for Ilparakuyo than Ilumbwa. The fact that Samburu call themselves "Iloikop" may lend some weight to the identification of Ilparakuyo as Iloikop. But Jacobs' insistence that the term is related to one of the Maasai words for "murder" (e.g. someone who has committed serious assault or murder is in a state of "taboo" and is said "to have iloikop", "*eeta iloikop*") is on shaky ground, at least in this context, when we note that Samburu deny any association between their own term for themselves and the word for the contamination of murder (Spencer 1973: 109, fn. 7). As Berntsen correctly maintains, all these usages and concepts have not remained historically consistent, and there is strong evidence to suggest that there were several groups of Maa-speakers referred to as "Wakwavi" (or its variants) in the 19th Century who have little or no connection with contemporary Ilparakuyo, apart from the common one of language.

It is clear that Ilparakuyo historical consciousness is expressed not as a "mythical charter" for a unique and *fixed* identity as such, but as a narration of past spatial movements associated with other peoples, both Maa and non-Maa, and adaptation to constantly changing circumstances, political, economic, ecological, and ritual. At all of these times, specific age-sets acting as warriors (and later as elders directing and advising new warrior groups) are conceived of as playing decisive roles of a historically unique kind. Ilparakuyo history does have elements of what can be called a "topological" chronology, but it also has much more. The spatial elements inseparable from Ilparakuyo time and historical concepts do not establish "exclusive spaces", since Ilparakuyo appropriation of their environment is *temporary* to the extreme, and subject to ever-changing politico-economic circumstances, more so than pastoral formations which do have contiguous territories, and much more so than cultivators (see also Chapters 2, 3, and 5, but particularly pp. 98-103; Marx 1973: 472, 474; Beidelman 1960: 259). Ilparakuyo do have a very explicit notion of the territoral segments of their social formation; these are not, however, seen, as "fixed", bounded units, but as constantly changing through loss and accretion and migration, a process stretching back through the whole period of the known historical development of the social formation itself.

Finally, age-set chronology and the genealogy of the senior Ilparakuyo religious experts place the most significant conflicts and *final* separation or disengagement from other pastoral Maasai sections in the period of about 40 years prior to 1832, precisely when other historical evidence indicates them to have occurred.[17] Since this period, and probably (but less significantly) even before, Ilparakuyo and other Maasai age-sets have had different though sometimes overlapping names, just as they have had their own branch of the clan and sub-clan of the great religious leaders. This historicity and the territorial and spatial connotations of Ilparakuyo and Maasai historical consciousness has been admirably expanded by Vossen on the basis of linguistic evidence, and his conclusion, with the exception of the final period which I would change to "early 19th Century", is in no way contradictory or incompatible with the interpretation I have presented in this chapter:

In summary, the following hypothesis is set up. The Baraguyu [Ilparakuyo] are either close relatives or at least former neighbours of the Sampur. Their separation might be dated back to the end of the 15th century, slightly before the southward migration of the Baraguyu. Coming through the rift valley, they settled down in what is now the L-Oitai region [now the western part of Kenya Maasailand bordering Tanzania]. There they lived side-by-side with L-Oitai from around 1700. By the end of the 18th century, both groups got into quarrels which resulted in the defeat and explusion of the Baraguyu. In the environs of Pangani river they formed a new political [and ritual?] center which was gradually destroyed by the Kisonko during the mid-19th century and ultimately ended up with the scattering of Baraguyu to their present settlement areas. (Vossen 1977: 13)

VI

Although in my previous chapter on Ilparakuyo meat-feast ceremonies (*ilpuli*) and the notion of *entoroj* (also spelled *enturuj*) I emphasized the real and symbolic role of age-sets in social reproduction, it should be stressed here that the succession of age-sets through the age-grade system should not be thought of as merely a repetitious cycle, the life-cycle writ large; the Ilparakuyo certainly do not think of age-sets as such. Each age-set, the circumstances of its formation, and the creativity and originality of its actions, are emphasized, making it unique in the annals of Ilparakuyo historical consciousness as well as a referent for historical interpretation and, ultimately, the future of the social formation itself. If Ilparakuyo have any "identity" as a social formation, it lies not merely in an endless repetition of the past (despite a strong emphasis upon adherence to certain basic social practices and their associated values) but in a consciousness of a developing entity, with a definite historical beginning, and moving in a specific historical manner. This movement is not towards a "destiny", but embodies both the relations of past and present in the creation of a future.

In this context, the specific temporal concepts of life-cycles, days, months, years, generations, and age-sets are incorporated in a very specific historical manner in a social formation which has managed to retain its unique identity *not* through "conservatism" and the mere reproduction of the past, but in the creative use of the past in the praxis required for adaptation to an always uncertain future.

What I am arguing here is that the specific elements of the pastoral Ilparakuyo and Maasai social formations and pastoral praxis enable the development of a theory of historical time, closely linked to the spatial relations of migration, conflict, and the temporary appropriation of nature, which has a very specific meaning for pastoral praxis itself. Any changes in spatial relationships, through loss of access to grazing, water, etc., and subsequent movement must inevitably reflect upon, and be reflected in, notions of time and history. The very "fluidity" of Ilparakuyo concepts dealing with time and history are therefore a condition of continuing and successful pastoral praxis.[18] History is not merely "a rationalization of customary behaviour" (Thornton 1980: 187), although it is that on one level; rather, it is a theoretical reaffirmation of material practice geared to the pastoral appropriation of nature, in the context (one might say "in the face of") of other forms of such appropriation, either by agriculture or hunting and gathering, accompanied by its ritual and symbolic elements (see Chapter 3). It is only in this total setting, which includes Ilparakuyo historical relationships with other Maasai and the numerous non-Maasai amongst whom they live, as well as the modern state of Tanzania and its development policies and practices, that we can understand the other temporal "rhythms" of days, months, years, etc., which Ilparakuyo and Maasai conceptualize.

Finally, while I am in general agreement with Bourdieu's sensitive analysis of time and practice of the Kabyle (Bourdieu 1963; 1977: 171-9), his elaboration of the notion of "symbolic capital" and his insistence upon the "interconvertibility" of symbolic and other forms of capital by broadening the definition of "economic interest" are ultimately reductionist themselves, and cannot be applied to the Ilparakuyo and Maasai case. At the risk of provoking the relegation of the present study to the category of "naively idyllic representations of 'pre-capitalist' societies" (Bourdieu 1977: 177), I must assert that the introduction of the concept of "symbolic capital" and its articulation with "real capital" would seriously distort any understanding of the historical development of Ilparakuyo concepts of time in relation to pastoral praxis, the latter now increasingly penetrated by capitalist relations of production. To assume that practice in such social formations as Ilparakuyo and Maasai "never ceases to conform to economic calculation even when it gives every appearance of disinterestedness by departing from interested calculation (in the narrow sense) and playing for stakes that are non-material and not easily quantified" (ibid.) would be to obscure the very historical process we are trying to grasp. An analysis of the kind suggested by Bourdieu implies a universal "symbolic commoditization" of time, and hence the ability to "accumulate" and "dispense" it, destroying our understanding of how this process of abstraction and commoditization comes about with the introduction of capitalist relations of production. Thompson ably demonstrates that between the years 1300 and 1650 the "intellectual culture of western Europe [underwent] important changes in the apprehension of time" (1967: 56, and *passim*), and the backward capitalist countries of Europe (such as Greece) are still undergoing this transformation towards the accumulation, use, and "budgeting" of time, as are peasant social formations elsewhere; in short, its commoditization (cf. Mead 1955: 70-2; Taussing 1980: 5 and *passim*).

The formation of classes and the penetration of capitalist relations of production and ideology have been more fully explored for Kenya Maasai, where these processes are further advanced than in Tanzania (e.g. Bonte

1975; Hedlund 1979; ole Sena 1981; cf. Chapter 5, below). While these transformations need much further elaboration for the Ilparakuyo and Maasai social formations of Tanzania, I have attempted in this chapter to provide a theoretical and historical background for such an account by locating Ilparakuyo notions of time and change in the specific historicity of this social formation at a particular historical conjuncture.[19]

Notes

1. Evans-Pritchard also considered in some detail Lévy-Bruhl's ideas while preparing, in 1934, *Witchcraft, Oracles, and Magic Among the Azande* (1937).
2. At some points in his argument, Lévy-Bruhl comes close to recognizing the social and economic conditions that engender the production of various temporal concepts, but his false epistemological position prevents him from grasping their significance. Commenting upon the issue that, as far as he knew, "primitive" peoples did not see a future event as "situated at any point on the line of futurity", he notes (1923: 124, fn. 1), "This is one of the principal reasons for that 'lack of foresight' so often observed and deplored by those who study uncivilized peoples. It is *undoubtedly also due to other* causes of a *social and economic order*; but it proceeds mainly from the mental habits of primitives" (emphasis added).
3. That Geertz, despite the richness of the analyses he achieves, makes the same error in this respect is evident throughout his work (e.g. see Geertz 1973: 361).
4. In an often neglected but frequently perceptive paper on what he calls "temporal orientations" among the Berens River Saulteaux, an Ojibwa speaking group of hunters and fishermen, Hallowell makes explicit his comparison with "western time concepts", commenting upon the "relativity and provinciality" of the latter. He notes the reificiation and commoditization of time in capitalist society, quoting from Mumford (1934): "Under capitalism, time-keeping is not merely a means of co-ordinating and inter-relating complicated functions; it is also like money an independent commodity with a value of its own" (Hallowell 1937: 649, fn. 9).
5. Leach's study of Kachin social structure (1954) is an excellent and in many ways pioneering analysis of the "time dimension" in social structure (cf. Friedman 1975).
6. It is pertinent here to note Robin Horton's much more accurate contention (1967: 176) that, "In traditional Africa, methods of time reckoning vary greatly from culture to culture", an observation in keeping with the analysis presented here.
7. Somewhat similar, but less "theological", versions of time reckoning among the Kamba are given by Ndeti and Lindblom (Ndeti 1972: 178-85; Lindblom 1920: 338-42).
8. In an extremely penetrating and too-often ignored analysis of Iatmul ritual, ideology, and social structure, Bateson (1958 [1936]: 111-14, and *passim*) emphasizes the importance of an historical approach to the study of pre-capitalist societies and their conceptual systems.

9. Lévi-Strauss (1963: 21) maintains that:

> Even the analysis of synchronic structures . . . requires constant recourse
> to history. By showing institutions in the process of transformation, his-
> tory alone makes it possible to abstract the structure which underlies the
> many manifestations and remains permanent throughout a succession of
> events. (1963: 21; cf. also Lévi-Strauss 1966 [1962]; 66-74, 245-69)

I show later why this position entails an unacceptable notion of "history": but
we may note here that the strong Hegelian influence underlying structuralist
theory accounts for the reification of time concepts and hence the emphasis
upon "experience" (cf. Dunayevsksaya 1973: 15-16, and *passim*).

10. Jean Hyppolite's contention that essentialism is "displaced forever" is
erroneous in that essentialism is in fact embodied in the very structuralist problematic he sees as displacing the "tide of neo-Hegelian existentialism"
(Hyppolite 1969: viii, 13).

11. That most concepts of time are inextricable from concepts of space is
admirably documented for the Iraqw by Thornton (1980); this is, of course, a
universal condition.

12. The implications of age- and generation-set systems for chronology and history are explored for a number of societies in Baxter and Almagor (1978) and
in such monographs on particular societies as Dyson-Hudson (1966: 2 8-70,
and *passim*) and Lamphear 1966: 258-70.

13. Some versions give Kidong'oi as the son of "ole Mweiya", but as Jacobs
points out (1965a: 321), this is not a proper name but an appellation to "the
first one" in any story or legend when the true name is not known. In his later
article, Jacobs (1968: 20) suggests that Sitonik was the "first ritual expert",
the third on Hollis's list.

14. According to Maasai and Ilparakuyo legend, a warrior of the Ilaiser clan
"found" ole Mweiya (Kidong'oi or Sigiraishi) on the mountain called
Enkong'u e Mbakasi, "the source (lit. the 'eye') of the Mbakasi (Athi) River".
The mountain is also called Oldoinyo lo 'Laiser ("of the Ilaiser clan") or
Oldoinyo lo 'leMweiya ("of Mweiya's place"), and is known as the Ngong
Hills by non-Maasai.

15. Mr Melkiori Matwi, of the Tanzanian Ministry of Information and Culture,
has prepared such an account; but access to it has not yet been possible.

16. I must emphasize the extremely tentative nature of this provisional outline,
which is subject to further verification from oral sources as well as comparative research. The version of Ilparakuyo historical relations presented here is
gleaned from cross-referencing my own research with materials from Beidelman 1960, 1961a, 1961b, 1962, 1968; Berntsen 1979 and forthcoming;
Jacobs 1965a, 1968a, 1968b,1975, 1979; Fosbrooke 1948, 1956; Lemenye
1956; Thomson 1885; Krapf 1968 [1860]; and Berntsen (personal communication). Other historical references are cited in the text.

17. In commenting upon a story told to Justin Lemenye by an Olparakuoni elder
in 1893, Fosbrooke places the final conflict between "Kwavi" and Maasai
and their final separation in the period 1825-39 (Lemenye 1956: 51, fn. 11).
The evidence from such writers as Baumann (1894), Thomson (1885) and
others is summarized by Beidelman (1960: 245-50) and roughly confirms
this period. There have been Ilparakuyo communities on and off since at least

1837 in the areas of West Bagamoyo District where I have lived with them.

18. I am in fact suggesting that Ilparakuyo and Maasai consciousness of "time in historicity" is dialectical, and to that extent it is antithetical to the "metaphysical mode of thinking" characteristic of bourgeois philosophy. It is similar, on the other hand, to what Engels identified as conceptions of history and time in "this primitive, naive, but intrinsically correct conception of the world" characteristic of ancient Greek philosophy, "first clearly formulated by Heraclitus: everything is and is not, for everything is fluid, is constantly changing, constantly coming into being and passing away" (Engels 1975: 27-8; cf. Galaty 1977; 1978b, for Kenya Maasai).

19. A somewhat different interpretation of the data on relations of production and their transformation in the Ilparakuyo social formation is given by Bryceson and Mbilinyi (1980: 95-8, and *passim*).

5. Pastors and Pastoralists

"*Menyanyuk otoputo tung'ani, o lotoputo Enkai.*"
The one chosen by God is not the one chosen by people."

"*Erisio Ilmaasai o Enkai.*" "Equal are the Maasai and God" – if you remain Maasai, you are as safe as you are with God.

The primary interest in this study is to make some contribution to the elaboration of a theoretical problem: what are the relations between certain forms of ideology and the social formations in which they are, or can be, realized? The consideration of ideology as a sociological category is of continual and growing concern (e.g. Moskvichov 1974; Bétaille 1978; Gellner 1978), despite the attempts of bourgeois social science to kill it off during the 1960s (cf. Lipset 1960; Bell 1960; Waxman 1968). But my present interest in it arises out of a particular historical question: why did the Christian missions fail so signally in their efforts to evangelize and convert East Africa pastoralists, most conspicuously the various sections of the Maasai peoples of Tanzania and Kenya?

Since my own research has been basically amongst Ilparakuyo of West Bagamoyo District, a section of the Maa-speaking peoples that has been virtually ignored by the missionaries in favour of the more receptive cultivators among whom these pastoralists live, I include a discussion of other Maasai sections in Tanzania and Kenya where more intensive efforts have been made by various, primarily Protestant, groups.

As a result of this theoretical focus, the extensive anthropological literature on conversion in Africa and the complex historiography of mission activity in East Africa (e.g., Horton 1971, 1975; Fisher 1973; Oliver 1952), while obviously relevant, do not provide the main basis for my project. Rather, the problematic I adopt is derived from recent developments in theories of ideology based upon the seminal work of Marx and Engels, and certain trends in structuralism (Marx 1973, 1975; Marx and Engels 1964, 1970, 1976; Althusser 1971; Feuchtwang 1975; Bonte 1975; Godelier

1977). Such a problematic treats religions and religious change as aspects of ideological production in general, as manifested in specific social formations and modes of production, marking the differences between the one type and another and the differences in their associated ideologies as "systems of practices" (Feuchtwang 1975: 68 *passim*; cf. Colletti 1972: 3-44). The argument is a causal one, and the formation of ideologies in specific modes of production becomes the crucial issue. Horton (1975: 396 and *passim*) notes the reluctance of those anthropologists whom he calls the Devout Opposition, and amongst whom he classes Evans-Pritchard and Victor Turner, to accept any causal arguments whatsoever in questions of religious change, criticizing what he calls the absurdity of their (sometimes) various positions. The present essay, while taking a somewhat different view of what constitutes causation in social and historical processes from that adopted by Horton, postulates that causal arguments are the only meaningful ones possible in attempts to explain the issues at hand.

Religious practice, and discourse about religious practice, are here treated as aspects of ideological and theoretical practice in general. Stephen Feuchtwang summarizes the position neatly:

> Marxist analysis produces a theory of the system of practices, a theory from which can be derived all the forms which make up the complex unity of the society [or social group] in question. This must involve marking its differences from other societies. A theory of a specific socio-economic formation shows it to be repeatable. That is to say it shows it to be the constitution of a specific set of conditions, and not any other set. But Marxist analysis neither starts from nor seeks to discover some universal object, like Human Nature, or Society, or Power or Ideology, or Religion, which is a non-historical "fact". (1975: 68)

Religions and ideologies, then, are produced by historical social formations in specific historical circumstances, and they form an *essential element* (as ideologies) of the dominant mode of production in any case. Thus an ideology, and religion as a form of ideology, has a "social and historical existence" but, even more important, "only by means of ideology are individuals constituted as subjects, that is to say, as sources of action, able to relate to the whole of which they are parts". The subject is the "constitutive element, not of society in general, but of ideology in particular" (Feuchtwang 1975: 68-9).

It is clear, then, that the historical materialist analysis of religions as ideologies does not confine itself to the notion of ideology as merely "false consciousness". Rather,

> ideology is a systematic totality of views, ideas and theories which first and foremost express the interests and aspirations of a given social group or class. Political, legal, and artistic views, morals and religion, to varying degrees and with varying completeness express the ideology and propagate it by various

specific means. (Moskvichov 1974: 67)

Hence, for Marx and Engels, ideology is a *necessary* part of praxis, even proletarian praxis (or any other relatively "less alienated" than bourgeois praxis), since although Marx and Engels "did not describe dialectical materialism as an ideology, it was they who . . . elaborated philosophical, economic, political, legal and ethical views which express the basic interests of the proletariat" (ibid: 65-6).

II

The historical development of Christianity in eastern Africa can be seen as the penetration not of some abstract entity that we can label "Christian religion", but of specific ideological forms related to late 19th and early 20th Century Europe (as well as the United States) and their dominant capitalist mode of production, and to their missionary institutions themselves as social groups with their own particular ideologies, within the overall context of the intrusion of peripheral capitalism in its colonial form. These forms of colonial Christian ideology, if we may use that term, were very different from, say, early Christianity or Islam, a point to which I return.

In the case of the pastoral societies, most specifically the Ilparakuyo and Maasai, this penetration was confronted by a socio-economic formation of a unique kind, with its own system of religious, ideological, economic, and political practices, with their associated forms of discourse and the constitution of subjects. The confrontation resulted in the marked failure of evangelization, despite strenuous efforts on the part of the missionaries. It is this historical clash and relative lack of articulation of social formations, modes of production, and ideological practice that is the subject of this essay.

That missionary efforts to evangelize the pastoral peoples was in the long run largely a failure is attested to by many different sources, both missionary and non-missionary. In an overall survey of Christian progress in Kenya in the 1930s, Horace Philp wrote that:

> the centre of missionary activity [among Maasai] is at the station of Syabei (Narok), which is under the Africa Inland Mission, but considering the number of years that the society has been at work among the people, the results are deplorably small.[1] (1936: 57)

In fact, Philp's interesting statistics show that by 1936 there were fewer than 200 Christians among the Kenya Maasai population of 47,000 – despite the lengthy and strenuous efforts, as we shall see, of the Africa Inland Mission (AIM) and the Church of Scotland Mission (CSM) in the area.

Among the Ilparakuyo and Maasai in Tanzania, although early work was directed by the Church Missionary Society (CMS) and even earlier contacts with Catholic missionaries had occurred, the Lutheran societies have been the most active. In a perceptive work entitled, "A Cultural Study of the Maasai to Determine an Effective Program of Evangelization", a Lutheran missionary who is now working full time in Tanzania with the Maasai, sees clearly the "difficulties" of evangelization among them. Despite the fact that his was a library study, he notes correctly that the Maasai

> tradition of life is molded deeply into the pattern of thought and behaviour of each of them, and to bring something new, unadapted to this pattern is to only ask for discouragement. (Simonson 1955: 114)[2]

The Ilparakuyo pastoralists of Tanzania, as previously noted, have received relatively little attention from missionaries until recently, the latter concentrating instead upon the cultivators amongst whom Ilparakuyo have lived for 150 years or more. Groups of Ilparakuyo had been in contact with Catholic missionaries in the Bagamoyo and Morogoro Districts from a comparatively early period, and with CMS missions in other areas such as Kilosa, Dodoma, Handeni, and Mpwapwa (Last 1882, 1883a, 1883b, 1885; Beidelman 1960, 1962a, 1962b). These contacts had virtually no effect upon Ilparakuyo religious ideas or pastoral practices, although the people have for a long time made use of mission medical facilities. More recently, Lutheran evangelization by Ilarusa (Maasai-speaking cultivators from Arusha, northern Tanzania) immigrants into Ilparakuyo areas has had some success, particularly among women (Hurskeinen 1975, 1977: 119-22; cf. Ndagala 1972, 1978; Parkipuny 1978; ole Saibull 1974; see Chapter 6).

Most attempts to explain the failure of missionary endeavour amongst East African pastoralists have attributed it to a generalized pastoral resistance to change, or to some inherent conservatism in pastoral societies. Such explanations tell us nothing as to how or why this conservatism arises and hence it is tautological: pastoralists are conservative because they resist change (conversion); they resist change because they are conservative. This "resistance to change" has in turn been variously attributed to such cultural, or even psychological, phenomena as the notorious "cattle complex", invented by Herskovits (probably in all innocence) in 1926, and later sometimes taking on the complexion of a psychotic syndrome, or to the simple fact that pastoral societies tend to be nomadic, semi-nomadic, transhumant, or at least highly mobile. "Sedentarization" of the Maasai and other pastoralists was an early aim of both missionaries and administrators in East Africa, and it still is. Far from aiding the proselytizing activities of the former, these policies actively alienated the pastoralists. At any rate, the low population densities and high mobility of pastoralist populations does not explain why Ilparakuyo and Maasai deliberately ignored or rejected evangelization while being extremely friendly and hospitable towards individual missionaries and even government officials who behaved in a reasonable manner, right from the earliest periods of contact.

There is more substance in the suggestion that certain sociological factors unique to pastoral societies may explain their resistance to Christian proselytism and other intrusive socio-economic forces (e.g., Monod 1975: 56-60, 150-6 and *passim*: Schneider 1958, 1959, 1975; Dyson-Hudson 1962; Jacobs 1965b; Rigby 1969b), but the identification of these sociological factors has remained largely superficial. In a recent example of this type of approach, P.H. Gulliver (1969: 238-41) makes the "marginal economic environment" of the Maasai, and hence their *inability* to practise agriculture, the "crucial factor" in their "conservative commitment". Thus, he argues,

> the Maasai have developed a social system, a pastoral regime, a family and territorial organization, which are fairly closely geared to the limitations of their rather severe environment . . . Changes from the established and proven regime are, or certainly seem to be, likely to endanger the constant struggle against poor, unreliable natural resources.

Furthermore, he claims that the Maasai "have combined an ostensible refusal to accept change with the appearance of an attitude of implicit superiority towards other peoples" (ibid.: 234). *Ipso facto*, the Maasai reject any form of conversion, Christian, Islamic, or otherwise.

Such explanations, while obviously having some limited utility, are faulty on several grounds. The notion that the crucial factor is the economic marginality of pastoral areas is at plain contradiction with the historical facts, particularly for the Kenya Maasai and the Ilparakuyo, as well as for other East African pastoralists. Prior to colonization, most of these peoples lived – and some still do – in areas perfectly suitable for cultivation. Most of those communities that now occupy semi-desert, drought-prone, and degenerating areas were pushed there during the colonial period (Rigby, in press). Maasai and Ilparakuyo were not "forced" by ecological factors to adopt pastoralism, and hence to their "conservative commitment", by a hostile environment; they chose, and still choose, to be pastoralists when they could easily be cultivators, or now even proletarians or petits bourgeois. Gulliver's first argument, then, is clearly an example of the functionalism of certain forms of cultural ecology in which social adaptations are "determined" by man's physical conditions since he is a victim of his environment: hence, "man maketh not his own history", a form of explanation inadvertently derived from Feuerbach's vulgar materialism while being far less sophisticated than the cultural materialism of Harris (1968, 1979).

The second element in Gulliver's argument, concerning the alleged Maasai attitude of superiority to all others, is constantly reiterated in the literature on these and other pastoral peoples without the slightest attempt at explanation or grounding in ethnographic context. In fact, as with

Gulliver, this statement is taken as a given which explains other things, such as the reluctance to accept the ideas of others. He himself notes that, "despite their seemingly implacable attitudes and their [derogatory] evaluation of others, the Maasai have for several generations recruited and accepted non-Maasai into their communities" (1969: 237), a historical fact true also for Ilparakuyo and other pastoralists, and one which seemingly contradicts his own conclusion. An examination of the deeper implications of this apparent paradox might have led Gulliver to the crux of the matter; but in any event, at this superficial level, none of this explains why Ilparakuyo and Maasai welcome and accept strangers whom they like into their midst, including missionaries, while rejecting the latter's ideological commitments. The real nature of Maasai identity *vis-à-vis* other peoples, and in terms of their own culture, which can be expressed only in dialectical terms, has been fully explored by Galaty (1977, 1978a, 1982).

III

Elsewhere in this book, I refer to some aspects of the seminal and excellent work of Pierre Bonte (1974, 1975, 1977, 1981; See Chapters 1 and 6) in considering East African pastoralist societies within the general framework of the "Germanic" mode of production as a "transitional" form. What emerged from the previous analyses was that the pastoral mode of existence, or the pastoral social formations of eastern Africa, have some unique features that distinguish them from other social formations in which more or less settled cultivation of land constitutes the basis of the Germanic, or "domestic", mode of production.

A mode of production is a specific articulation of relations and forces of production in a particular historical conjecture, i.e., social formation; the nature of the articulation determines the nature of the mode of production and the social formation in which it is dominant. While I would agree with Hindess and Hirst's earlier (1975) formulation that, in conditions of transformation, this articulation is "structured by the dominance of the relations of production", *particularly* for the pastoral formations under discussion, radical differences in the *nature of the forces of production* are marked by specific forms of articulation, giving rise to distinct modes of production.[3]

It is evident that there are significant differences in the major means of production (as aspects of the forces of production) and, consequently, differences in the forms of access to, control of, and labour processes involved with these means of production (i.e., basic elements of the relations of production) in predominantly pastoral societies on the one hand, and agropastoral and agrarian or "horticultural" societies on the other. It could thus be argued that the articulation of relations and forces of production in the two cases is significantly different, even if both qualify for inclusion in the wider category of the Germanic mode of production. This is particularly so, it is maintained here, in the context of radical transformation engendered by the penetration of capitalism and its related ideological practice.

Some of these instances are discussed in Chapters 1, 3, and 6, as are certain aspects of the dominant ideologized instance (the age-set organization, as opposed to kinship organization characteristic of most agro-pastoral or agrarian formations). Here, I wish to pursue further the particular nature of other ideological elements in pastoral social formations in regard to religious and symbolic practices and, at this level, their distinctiveness from non-pastoral societies becomes even more evident.

In a short but extremely concentrated introduction to a recently published collection of papers on pastoral production and society, Claude Lefébure makes a number of penetrating comments which provide the next step in my theoretical discussion. Submerging for the moment the distinctions I have drawn between types of formations within the general concept of the Germanic mode of production, the crucial importance of the dominance of the ideological instance (in the articulation of the economic, politico-juridical, and ideological instances) characteristic of such formations is succinctly expressed by Lefébure:

> there is reason to think that it is because the community only really exists on the basis of relations established by the domestic groups, because its territorial status itself is merely a consequence, that *it requires some form of ideological guarantee* and that its conditions of reproduction call for some basis *external to the objective conditions of production*.[4] (1979: 5, my emphasis)

The *de facto* character of the community relations of production, beyond the domestic groups, is expressed in the ideological organization of age-sets, or kinship groups, or both. "This trait", adds Lefébure significantly,

> goes hand in hand with the *pre-eminent function* of the *community's own ideology* in the reproduction process. Seen thus, this specificity seems to us to constitute an original historical evolutionary path of which . . . still undifferentiated nomadic pastoral societies may be regarded as a typical product. (1979: 6, my emphasis)

Thus although Lefébure is not arguing explicitly for a "pastoral mode of production", the elements of such a notion are there, especially for the historical conjuncture in which undifferentiated (non-class) pastoral societies exist as actual social formations, as in the eastern African case. There are two other indications in his overview which mark the specificity of pastoral formations within the overall Germanic mode of production. They both concern the transformation of undifferentiated societies into differentiated (class) societies. Here, those societies in which the ideological foundations of the community's relations of production, and hence the reproduction of the community, are based predominantly upon kinship – and these tend to be societies with relatively greater dependence upon agriculture, at least in the East African context – certain contradictions *do not arise* in the transition to class structure. Lefébure states that:

> because the discourse of members of a segmentary society is rooted in kinship relations which are consubstantial with the group, the alteration in the conditions of the realization of the community [to dominant-dominated groups] does not render it obsolete, even though this alteration may necessitate certain modifications. (1979: 10)

Such a transformation is, however, patently impossible without total breakdown in the case of those pastoral social formations, with least dependence upon agriculture, in which the conditions for the realization of the community are expressed in the dominant ideology of age-set organization and the consequent subordination of kinship categories.

Finally, transformation through commoditization and the penetration of peripheral capitalism (i.e., the articulation of the capitalist and Germanic modes of production) further distinguishes "more pastoral" from "less pastoral" formations, as the crisis engendered by this articulation,

> which reflects the difficulties standing in the way of community control over the domestic units, is *characteristic* of the contradiction between forces of production and relations of production in *pastoral societies*. (Lefébure 1979: 7, my emphasis)

Hence this *form* of "contradiction in transition" is specific to pastoral social formations within the Germanic mode, and is *not* characteristic of the agro-pastoral or settled agricultural formations. The unique manner in which the Ilparakuyo, for example, handle the problem of commoditization is explored in Chapter 6, and similar processes have been confirmed for pastoral Maasai (Jacobs 1978).

Having established the notion of a relatively distinct pastoral formation of the Germanic mode of production, and having realized the dominance of the ideological instance in such formations, I now proceed to a further examination of the nature of these pastoralist ideological forms. This is necessary in order to contrast them later with intrusive 19th and early 20th Century forms of Christian missionary ideology and its variations. In doing this, I must set the Ilparakuyo and Maasai data in a broader comparative context, and this is provided by P. T. W Baxter's excellent paper on why witchcraft accusations are rare among East African pastoralists (1972). The theoretical problematic I have adopted is quite distinct from Baxter's, but his insights are crucial to much of the argument presented here.

Baxter compares in detail the evidence on witch beliefs and witchcraft accusations amongst nine eastern African pastoral and semi-pastoral peoples, including the Samburu (Isampur), a group closely related to Maasai.[5] All but one of these societies (the Mandari, who had chiefs and land-owning clans, are the exception (cf. Buxton 1963) could be characterized by the dominant Germanic mode of production.

Baxter's conclusions on these specific aspects of ideological belief and practice generally known as witchcraft are as follows (1972: 171):

1) Although beliefs in witches are widespread, the attribution of affliction and misfortune to witchcraft is not frequent.

2) Accusations are rare and very seldom intrude into the cracks and crevices of close social relationships.

3) Accusations appear to be most frequent where cultivation is essential to subsistence and rights over land have economic importance.

4) Such accusations as do occur are likely to be directed against "outsiders" or "strangers", that is persons identified by their peripheral status.

All of these points are relevant to our discussion, but the most immediate is item 3, in which Baxter finds that the frequency of witchcraft accusations is directly related to the relative importance of cultivation and hence rights in land, that is, land as the most important means of production. Those societies in which livestock are the major means of production, "land" (grazing, water, salt) being "given by God" to all people, are characterized by a negligible frequency of witchcraft accusation, religious practice being dominated instead by the power of the elders to "bless and curse" and to "ensure the ritual which maintains health and fertility" (Baxter 1972: 173; cf. Rigby 1971). These religious practices of the elders, which are in effect an aspect of the ideology of age organization, "are open and not covert, public and not private", and hence antithetical to the alleged practices of witches and sorcerers.

In pursuing what is in effect our distinction between the pastoral versus the cultivator social formations of the Germanic mode of production, Baxter perceptively notes (1972: 172) that "cultivators . . . commonly see themselves in competition for a common and limited pool of resources; so that one man's gain inevitably involves another man's loss, and a type of occult mercantilism prevails". Witchcraft and sorcery are used to "steal" fertility or plants from neighbours' fields into one's own, and "even where land is plentiful the production of surplus subsistence needs is limited by the work performed by the hands of the cultivator and his dependents" (cf. Sahlins, 1972).

Among pastoralists, on the other hand,

cows, camels, sheep, and goats . . . visibly breed and multiply, and a herd which increases brings dependents and affines. Surplus milk and meat, where there is no market, have to be distributed. Grazing and water are limited, but title to their use, with negligible exceptions, is open to all members of the political community and is not vested in individuals. (Baxter 1972: 173)

Labour is a problem in pastoral societies, a point Baxter fails to take up (see Chapters 6 and 7), but even this is solved by co-operation rather than competition, and I think Baxter's comparisons of the two types of social formation and those aspects of their ideologies related to witchcraft beliefs and practices are valid. The causal connection, however, remains unexplored.

Put in a more generalized fashion, the relation between the ideological aspect of the mode of production and the specific form of the means of production in predominantly pastoral, versus predominantly agricultural social formations of the Germanic mode of production, is influenced by a further crucial factor. Although land is controlled communally in the latter formations, usually on the basis of descent group affiliation, the *actual* appropriation of nature (i.e., land) is effected through rights in usufruct vested in individuals, both men and women. In such a situation, then, the "objectification" of nature involves the polarization, albeit in the context of temporary usufruct, of the subject (individual cultivator) and object (land/nature), resulting in a particular influence upon the formation of the subject and discourse about relations between man and nature, and hence amongst men.

In the predominantly pastoral social formations, on the other hand, since the major means of production is not land but the herd, and the herd is not unequivocally a part of nature, being instead a "mediator" between man and nature (Rigby 1971), the appropriation (and hence objectification) of nature assumes a distinctive form which excludes a simple subject/object dichotomy. In pastoralist ideology and praxis, men appropriate nature *only* through the mediation of the herd, which is a *product* of man's labour in the context of a universally accessible world: hence the Ilparakuyo and Maasai rejection of cultivation of the soil or hunting (Galaty 1977, 1978, 1982), as the latter are both destructive of nature through one form or another of "exclusive appropriation".

Although the necessity of avoiding a "nomadic pastoral mystique" is noted, Baxter concludes his discussion with the statement that

> Boran . . . perceive their herds, given good management and God's blessing, as always containing the potentiality of increase which is not at the expense of other Boran but depends, rather, on their active and amicable co-operation. The activities of elders are constantly directed to maintaining those co-operative social relationships which are subsumed in the "peace of the Boran", which is an expression of God's peace visible in active economic and social co-operation. (1972: 173)

Such a notion could be translated without alteration into the "peace of the Maasai", as expressed in the second proverb of the epigraph to this chapter. For Ilparakuyo, as for other pastoral Maasai, the close relationships of co-operation between men created by the periodic founding of new age-sets (*ilporori, ilajijik*), the associated practices of *olpul* and *entoroj* (also written *enturuj*; see Chapter 3), and the passage of age-sets through the system of grades, are conceived of as the essential reproduction and survival of the community. That closeness, co-operation, sharing, and the associated religious beliefs and practices *are* the peace of the Ilparakuyo or Maasai, and, as with the Boran, when "God is capricious and acts in ways that are hard for men to understand", and men are confronted with misfortune such as drought or epidemic disease, "they examine their own conduct, offer prayer and sacrifice", and so re-establish the blessings of that peace. (cf. Baxter 1972: 186)

Such are the ideological conditions necessary for the reproduction of the pastoral social formation, and they give rise to immediate religious practices and beliefs that involve the whole community and in which, in a sense, the efforts of men and God are conjoined and equal in a common enterprise. In such a context, God can hardly be an alienated, "omnipotent, omniscient, and omnipresent" deity. In some vague sense, God may have the ultimate power to destroy what he has created, but he would only do so if men fail to ensure their own regeneration through co-operation, good herd management, and the correct ideological practices in relation to age organization as well as kinship.

Ilparakuyo and Maasai identity, then, is at once correct pastoral and associated ritual praxis, both within the community and in its "correct" (dialectical and complementary) relations with other, "different", communities. I have explored elsewhere Ilparakuyo notions of interdependence with the Bantu cultivating neighbours (Ilmeek) and the Iltorrobo hunters and gatherers, as expressed in myth as well as *ilpuli* meat-feasts. The ultimate interdependence of *all peoples* in their *varied forms of praxis* is ideologically expressed in Maasai (and Ilparakuyo) myths of common origin, the implications of which are neatly summarized by Galaty:

> The mythical differentiation of Maasai, Torrobo, and Meek signifies the concurrent fissioning of symbols of economic practice, social and cultural tradition, and spatial proximity. Here is the Maasai counterpoint of the conventional anthropological notion of the unity of the "ethnic" unit or the "tribe", as representing a biological, social, cultural and linguistic entity. Yet the mythical unity of the three basic types is affirmed in the aboriginal oneness which preceded the division of the world. (1982: 7)

Put another way, the ideological practices of Ilparakuyo and Maasai – their religious beliefs and rituals – viewed as aspects of a cosmological theory, are perceived *by the subject* as being one with pastoralist economic and political praxis; in this sense, despite its ideological nature, it is a relatively "nonalienated" form of ideological praxis. *Objectively*, the notion of unalienated pastoralist praxis, including its ideological forms, can be related dialectically to the relative absence of exploitative relations in these social formations in the most specific as well as the broadest sense of the latter: man's appropriation of the world and "other men". This pastoralist unity of theory and praxis affords the subject a firm basis from which to perceive "the other", who can be fully assimilated into the community on the grounds of his dialectical "difference", as long as he does not initiate a discourse which threatens that unity, for example, by advocating agriculture (antipraxis) or by positing an alienated mystical force which controls the immediate destiny of men (ideological antipraxis). The dialectic of oppositions perceived by Ilparakuyo and Maasai in their unified pastoral and ideological praxis would collapse should any such intrusion be successful, removing the conditions under which the community can reproduce itself and the manner in which it "appropriates the world". As Galaty notes (1978b: 25), "The ethno-sociological structure [the dialectic of oppositions and their mediation] does not, then, merely reflect social forms, but plays a dynamic role in their systematic perpetuation, representing a code for social praxis", the social praxis of pastoralism itself.[6]

IV

It has been necessary to outline the theoretical argument thus far in order to situate the discussion of Ilparakuyo Maasai-missionary relations which follows. Without a sound theoretical problematic, the historical evidence would present us with an unresolvable contradiction: namely, the Maasai and Ilparakuyo accepted with open arms missionaries and other strangers as individuals, yet ultimately rejected the ideologies and other practices to which the strangers began to demand conformity.

Although missionary activity had begun much earlier on the coast of East Africa, the first real experience both Ilparakuyo and Maasai had of missionaries came at the time of intensive slave-raiding and internecine warfare in the interior during the 1840s and 1850s. It should not be thought, however, that the exploitation of eastern Africa in the middle of the 19th Century was entirely in the hands of the Arab traders and slavers who had brought Islam to the coast. Portuguese influence on the East African coast north of the Ruvuma River had, indeed, been broken by the Arabs of Oman in 1750, but after about 1800 the commercial activities of various European nations and the United States played a critical role in the penetration of mercantile capitalism and Christian influence, the former soon becoming the fully fledged exploitation of colonies by industrial capitalism in those countries.

Seyyid Said, the Sultan of Zanzibar and Muscat, headquartered in Zanzibar since 1840, had encouraged European and American traders even before this, making treaties with the United States in 1833, Britain in 1839, and France in 1844. These countries established consulates in Zanzibar in 1837, 1841, and 1844, respectively. Groves (1954: 93-4; cf. Bridges 1968: 16-24) notes that "the Americans held the lead in commerce at Zanzibar, and traders from Salem, Massachusetts, at first enjoyed a monopoly".[7] The active and leading role played by United States commercial interests in East Africa was undoubtedly the reason why the American Board of Missions was the first to plan activities in Seyyid Said's domains. But it was Johann Ludwig Krapf and his assistant, Rebmann, German missionaries who were Lutherans trained in Basel but working for the British CMS (Oliver 1952: 5-7), who were the first to come into contact with both

Maasai and Ilparakuyo.[8] They were established at Rabai, some 12 miles from Mombasa, by 1846, and from 1847 to 1849 and after they both made major journeys to Uchagga on Mt. Kilimanjaro (Rebmann was the first European to see the snows on Kilimanjaro), Usambara to the south, and Ukambani to the north-west. On most of these journeys, there were contacts with both Ilparakuyo and Maasai, so that by the "first and second journeys to Ukambani", Krapf could write a description of these peoples, referring to the former as "Wakuafi" (Krapf 1860: 355-66).

Krapf had come to East Africa from Ethiopia, where he had become fascinated with the task of evangelizing among the Galla, whom he thought were relatively "unaffected by any false religious principles" (Bridges 1968: 13-14) and hence capable of resisting "Muslim onslaughts". "I consider them", said Krapf (1860: 72), "destined by Providence after their conversion to Christianity to attain the importance and fulfil the mission which Heaven has pointed out to the Germans in Europe." But owing to the hostility it had encountered from both Ethiopian and Catholic clergy, the CMS finally abandoned its Ethiopian mission in 1843.

Although he never managed to work among Maasai or Wakuafi (Ilparakuyo) either, Krapf's interest in them was also strong, and was related to his infatuation with the ever-distant Galla. This was because, first, if the Galla were strong enough to have "taken possesion of a large section of Eastern Africa", the Maasai and Wakuafi were even stronger. For, as Krapf noted:

> The two kindred tribes, the Wakuafi and Masai, hate each other mortally, which is, however, a fortunate circumstance for the weaker African tribes; since, were they united and ruled by one supreme head, there would be an end to the existence of the other East African tribes, who could not possibly resist them, the savage Galla themselves not excepted, for the latter fly before the Wakuafi and Masai, and at most only prove dangerous enemies to them by stratagem and cunning, but never cope with them in a fair and open field. (1860: 361)

Second, Ilparakuyo and Maasai became in some sense a substitute for the Galla in Krapf's fading ambition to convert the latter, not least because of their physical appearance:

> As regard the physical conformity of the Masai and Wakuafi, their forms are tall and slender, with handsome and rather light features. Their greatest resemblance is to the Somali, who are considered Mohammedanized Gallas...[9]

Given the violent and unsettled circumstances of the times, it is not surprising that Maasai and Ilparakuyo were cautious and relatively hostile towards any intruders, and both Krapf and Rebmann were constantly warned against the dangers of the pastoralists.[10] Nevertheless, his ambition to evangelize the interior, coupled with his relative failure among the coastal people at Rabai, encouraged Krapf to dream of Christianizing Ilparakuyo and Maasai, a dream which was never fulfilled. While pursuing his labours with Rebmann among the Wanika tribes (Duruma, Digo, Giriama) of the coast near Mombasa, Krapf wrote that

> in course of time it became ever more evident to us, impressing itself upon us with all the force of a positive command, that it was our duty not to limit our missionary labours to the coast tribes of the Suahili and the Wanika, but to keep in mind as well the spiritual darkness of the tribes and nations of Inner Africa. (1860: 159)

This was as early as 1844, before his and Rebmann's journeys inland; by 1847 it was quite clear to Krapf that conversion of the Ilparakuyo and Maasai was essential to the achievement of his plan. After his brief description of the Wakuafi and Maasai tribes, which included an attempt to ascertain their "religious notions", Krapf is constrained to remark:

> May it soon be granted to our Protestant Church, to send missionaries to the millions [sic] of Wakuafi and Masai, to proclaim to them the Word which preaches reconciliation, so that these worst of heathen, "a nation scattered and peeled, a people terrible from their beginning hitherto," may be brought as an acceptable offering in the sight of the Lord God of Sabaoth to Mount Zion, and taught to know, to love, and to honour the true Naiterkob,[11] "the shining light of the world", and cease to murder and extirpate their fellow men. (1860: 366)

The full and lasting significance of Krapf's attitudes towards Maasai and Ilparakuyo will appear later; for the moment it should be noted that both Krapf and Rebmann soon found it more expedient to concentrate their inland efforts upon those peoples who had some form of centralized political organization, with chiefs or kings, such as the Chagga and the Shambaa (Shambala). Although Krapf explicitly criticized the Catholics for their attempts to "work first on the prince of a country, and through him influence his subjects" (Krapf 1860: 407), and emphasized the necessity for individual conversion, he later became highly suspicious of the "republican tendencies" of East African peoples, especially the egalitarianism of the pastoralists.[12]

While disagreeing with Rebmann and J.J. Erhardt, another German colleague, that the imposition of European rule was a necessary precondition for successful evangelization (a notion wholeheartedly adopted later by missionaries of all persuasions), Krapf believed the Africans to be "fallen men" who had to be civilized as well as converted (Bridges 1968: 52; Oliver 1952: 9). He was unable to distinguish conversion to Christianity from the "civilized nature" of 19th Century European culture as he knew it and to which he thought Africans should conform. He therefore ultimately became an outspoken advocate of European (particularly British and German) political intervention in this area, with its implicit economic imperialism.

But what of Ilparakuyo and Maasai? To summarize my argument thus far: the pastoral social formations of these peoples allowed the easy acceptance of strangers into their society, as pastoral and ideological praxis form a unity in which identity is expressed in a dialetical fashion, a balance of complementary oppositions which include non-Ilparakuyo/Maasai. Assimilation is related to adoption of this "unity in praxis". The historical evidence for such relations of interdependence in the pre-colonial period, at least as far as Maasai and Ilparakuyo are concerned, is well established (e.g., Muriuki 1974; Jacobs 1979 *passim*; Galaty 1978a, 1982; cf. Chapter 3), as is the exaggerated nature of the alleged aggressiveness and hostility of the Maasai in the 19th Century (Jacobs 1968, 1979); although, in the latter case, the historical conditions external and internal to Maasai society at this time were certainly capable of encouraging hostility towards strangers. Paradoxically, however, once individual European travellers and missionaries made peaceful contact with Ilparakuyo and Maasai, they were somewhat surprised by the friendliness and openness of the pastoralists. This point needs substantiation, first for the 19th Century and then for later missionary contacts, since it is crucial to the argument presented here.

The first European to travel through Ilparakuyo and Maasai country without firing a shot in anger was Joseph Thomson, whose expedition of 1883-4 is described in detail in his book, *Through Masai Land*, first published in 1885. Despite the fact that the journalist-explorer, H.M. Stanley, had declared in 1878 that the Maasai were a "tribe ... that specially delights in blood"[13] and had compared them with the Comanche and Apache of North America, and that a German naturalist, Dr Gustave A. Fischer, had just preceded him through Maasailand in the customarily aggressive fashion, killing many Maasai (Fischer 1885), Thomson stuck to his resolve to establish peaceful relations with the Maasai (Rotberg 1968: viii-x). Soon after Thomson returned to the coast at Mombasa in June 1884, Bishop James Hannington arrived in East Africa in January 1885 to take up his post in Uganda. He lost no time in preparing his expedition to Uganda, deliberately following in Thomson's footsteps. Hannington was "fired with the holy ambition of opening Maasailand, establishing a station and shepherd somewhere in the midst of those unruly flocks whose fine promise had strongly attracted him" (Dawson in Hannington 1886: 141). He was fated neither to establish such a mission nor to reach his destination in Uganda – he was murdered in Busoga – but his experiences with the Maasai and Ilparakuyo are highly illuminating.

Commencing his journey from Rabai in July 1885, Hannington soon learned that he had little to fear from the Maasai. His curious blend of naivete and righteousness is patent in his last journals, published in 1886; but he was also a gentle and sensitive man, and the Maasai and Ilparakuyo ("Kwavi") he met clearly warmed to him. Arriving at Ngong on the borders of Maasai country in August 1885, Hannington perceptively noted the friendly relations which existed between Maasai and Kikuyu when he wrote (1886: 161), "At one point there was an alarm of Maasai, who proved to be some Wa-Kikuyu women returning from a Maasai kraal. They say that the Maasai have all gone to Naivasha ... " Then, on Sunday 30th August:

With a sigh of relief [that they were not Kikuyu] I caught sight of the glittering spears of some Masai – the first I had seen! Confidence being restored, I advanced to meet them. About seventeen young warriors appeared, and I at once saw their spears were stained with fresh blood. I went round amongst them, and soon we were the best of friends. Their look was enough to paralyse my men with fear.

Hannington's attempts to obtain meat for his caravan from the Maasai, a notoriously difficult task (cf. Jacobs 1979: 46), led him to his most enlightening experiences with them. I quote him in full, since the entry in his journals indicates how open and friendly the Maasai were, despite the difficulties of the times. On camping one evening in the heart of pastoral Maasailand, from which most of the population was absent, probably owing to the outbreak of cattle disease and the exigencies of grazing and water, he noted in his journal:

No traces of Masai . . . but then three came along with a magnificent ox to sell.[14] The day was far spent before a somewhat dear bargain (though cheap to us at any price) was concluded, when what to my horror as I said as a matter of course "You will sleep in camp?", a thing which warriors never do, to hear them say, "Yes, we will." However, they seemed so amiable, that I began to feel pleased; and to keep them in view, I invited them to sleep in my own tent, an offer which they to my astonishment accepted gratefully. In spite of Jones declaring that I should be most miserable with three such evil bedfellows, I felt I would rather have them under my own eye than chance their prowling about the camp. The warmest friendship now seemed sprung up between us, and, having strewn the floor of the tent with the leaves of the sweet-smelling caleshwa,[15] a herb which the Masai use for beds, we laid us down to rest, their spears and shields at their sides. They packed themselves away like sardines in a box, and I covered them over with a leopard's skin, then with a grass mat and finally a waterproof sheet. They fell almost instantly into a most gentle sleep. I followed their example, and with one exception, I did not wake until time to start. Whenever we meet we are to be brothers. (1886: 188-9)

Later, near Lake Baringo, Hannington met groups of "Wakwafi refugees", who were probably Ilparakuyo sections which had gone northwest instead of south during the internecine battles of the early and mid-19th Century (Jacobs 1979; Thomson 1885: 240-3). He notes of them that the "Wakwafi . . . a tribe of the Maasai, . . . are most friendly, but our attempts to purchase food were futile".

It is clear, then, that even during troubled times, Maasai and Ilparakuyo were open and friendly to this gentle missionary, as they were to others who did not approach them aggressively. Jacobs' conclusion (1979: 46) that "although at the height of their power . . . at no time did Maasai attempt to dominate surrounding non-Maa-speaking tribes or prevent peaceful caravans from entering their country" is fully justified, as is Arnold Temu's more general comment (1972: 36) that "a close examination [of the period of missionary intrusion] reveals beyond doubt that the missionaries were able to survive only because they were treated well by the Africans."

For early Ilparakuyo–missionary relations further south in what is now Tanzania, the most significant source is the autobiography of a remarkable Olparakuoni, Sameni ole Kivasis, who was later known as Justin Lemenye, the Chagga corruption of Maasai *Olomeni*. Sameni's childhood was very unsettled, and he was soon to become cut off from his society, hence the nickname "Olomeni". Hollis correctly notes (1905: v, n. 1) that "Ol-omeni means He who is despised. When the name was given to him, he was a small, sickly child, and not expected to live" (cf. *olomen kewan*, "a diffident person", "one who despised himself"). It is highly unlikely that Sameni would have become a Christian had it not been for the tragic circumstances of his early years.

Sameni was born in 1878 and was ten to twelve years old when the rinderpest epidemic hit the Ilparakuyo and Maasai areas of northern and eastern Tanzania in about 1890. Around 1885, Sameni had been "captured" by a pastoral Maasai raiding party at the age of about seven, had escaped, and returned to his parents in Upare. However, famine continued, and in 1887, at the urging of his father, he went to live with a pastoral Maasai family (Lemenye 1956: 37-40).[16]

When the rinderpest epidemic devastated the Maasai herds, Sameni and a Pare youth his father had "captured", fled to Uchagga and threw themselves upon the mercy of Chief Rindi of Moshi. Perhaps owing to the terrifying experiences of his early years and the Ilparakuyo relations of interdependence with Shambaa, Zigua, and other Bantu people in the area, Sameni was constantly awed by chiefship, first in Shambaa and then in Chagga. This feeling of dependence he later transferred to his surrogate fathers, the two CMS missionaries, Steggall and Baxter, who had set up the mission at Moshi in 1885 and to whom Sameni was "given" by Chief Rindi in 1891 (Lemenye 1956(i): 48). The Germans had recently taken over Tanganyika, their new colonial possession. In 1892, the British CMS mission at Moshi were asked to leave as they seemed to have "too much influence" with the Chagga over a conflict with the German administration. In 1893, the CMS mission moved back from Moshi to Taveta, on the British (Kenya) side of the border, and Sameni went with them. He was baptized at Taveta on 2 April 1893, and became Justin Lemenye.

Justin Lemenye, probably the first of the very few Ilparakuyo converts to Christianity, went on to play a most significant role in Maasai and Ilparakuyo relations with missionaries and administrators alike in both Tanganyika and Kenya. He had been completely cut off from his Maasainess and pastoral praxis at the early age of 13, even submitting to what was the most humiliating of activities to the Ilparakuyo and Maasai, digging the soil. In a half-starved state, his first experience at mission school was the association of food and agricultural labour. He records:

Each child was given two bananas and issued with hoes and so we went off to the *Shamba* [Kiswahili "field"]. Although I knew nothing about cultivation, I was not at a loss, as I just copied what my companions did. After the few days, we became used to the routine of the place. The two compulsory tasks were firstly to cultivate the *shamba* every morning till eight o'clock, the second was school from nine to twelve and two to four; but nothing worried me. I performed all my tasks happily. (1956: 48)

That this recorded sense of well-being was not an entirely accurate description is revealed in Sameni's comments on the move from Moshi to Taveta when he states that

our safari to Taveta was a secret one. Every night we took our possessions into the bush and others received them to take them to Taveta. For us the move was not difficult and none of the children refused to go *because we had no country, all being captives*. (1956: 51, emphasis added)

Justin left his mark on Maasai history, in a number of ways. He was the main informant and research assistant to A.C. Hollis during the preparation of the book *The Masai: Their Language and Folklore*, first published in 1905. At this time he lived in Nairobi, met the famous Maasai *oloiboni kitok* (religious and political leader), Lenana or, correctly, Olonana, who played a critical role during the period of British alienation of large parts of Kenya Maasailand, and acted as interpreter for the British administrators "Collier" (Collyer), Hobley, and Ainsworth in Laikipia Maasai before the Maasai moves of 1904 and 1911 (Lemenye 1956(ii): 26-7). He also worked for the AIM (African Inland Mission) at Kijabe in Kenya from 1909-11 with its field director, Dr C.E. Hurlburt (Lemenye writes "Hulbert"); there he had the dubious distinction of meeting President Theodore Roosevelt when the latter was on his notorious East African safari in 1909. During this period, he must also have met Mulunkit ole Sempele of the Ilkeekonyokie section, as well as the AIM missionary John Stauffacher, who is discussed below, but he does not mention them. There is no doubt that, by this time, Lemenye had not only become disillusioned with his own role in the mission, but he had also become acutely aware of what the Europeans were doing to the Kenya Maasai by betraying the treaties that had been made with them, and by alienating their best pastures, including Laikipia. His growing impatience with the white man is indicated in the following comment on his trip to Laikipia, at Olomuruti ("Rumuruti"):

Here we slept, and in the morning our departure was delayed because the Europeans liked to play like children chasing after ducks which were swimming in some shallow lakes nearby. In spite of this, we got off at nine-thirty and arrived at the Boma [administrative centre] at noon. (Lemenye 1956(ii): 27)

109

Certainly, at the age of only 33, Lemenye had tired of his association with both the CMS and AIM. He had returned to Taveta after three years with the AIM at Kijabe, but he was given no work or status at the mission. He notes (1956(ii): 28) that "at that time I began to remember that I myself was Kwavi [Olparakuoni], so I left Taveta going in the direction of Mombo hoping to meet up with some of my relatives". He did, and took up again the threads of his Ilparakuyo existence for the rest of his 43 years of mature life.

On his return to Tanzania in 1911, then, Lemenye became fully involved in political activities and the administration, acting as go-between for the Ilparakuyo *oloiboni* (ritual leader) Maitei and the Germans at Lushoto in Usambara. When Maitei "resigned" in 1918 after the British took over the administration of Tanganyika,[17] Lemenye was chosen to be "Jumbe", or paid local administrative official, of the "Kwavi", a position he held for 35 years until he resigned in 1947 (Fosbrooke 1956: 36). He died in 1954 at the age of 76.

It would be reasonable to conclude that Justin Lemenye's conversion to Christianity was the result of historical circumstances in which famine, warfare, and disaster made him a refugee and a "captive" at an early age. From his autobiography, it seems likely that he was never a fully integrated member of his age-set among the Ilparakuyo or the pastoral Maasai, and only in later life did he have the opportunity or feel the need to reintegrate himself into Ilparakuyo society, albeit as a "mediator" with the external, colonial world. The point of his reintegration marked the end of his active involvement in mission affairs.

Mulunkit Olokirinya ole Sempele (hereafter referred to as Sempele), on the other hand, whose lifespan (1880-1955) covers much the same period as Lemenye's, approached his conversion with his eyes wide open and as a fully integrated member of the Maasai social formation.[18] He was to suffer deeply for this later on. Although his involvement with the AIM was to hamper his full participation in the ongoing age-set rituals and ceremonies which were a part of the Maasai religious practices, he was an elected *olaiguenani*, or spokesman, for his local age-set, a position of great trust among Maasai and Ilparakuyo alike (cf. Jacobs 1958, 1965a: 309-14, and *passim*). He was also marked for election as the *olaiguenani kitok*, "great" spokesman, of his entire age-set. Iltareto. Sempele was, as Kenneth King states (1971a: 1-2), "someone whose changing vision of the compatibility of Maasai culture and Christianity" was of major historical and contemporary significance.

Sempele's first 17 years, then, were spent in the mainstream of Maasai life, what I have called the "unity of pastoralist and ideological praxis". But owing to the aftermath of the same rinderpest epidemic that had driven Sameni from Tanzania Maasailand in the 1890's, Sempele's father, Sempele ole Ntokoti, had lost his considerable herds and had died, leaving nine wives and a large family. Sempele had been forced to engage in "trading activities", travelling as far as Uganda at the age of 19 or 20. During this trip, he met an unidentified missionary who made a great impression upon him.

As a result of this earlier experience, his knowledge of Kiswahili, and his already developed orientation towards economic activities other than pastoralism, Sempele was the ideal contact for a missionary. He was presented one in the form of John Stauffacher, whose commitment to his Maasai mission has already been mentioned. The young Stauffacher was obviously a sincere and open-hearted man, in the mould of the ill-fated Bishop Hannington. On this basis, the Maasai *ilmurran*, warriors, Sempele among them, welcomed him with customary openness and candour. This candour in accepting strangers, far from being idiosyncratic among Ilparakuyo and Maasai, is, I have suggested, characteristic of the ideological constitution of the subject in these social formations. Thus in November 1903, Sempele and a friend, Naguldu, arrived at Stauffacher's camp and told him they wanted to live with him and teach him the Maasai language, so that he could then "explain to the Maasai the word of God". As King notes,

> This first meeting with young men almost of his own age – open, courteous, welcoming – convinced Stauffacher that in a very short time he could be accepted and understood by the ordinary Maasai. (1971a: 4)

He also, however, reacted in typical European fashion, giving Sempele and Naguldu "2 rupees each for their instruction and help", and remarking in a letter to his fiancée, despite his delight at their friendliness, "Of course, there are some things about the Masai that are not just agreeable to think of but I think if we treat them kindly . . . these things can be overcome."

It was not only Sempele and Naguldu who welcomed Stauffacher; the whole Ilkeekonyokie community was delighted with this young stranger who was prepared to live with them, even moving about with them when they went in search of new pastures. They gave him a free supply of fresh milk and fruit. The affection between Sempele and Stauffacher grew stronger by the day, and with it Sempele's determination to "embrace Christianity". This very strong personal tie withstood to some extent the great rift that grew between them later as Sempele began to see more closely the collusion of the missionaries in the dispossesion of the Maasai of their best areas in favour of the white settlers and the government in Kenya, and as Stauffacher became more and more intransigent (sometimes at the instigation of his wife) about the kind of Christianity he was trying to impart to the Maasai. Some of these ominous developments form the subject of the next section. But we must first mention a point of major importance, noted perceptively by King:

> In later life what would distinguish Sempele from other Africans of his generation was his way of treating all white men and particularly missionaries as mere men, never dignifying them with the title *Bwana* (master), but looking them straight in the eyes as an equal. (1971a: 5)

The fact that Sempele was like this, says King, "may perhaps be partly explained by the fact that his first white friend was able to regard him not merely as an equal but someone to be loved and cherished". Certainly, up to a point. But this does *not* explain subsequent events, the fact that most Ilparakuyo and Maasai treat whites and missionaries in this same way, and that Stauffacher ultimately failed in his evangelizing effort, even with Sempele himself. For this, we must turn elsewhere, to the political economy of European imperialism in East Africa, and missionary involvement in it, as well as to its confrontation with the pastoral social formations.

V

We have seen that, despite his ostensible quarrel with fellow missionaries Erhardt and Rebmann over the necessity of European colonial control as a condition for successful evangelization, Krapf eventually advocated it himself. This was not diffcult for him, as he believed sincerely in the "civilizing mission" of European capitalism, as did most of the European and American bourgeoisie of that time. As R.C. Bridges notes (1968: 49), "When Krapf died [in 1881], a new age had begun in Africa. The number and scale of missions had increased and the 'scramble' by Europeans for political control was beginning." The period leading up to this would be called one of "informal European influence", and "Krapf was one of the key figures of this period; by his active work as missionary and explorer, and no less by his scholarship, he brought Africa and Europe close together."

Thus it was implicit in Krapf's thinking, as it was in that of most other missionaries, that

> Europe must eventually come to have a major influence on East African peoples . . . . The fact that Krapf turned to travel and discovery as a means to opening the way for the Gospel made it impossible for him completely to disregard the question of the secular basis for the introduction of Christianity, as he himself wrote. (Bridges 1968: 52-4)

Krapf's awareness of the economic and commercial content of this secular basis is amply evident from his writings. He believed that European imperial control in East Africa would "pay for itself" and that "great return would result from the application of European capital and enterprise in East Africa", and he even advocated the construction of a railway. This later became a key strategy in both British and German exploitation of East Africa.

It would be accurate to say that Krapf, this dedicated missionary, had a very sound grasp of the political economy of imperialism as it impinged upon East Africa, and he manipulated this knowledge to his own advantage. Bridges states that Krapf pointed out what was later to become conventional in British strategic thinking – that "the fate of India will some day be decided in Africa." Yet he wanted British rule as much as anything to prevent French Roman Catholics from supplanting Protestants in East Africa as they had in Ethiopia. (Bridges 1968: 54)

In the long run, then,

Krapf's influence on the European powers who were currently or later to be concerned with [the political and economic exploitation of] East Africa was more important than his direct impact on the region itself. Britain, Germany, and France were the countries most involved. (Groves (1954: 50)

Other missionaries in the latter part of the 19th Century, while perhaps lacking Krapf's global view, were also consciously aware of the close interconnections between their evangelistic activities and the penetration of capitalist enterprise and European political control. Dr S. Tristram Pruen, a medical missionary at the CMS station at Mpwapwa (Ugogo), Tanzania, displays a somewhat typical attitude of the time, both in his patronizing view of "the African" as well as in the blessings he gives to capitalist enterprise. Writing of the period when the "scramble" was on, he says:

The East Equatorial African is not a warlike individual; he is timid and suspicious, and these characteristics often urge him on to acts of violence which he would not naturally commit . . . the courage and ferocity of the Masai have been, I have no hesitation in saying, very much overrated by travellers, and I believe his reputation for bravery arises solely from the fact that he is less peaceable, and perhaps somewhat less timid, than the tribes by which he is surrounded. He has a wholesome dread of the white man, and is not likely to cause much trouble to the Imperial British East Africa Company in whose sphere he chiefly lives. Indeed, he would probably be glad to come to terms with this company at the earliest opportunity, and may prove a very useful ally. (1891: 87-8)

How wrong he was, and how wrong the Ilparakuyo and Maasai were to trust such men they were only much later to learn to their cost.

Willis R. Hotchkiss, a Protestant fundamentalist missionary from America who first arrived in East Africa in 1895 and was the first missionary to work among the Kipsigis of Kenya, was even more candid about the relation between Christianity and the penetration of capitalism. Writing mainly for American audiences in 1937, he says in his memoirs of his East African experiences:

Trade always follows the missionary . . . . It seeems incredible, therefore, that any intelligent man can fail to be interested in the Christian missions, when every pagan brought to Christ becomes in the very nature of the case an asset in the economic structure instead of a liability. These very Kipsigis who but a few years ago were a drain on the British taxpayer, are now buying everything from needles to automobiles. By every consideration of good business sense, therefore, Christian men ought to get back of the missionary enterprise instead of leaving it to the women, as they have done hitherto. (1937: 101)

The Maasai, alas, remained outside this capitalist utopia of joint enterprise between missionary and merchant, for Hotchkiss remarks that

with the possible exception of the Masai, who have resisted all efforts towards their regeneration, every native tribe is vastly better off now [1935], materially at least, than in [1895]. (1937: 45)

Hotchkiss is, in fact, even more egregiously patronizing in his attitudes towards the predominantly pastoral Kipsigis as well as towards other non-agricultural groups. Speaking of his "wards in Christ", he states:

Possibly there may be tribes who habitually live on a lower plane than the Kipsigis, but they are very few. The Pygmies of the Congo forest, the Wanderobo [sic] of our own Kenya forest area, and possibly the Masai, are among them. But they are relatively few in number. (1937: 102)

By the time colonial administration had been firmly established at the end of the 19th Century, pastoralists in both Kenya and Tanzania had begun to see the clear connections between the missionaries' evangelical activities, capitalist penetration, and eventual political domination by white colonial governments. We have seen how the Olparakuoni convert in Tanzania, Justin Lemenye, had realized the existence of these connections, largely through his Kenya experience but also from events in north Tanzania, and eventually broke his ties with the missions in 1911. The problem was most acute in Kenya, where missionary collusion with the government and settlers leading to the loss of land and political independence was certainly becoming known to the Maasai, partly through the activities of such politically conscious individuals as Mulunkit ole Sempele.[19]

The 1904 "agreement" between the British and Maasai had resulted in the loss of the best Maasai grazing lands in the heart of their country, near Lakes Nakuru, Naivasha, and Elmenteita. Some Maasai sections had been "given" the Laikipia plateau (previously occupied by a now defunct section, the Ilaikipiak) to the north "in compensation", others were pushed south into the present reserve.

By 1909, however, the influx of white settlers coupled with the fact that enormous areas of central Maasailand had been given at minimal rates to such powerful figures as Lord Delamere, generated mounting pressure to remove the Maasai even from Laikipia and make those sections already there "rejoin their brethren" in the "southern reserve". The top levels of missionary organization were in full support of these further dispossessions of the Maasai as Temu succinctly puts it:

The government on the spot, with the backing of the missions, seemed in favour of establishing a reserve for the Masai. The missions in the highlands believed that the concentration of the Masai and for that matter, of any tribe, into one reserve would given them large concentrations of people whom they could easily reach. (1972: 98)

We may note that they were no more successful in making converts even when Maasai were concentrated in their southern reserve, a state of affairs that missionary collusion with the government and the settlers had no little role in bringing about.

This collusion was of such enormous significance in creating Maasai and Ilparakuyo awareness of the apparent bond between Christian evangelism, capitalist penetration, and the threatened end of their pastoral praxis and ultimate identity that it cannot be overemphasized. That Protestant and Catholic were equally involved is clear, and the tenor of the times is admirably expressed by Temu:

> The Protestant missions fully supported the concentration of the Maasai into one reserve, thus giving a blessing to the demands of the settlers and the pro-settler administration . . . . They supported the policy from what they argued was a moral point of view . . . . Bishop Peel [of the CMS] put this moral Christian point of view even more sharply . . . . To put the Maasai into one reserve was, according to the bishop, "sound administration and a wise step in the moulding of these remarkable people afresh in civilization, Western and Christian, but admitting of conservation of anything good in the end of keeping them from all the peculiar evils of their present system and customs."[20] The Vicar Apostolic of Zanzibar and British East Africa seized the opportunity to warn the Governor that if the Maasai were not confined to one reserve they would be a major source of trouble for the administration in the future. Echoing the Protestant missions' view, he wrote, "you are only aware of the moral condition of a people if they are brought together and firmly controlled by government." Thus far it had been difficult to evangelize the pastoral tribe so the missions believed that work among them would be easier if they were restricted to one area. (1972: 100)

In Tanzania, German policy was also to alienate for European settlement the best areas of Maasailand, including the central areas of Monduli, Longido, Ngorongoro, and Loliondo (Fosbrooke 1948: 10–11). The Lutheran and other missions in the area did nothing to prevent the loss of the best grazing and water by both Maasai and Ilparakuyo and the consequent social upheavals which affected both peoples so soon after the droughts and epidemics of the late 19th Century. Most of these lands were later returned to the Maasai after the British took over administration of the territory in 1916.

By the time of the second Kenya Maasai "treaty" and move, which was completed by 1911 and in which they lost even Laikipia to the white settlers, even the most isolated of Maasai would have known of the missionary complicity in the advancing destruction of their mode of existence. Sempele, still a close friend of the American missionary Stauffacher, resolved to help his fellow Maasai who had decided to take legal action against the government over the abrogation of Maasai rights and the earlier treaty. He had just returned in 1912 from the United States, where he had seen how American blacks were treated, and from then on he consistently warned Maasai and other Kenyans about the possibility of such conditions appearing in East Africa (King 1971a: 15-16, 1971b: 66-7). Justin Lemenye, who had just left Kijabe for Tanzania, was undoubtedly party to all of these events, and was transmitting them to the Tanzania Maasai and Ilparakuyo.

However, Sempele was prevented from acting as a witness on behalf of the Maasai by Lee H. Downing, then acting head of the AIM, who "spoke most disapprovingly" to him, adding that "as a mission we do not for a moment approve of one of our boys championing such a cause. Our policy is to work in harmony with the administration". Stauffacher was not in Kenya at this time, and Downing made it clear to counsel for both Maasai and administration that the mission could not allow "one of our boys" to take any action antithetical to administration policy, largely in order to prove to the latter and to the settlers that the AIM was "a responsible society". As M.P.K. Sorrenson notes:

> But acting in a "responsible" manner towards government on such an important issue was not likely to win the mission Maasai converts . . . . It is perhaps significant that after 1913 the Maasai refused to allow missions to open stations in the southern reserve.[21] (1968: 266-7, and n. 40)

This Maasai ban remained in effect until the 1930s.

Thus the alienation of Maasai land and the white man's duplicity, with overt missionary collusion and even blessings, were to play a major role in Maasai and other pastoralists' disillusionment with Christianity and evangelical activities. But the real reasons for the rejection of Christian teachings by Ilparakuyo and Maasai go much deeper than this, as I have suggested. Loss of land and political independence was also true of most other East African peoples, the Kikuyu, Chagga, Kamba, Pare, Shambala, and other Bantu cultivators, who nevertheless were eager to convert, and gain the white man's education and culture, hoping to use it to their own advantage. The Ilparakuyo and Maasai were not, preferring instead to cut their ties with even those friendly missionaries who were ultimately powerless if not actually involved in colonialist conspiracy. Even Stauffacher, who had worked so hard to persuade the Maasai to reject both moves, later became increasingly hostile to Maasai social and cultural characteristics and values, leading eventually to his rift with Sempele (King 1971a).

The crux of the argument proposed here is as follows. We have seen that the identity of interests between missionary, settler, and administration was explicable in terms of their common commitment to 19th and 20th Century bourgeois values engendered by the development of capitalist society in Europe and North America. There was little difference between the excuses made, for example, by Philp for the loss of Maasailand by the Maasai in 1936 and the colonialist ideology propounded by Elspeth Huxley in her paean to Lord Delamere in 1935 (Philp 1936: 56, 125: Huxley 1935 [1953]: 72-3, and *passim*). But to Ilparakuyo and Maasai there was a difference, in that the settlers and administration did not, on the whole, preach one thing and do another; the missionaries did. In fact, the ideological discourse of the missionaries was in flagrant contradiction to their behaviour in conspiring with the settlers and government to defraud the pastoralists, and even the western education so eagerly seized upon by other East Africans turned out to be "education to work for the white man", ultimately a denial of the unity of pastoral praxis and ideology in a egalitarian social formation. And the missionaries compounded the alienation of their ideological discourse in their other "moral stand", that concerned with the "labour problem".

During the period of settler consolidation after the First World War, the most perceptive foreign commentator on the scene in Kenya was an English doctor named Norman Leys. While Huxley was perpetrating her colonialist mythology in the 1930s, as well as attributing the labour crisis being faced by the settlers in Kenya to a "lack of incentive to work" on the part of the Africans and thus exposing her racist attitudes (Huxley 1953(i): 231),[22] there was already available a brilliant exposé of settler strategy and missionary involvement by Norman Leys, first published in 1924 and again in a revised edition in 1926. Huxley does not mention Leys because, from the settler's point of view, he had to be obliterated; his outspokenness over the Kenya administration and alienation of Maasailand had caused his dismissal from the colonial government (King (1971b: 129).

Despite minor intrusions into Leys's work of the patronizing attitude of the liberalism of the period, he provides a clear indictment of the duplicity of the government, settlers, and missions in the loss of Maasailand and other pastoral areas to their inhabitants. But not only this: he also recognizes the basic elements in the Maasai social formation and its associated ideological system with unusual perceptiveness for the time. For example, although he mishandles the structure of the elderhood, or age-set, system, he correctly notes that

> it was impossible for the tribe to develop into a monarchy or an aristocracy, as is the usual course of political growth, and as conquest could neither enrich nor add to the glory of the warriors, it was never attempted. (1926: 106)

While Leys gives no indication of having read Marx, his categorization of the Maasai as similar to "our German ancestors" is so close to the notion of the Germanic mode of production and the pastoral social formation given in this book that it bears repeating. Commenting upon Maasai cattle-raiding, he notes that raids were undertaken, not by the tribe, but by one or more warrior bands, with the approval of the medicine man [*oloiboni*]. Each band, like the *comitatus* of our German ancestors described by Tacitus, consisted wholly of the youths and young men of a single sept, or sub-sept, who lived together when at home, and fought with mutual rivalry in war.

In proceeding to a discussion of the ideological relations characteristic of pastoralism it is almost as if he were using the *Grundrisse* as a model – a chronological impossibility[23] (cf. Chapter 7).

The Masai could not be induced [to work for the settlers or become involved in commodity production]. Like all purely pastoral people, they held [the use of agricultural tools] to be degrading . . . . Most if not all primitive peoples agree with the author of Genesis that labour on the soil, and indeed the use of tools in general, as distinguished from the free pastoral life, was imposed on mankind by some primeval curse. Mohammed is quoted by Peisker, in the *Cambridge Mediaval History*, as having written, "Wherever this instrument (i.e. the plough) has penetrated, it has always brought with it servitude and shame." (Leys 1926: 112, n.I)

The pastoralists' temporary appropriation of the world for the purpose of reproduction (Marx 1973: 472, 474) is expressed in their ideological system as a rejection of *certain forms of labour*.

Thus, as far as the settlers and administration were concerned, and with the moral backing once again of the missions, "the reason that the [Maasai] present a problem at all is simply that they have failed to fall in with the accepted idea about the status and duties of Africans in Kenya" (Leys 1926: 132); that is, they refused to work on plantations or to involve themselves in commodity production.[24] Not only that; they refused also to disband the age-set system, particularly the organization of the *ilmurran*, junior warrior age-set, and declined to fight for either side in the British–German conflict in East Africa from 1914 to 1916 (cf. Huxley 1935(ii): 39-49; King 1971a: 17).

VI

Tragically, and because of their 19th and 20th Century capitalist ideology, the missionaries dealt the *coup de grace* to their evangelizing efforts among the pastoralists by their moral support for all the methods used to make East Africans labour for them, the government, or the settlers, even to the use of forced labour. Most missionaries "welcomed European settlement in the belief that settlers, by introducing improved methods of cultivation and employing labour, would assist in the civilizing process" (Sorrenson 1968: 264). Some, particularly those of the Church of Scotland Mission, which was based in Kikuyu from where it did some work in Maasailand, advocated "commercialization" and were involved first hand. "Ever since Livingstone's day, the Scottish missionaries had looked on commerce as a necessary means of spreading Christianity." The "moral viewpoint" that both Protestants and Catholics had had in support of the alienation of pastoral land was extended to moral support for small reserves for the Kikuyu, for example, so that they would be forced to work for the settlers and participate in the "dignity of labour". One CSM missionary, D.C.R. Scott, saw "industrial work as a means of preparing Africans for conversion to the faith"; he became a vice-president of the Kenya Planters and Farmers Association and campaigned for the expansion of settler rights in land, using mission buildings for settler political meetings (Sorrenson 1968: 264).

"Work", which meant Africans working for settlers, missionaries, or government, was hailed as a virtue in itself, a moral naturally taken up by the settlers to justify their demands. Huxley records approvingly that the "Heads of the Church" had objected to a government circular advocating forced labour on the grounds that "it did not go far enough", and that the "Bishops' memorandum recommended a system of carefully controlled and legalized compulsory labour" (Huxley 1953(ii): 63-4; cf. Sorrenson 1968: 367-8).[25]

The missionaries, then, became the moral apologists for the expansion of capitalist settler interest not only over land but also labour. The Protestant missions in Kenya and Tanzania, whether CMS, CSM, the largely American-sponsored missions with a loose ecclesiastical organization such as the AIM, or the Lutherans, all derived from the Puritan strain of European life. Despite the fact that this strain was, *in Europe*, committed initially to egalitarian and socialist ideas, the missions' dominant commitment to a 19th Century capitalist ethic determined their response to the pressure of the strongly bourgeois elements which made up the settler population in East Africa, and led them to wholehearted support for the penetration of capitalism and its ideological concomitants.

The missionaries' presentation, through control of African education, of this essentially alienated form of ideology and practice to the pastoralists, combined with their obvious identification with settlers and government (their "praxis"), presented the Ilparakuyo and Maasai with an unresolvable problem. Viewing the discrepancy – one might say gulf – between missionary ideology and missionary praxis from the fundamental unity of pastoral ideology and praxis engendered by the unique relations of production of the pastoralist social formation, they could accept in sincerity the friendship of individual missionaries, but not the ideological content of the *kind* of Christianity the latter espoused.

This ideological content was basically capitalist, individualist, and tied to the essentially inegalitarian notion of the benefits to be derived from labouring for someone else. Since the missionaries had already demonstrated their willingness, even eagerness, to act as the harbingers of land alienation, commoditization, and labour exploitation, all antithetical to both pastoralist praxis and discourse, and leading inevitably to their destruction, the only answer was to break off discourse with the missionaries. For the pastoralists this was historically possible, first, because they had already been relegated to the economic margins of the colonial political economy, but more important, because the unit of ideological and economic practice characteristic of their social formation perhaps encouraged an awareness deeper than that attained by their agricultural neighbours (until it was too late) of the consequences of missionary penetration. One cannot help but wonder whether, had the missionaries brought to East Africa the revolutionary ideology characteristic of early Christianity rather than the bourgeois economism of 19th Century Europe (cf. Leys 1926: 227-71; Engels 1957 [1894-5]: 316-47), perhaps the Galla, Maasai, and Ilparakuyo might have become the evangelical crusaders of Krapf's dreams.

Notes

1. Sir Charles Eliot, the East Africa Protectorate's Second Commissioner from 1900-4, hated the Maasai with an intensity difficult to exaggerate. It was he who repeatedly commented upon the "abominable habits" of the Maasai, an idea later adopted eagerly by both missionaries and settlers, making this an excuse to dispossess them of their land. He wrote of the Maasai that "their habits may be of interest to anthropologists, but they are socially and politically abominable".
2. The Revd J. Davis Simonson very kindly gave me permission to see and quote from his thesis in this paper. It was submitted in partial fulfillment of the Master of Theology degree at the Luther Theological Seminary, St. Paul, Minnesota, in 1955. I am also indebted to the librarian of that institution, Mr Ray Olson.
3. In their "auto-critique", Hindess and Hirst maintain that the effects of their critique of the concept of mode of production as expressed in *Pre-Capitalist Modes of Production* (1975) "are not . . . the displacement of one conception of mode of production (dominance of the forces) by another (dominance of the relations) but rather the displacement of the mode of production itself as a subject of analysis" (Hindess and Hirst 1977- 55; Marx 1973: 472-4; Melotti 1977). This does not materially alter the substance of the present discussion, which can easily be assimilated to one about specific *social formations*.
4. It is generally accepted theoretically that it is only in the capitalist mode of production that the economic instance determines its own dominance. In all other known modes of production, the economic instance determines the dominance of one or both of the other two.
5. The Samburu are considered peripheral by central pastoral Maasai, just as are the Ilparakuyo and even the Tanzanian Kisongo section of pastoral Maasai. The notion of the "peripherality" of these groups is examined in detail in Galaty (1982: 8ff). The older eight societies surveyed by Baxter are the Boran, Nandi, Turkana, Karimojong, Somali, Nuer, Mandari, and Dinka.
6. Although I have not yet examined the issue in detail, the theoretical position adopted here is not inconsistent with the much more far-reaching analysis presented by Lucien Sève in his treatment of Marxist theory and the psychology of personality (Sève 1976 [1974]).

7. It was as a result of this activity that the cheap cotton cloth known to this day as Merikani in East Africa became a major part of clothing throughout the area.

8. When the Germans eventually established colonial control in Tanganyika, a process which spanned the period 1885-91, there were no Germany missionary societies in the area. Apart from contacts with the CMS described here, it is likely that Ilparakuyo had earlier experience of the Catholic mission of the Congregation du Saint Esprit, also known as the Black Fathers, who were based at Bagamoyo on the coast and who had opened missions at Mandera (1880), Mhonda (1877), Morogoro (1883), Tungwe (1884), and Kondoa (1885) (Groves 1954: 72). There are Ilparakuyo in most of these areas, and they have probably been moving in and out of them since at least the 1830s. The Ilparakuyo community in which I lived is adjacent to Mandera, with another Catholic mission at Lugoba a few miles away. There is currently a large Ilparakuyo population also in Morogoro District.

9. Krapf's speculations on this point are curiously akin to Ilparakuyo and Maasai notions of their relatedness to the Somali, whom they consider their closest relatives among non-Maa-speaking peoples, although they are linguistically, historically, and culturally distinct (cf. Galaty 1982:7).

10. On hearing of Rebmann's plans to visit Uchagga on Kilimanjaro (which Maasai called *oldoinyo oibor*, "the white mountain"), the Governor of Mombasa warned Krapf of the "risks the journey involved from warlike tribes, among them the Masai" (Groves 1954: 101, n. 1). Rebmann, however, successfully completed his journey with only nine men and "weaponed with only an umbrella". Yet, much later, when Krapf was in Europe in 1856, Richard Burton and John Speke visited Rabai and insisted that there was a threat from the Maasai (and Ilparakuyo) civil war refugees. In January 1857, they returned to Rabai, "swords in hand to help", when they "insisted on the evacuation of Mrs Rebmann and she and her husband finally retreated to Zanzibar for a period of several months" (Bridges 1968: 41; Burton 1872(ii): 57, 68-71).

11. Naiterukop, which means literally "the one (feminine) who begins the earth", or "the first on earth" from *a-iteru* ("to begin") and *enkop* ("earth, country") cf. story by Justin Olomeni (Lemenye) in Hollis 1905: 266-9.

12. Krapf's mistrust of republicanism applied equally to what was happening in Europe. Later in his life, as Bridges perceptively remarks:

> Krapf . . . appears to have found the general development of Europe outside Kornthall (the pietist settlement near Stuttgart where he had lived on his return from East Africa in 1855) not altogether to his taste. He had deplored the popular commotion of the 1848 revolution and disliked what he saw as analogous republican tendencies among East African tribes. (1968: 43).

13. In an address to the Royal Geographical Society in 1878, Stanley told his audience:

> If there are any ladies or gentlemen in the Society this evening who are especially ambitious of becoming martyrs, I do not know in all my list of travels where you could become martyrs so quickly as in Masai.

14. The sale of such a beast at this time is another indication of the extreme hardship the Maasai must have been facing.
15. Maasai *elelshua*, a variety of plants including *Helichrysum spp.* and *Gnaphalium luteoalbum* (cf. Kokwaro 1976).
16. Sameni went with his patrilateral cross-cousin, Simel; the latter's father, who came from a pastoral Maasai section of the Kisongo to the west of the Ruvu river, had married Sameni's father's classificatory sister. The bond between cross-cousins among Ilparakuyo is very strong, especially if they are of the same age-set. Sameni recalls:

    When the time for departure came, my father called me, and said, "Tomorrow Simel's father will migrate and I want you to help Simel to herd his goats." Since Simel was a great friend of mine, I was very pleased with this arrangement. (Lemenye 1956: 39)

17. Maitei, of course, remained principal *oloiboni* of the Tanzania Ilparakuyo until his death, when his son Moreto took over from him. The present *oloiboni kitok* of Ilparakuyo, who lives near Mvomero in Morogoro District, is Moreto's son.
18. The following account is taken substantially from King's excellent article (1971a).
19. Since Maasai straddle the border, the flow of people, herds, and information between Kenya and Tanzania sections of Maasai, as well as Ilparakuyo, is a permanent feature of the pastoral social formation.
20. The missionary attitude here is reminiscent of Sir Charles Eliot's distaste for Maasai society, as mentioned in note 1 above.
21. Sandford 1919: 67.
22. The settlers' racism extended also to Asians and Jews, and in this they yet again had "moral" support from the missionaries.
23. Marx's *Grundrisse* was first published in a limited edition in 1939 and 1941, but a full edition was not available until 1953 (Nicholaus 1973:7).
24. The only exception were those few Maasai who agreed to remain with Delamere, who had taken over an enormous part of central Maasailand's best grazing areas. They stayed on at his ranches on condition that they could herd their cattle with his; but this is not the place to deal with this interesting exception.
25. Sorrenson notes further (1968: 270) that "no matter how genuine their motives, the missionaries could not avoid the African suspicion that a missionary was no better than a settler", and he quotes from Welbourn (1961: 111) a Kikuyu proverb, "*Guitiri mubea na muthungu*, 'there is no difference between a missionary and a settler.' "

6. Pastoral Production and Socialist Transformation

> *"Ore olonoto enkitok supat, nenoto olpusii ogol enkinyiang' a."*
> "And the one who has a good wife is as he who has a precious stone."
> *"Meoro enkaji nabo."*
> "One (wife's) house cannot be divided."

Numerous and often excellent descriptions and analyses exist of "pastoral cultures" or the "nomadic way of life", as well as many comparative studies of pastoralism in general. Among the former, few are informed by developments in the historical materialist and structuralist problematics, most adhering to fairly "classical" forms of anthropological functionalism; among the latter, a number of efforts have been directed towards dispelling various myths about the "peculiar" attributes of pastoral social formations (e.g. Jacobs 1956a; Rigby 1969b), while others seem devoted to creating new, and perhaps more "attractive" myths about them, for example the notorious "cattle complex" attributed to East African pastoralists (Herskovits 1926; cf. Klima 1970: 4-5). Recently, volumes of collected papers and proceedings of conferences upon pastoral peoples have immeasureably advanced our general knowlege of pastoralism (e.g. Irons and Dyson-Hudson 1972; Salzman 1971; Monod 1975). International study groups and commissions have been organized to further studies in pastoral and nomadic groups.[1]

Despite a number of themes common to many of these studies (such as the close interrelationships among pastoral economies and various ecological factors), there is often a serious lack of concern, with a few notable exceptions (e.g. the excellent work of Dahl and Hjort 1976), with the actual processes of production in pastoral societies. For example, the theoretical problematics employed often emphasized such factors as "private versus communal *ownership*" of the herds, "rights in" grazing and water, notions of "private and individual property", and so on, resulting in considerable semantic confusion and error which tend to leave the debate at what may be called an ideological level. As a result, much of the argument about what *really are* pastoral societies as opposed to non-pastoral societies, or what pastoralism really *is*, or what is unique to the pastoral mode of existence, is conducted at a superficial level, *because* generalizations are made upon the politico-juridicial and ideological levels of each social formation, rather than upon the issues of the levels of control of the basic means of production, *as well as* (and this is critical) the concrete elements of the *process* of pastoralist production itself, and how people relate to each other in carrying out this entire process. This in turn leads to contradiction and confusion when discussion is directed to problems of the transformation of pastoral societies and their articulation with the broader social formations of modern nation-states, whatever their political hue.[2] Let me provide a brief example of statements on two pastoral societies which relate "rights in grazing and water" to the basic conditions necessary for the reproduction of the pastoral community itself. The first is taken from the work of Frederik Barth, whose contribution to pastoral studies has been immense and deservedly seminal. Writing of the Basseri pastoral nomads of Fars, South Persia, Barth states:

> A pastoral nomadic subsistence is based on assets of two main kinds: domesticated animals and grazing rights. The recognition by the sedentary authorities of traditional grazing rights vested in distinct tribes is basic to the pastoral adaptation in Fars. Such tribes mostly have centralized political organizations based on chiefs, as do the Basseri, and are further united into large confederacies, which were formerly integrated into the semi-feudal traditional organization of Persia, and which are still recognized by the authorities. (1964: 415).

Here, the politico-juridicial recognition of "grazing rights" by an *external* authority is a *condition* of the ability of the community to reproduce itself. Compare this with the following statement concerning the specific social formation of the pastoral Maasai:

> Within the sub-tribal land, pasture and water are *used* communally. The local society has communal *right to the use* of these resources, but the sense of *ownership* even communally does not seem to be entertained. So when a stranger moves in with his cattle or to cultivate the land, the local people will complain of the danger of disease and depletion of pasture in the first case, and the *appropriation* of *pasture* in the second; but not against the appropriation of soil, land as such, or even the *presence* of the stranger on land on which he has no rights communally with others. (Parkipuny 1975: 27, my emphasis)

Perhaps needless to say, the Maasai have no centralized political organization, nor have they ever been integrated with a semi-feudal social formation, unless the present inroads of capitalism can be construed as creating such a condition. But the point is that Maasai do not conceive of rights over any *particular area* as being a condition of their reproduction; this is even more true of the Ilparakuyo Maasai, whose pastoral economy provides the basis for the present discussion.

The aim of this chapter, which is confined largely to a comparison of pastoralists in contemporary Tanzania, is to employ a specific problematic in an analysis of the processes and relations of production in the pastoral mode of existence and its transformations, commencing with my own studies among the pastoral Ilparakuyo. At the outset, however, I must note that I am not advocating a concept of a "pastoral mode of production"; to my mind the proliferation in the literature of new varieties of modes of production has seriously deprived the concept of much of its utility (cf. Hindess and Hirst 1975, 1977). But what I do emphasize is that the production process and the relations of production in these Tanzanian (and other) pastoral societies have a number of unique characteristics that have either been overlooked or seriously misunderstood, *particularly* in regard to their transformations. Bonte relates this "uniqueness" to two basic conditions evident in the pastoral and agro-pastoral societies (Jie, Karimonjong, Turkana, and Samburu) which are the subjects of his study, precisely in the area of the articulation of the domestic units of production and wider community relations of production in which they are set. He notes:

> On peut parler dans les sociétés étudiées d'un même mode de production subsissant un certain nombre de transformations correspondant à celles: – des forces productives: variations de la productivité des activités pastorales et degré de spécialisation de ces activités; – des formes sociales de la production dans les limites d'un système des rapports de production défini par une articulation spécifique de la forme domestique et de la forme communautaire de la production.* (Bonte, 1974)

I return to a discussion of this hypothesis later.

The problematic I attempt to utilize here is basically derived from Marx's *Grundrisse*. Although considerably more focused upon relevant sections of the *Grundrisse*, I see the present essay as developing further several points made in my three earlier publications in Ilparakuyo/Maasai studies. These are: a) the necessity for the theoretical development of specific points of articulation between the historical materialist and structuralist problematics (cf Glucksmann 1974); b) further articulation with phenomenological theories in social science; and finally c) the illumination

---

*In the societies studied it is possible to speak of the same mode of production, undergoing a certain number of transformations in correspondence with:
– the productive forces: variations in the productivity of pastoral activities and the degree of specialization of such activities;
– the social forms of production within the limits of a system of relations of production determined by a specific articulation of domestic and communal forms of production. (ed)

such theoretical developments may provide towards an understanding of pre-capitalist social formations in which both kinship structures *and* age-set and age-grade structures *function* as relations of production, even during the transitional processes engendered by the penetration of capitalism and incipient class formation (Godelier 1966, 1972a, 1972b, 1972c, 1972d, 1973; Alavi 1974), and which may even be said to "mediate" such transformations (Alavi 1974: 59, Bonte 1975, 1977, 1981; see also below).

The importance of the *Grundrisse* for the development of Marxist theory is by now common knowledge, even if that knowledge has only recently begun to be applied to the analysis of specific social formations and their transformations. For example, David McLellan notes that the old controversy stirred up by the publication of the *1844 (Paris) Manuscripts* about the relation between the "early (Hegelian) Marx" and the later "mature Marx" has been greatly illuminated by the general access now available to the *Grundrisse*. He goes on:

> [The *Grundrisse*] is a rough draft not only of *Capital* but of his other books that he intended to write. Richer in many ways than either the *Paris Manuscripts* or *Capital*, it makes plain that there is a continuity in Marx's thought, but that it was not precisely of the nature so far advanced . . . Hence the importance of the *Grundrisse*, which contains a summary not only of the basic themes of *Capital* but also, as Marx himself said, themes that would have been broached in [another] five volumes . . . And to this extent it is the most comprehensive thing that Marx ever wrote . . . The centrality accorded to the *Grundrisse* on an examination of the external evidence is more than supported by its contents . . . (McLellan 1972: 11)

To which Martin Nicolaus, in the excellent "Foreword" to his translation of the *Grundrisse*, adds (1973: 7), "The *Grundrisse* challenges and *puts to the test*, every serious interpretation of Marx yet conceived" (My emphasis).

It is perhaps in the very fact that the *Grundrisse* points to the volumes that Marx *did not write* that at least some of its great significance lies. Like all great scientists and theoreticians, in his rare summaries of his methodology, Marx frequently makes statements that clearly contradict the analyses he achieves of specific historical social formations. It has been pointed out by many commentators that Marx fails to *elaborate* a theory of the *mediators* which provide man's "motive" to produce, and how he produces, the specific objects he may consume. In the Introduction to the *Grundrisse*, Marx states:

> Consumption creates the motive for production; it also creates the object which is active in production as its determined aim. If it is clear that production offers consumption its external object, it is therefore equally clear that consumption *ideally posits* the object of production as an internal image, as a

need, as a drive and as purpose. It creates the objects of production in a still subjective form. No production without a need. But consumption reproduces the need. (1973: 91-2, original emphasis)

In commenting upon this passage and subsequent sections, Sahlins correctly notes:[3]

In providing consumption with its object, production not only in turn completes consumption, but determines its actual form – that is, a definite good which defines the manner and content of consumption. Otherwise, consumption only has the *shapelessness* of a biological want [need]. It is production that creates the specific desire through the mediation of an object form. (1976: 154)

In other words, the "mediator", *culturally and historically* defined, between the processes of production and consumption, is lacking in Marx's formulation.

Despite this lapse, the *Grundrisse* can still be seen as pointing in many passages to the cultural mediators of this basic unity of production and consumption in all their variations, as a fundamental element of the materialist dialectic. As Nicholaus remarks elsewhere:

Marx's investigation of the confrontation between the process of equivalent exchange and the opposite process of accumulation [i.e., exploitation] occupies [a large section] of the *Grundrisse* manuscript; and, as always, the social, political, historical, legal, and even social-psychological aspects of the underlying fundamental question are brought out. (1973: 22)

And he adds (1973: 40), "The study in detail of the materialist dialectic in the *Grundrisse* would have to be a study of Marx's *mediations*."

This is not the place to continue further this theoretical discussion; I have already dealt with some aspects of it and return to it in relation to some of the material presented in this chapter. But even if we are to concede that in the Introduction to the *Grundrisse*, "Marx makes culture as a whole a *sequitur* to the nature of things" (Sahlins 1976: 158), there are sufficient brilliant and seminal insights in sections of the "Chapter on Capital", and elsewhere, to invest the skeleton of the *formen* with the body of concrete historical and anthropological elements derived from contemporary East African pastoral societies. Hence, in what follows, constant reference is made to passages from the *Grundrisse* to provide a theoretical underpinning, a problematic, for the analysis of pastoral production.[4]

II

I am not proposing anything new in this use of the *Grundrisse*; Bonte, for example, has employed sections of the work extensively in his writings on pastoralist, semi-pastoralists, and pastoralism, particularly in East Africa (Bonte 1974, 1975, 1977). Neither am I claiming that the methodology used here is the only one appropriate to the analysis of pastoral societies; other problematics have yielded interesting results on their account of pastoralism and "economic anthropology" generally (e.g. various papers in LeClair and Schneider 1968; Firth 1967; but cf. Godelier 1972, 1973). What I do maintain, however, is that the problematic of the following analysis illuminates' aspects of pastoral production as no other does, and that this may lead at least some way towards a deeper understanding of pastoralism and its transformations.

First we must recognize that the concepts Marx presents in the *Grundrisse* as "the forms which precede capitalist production" (1973: 471-97 and *passim*) are posited primarily as "working hypotheses" leading up to the development of capitalism; they are not presented as analyses of particular historical formations as such, at particular historical conjectures. Nevertheless, they represent such penetrating insights that they can now be developed within the context of the vast amount of anthropological knowledge now available to us, accumulated mostly since Marx's time. That Marx himself thought that this development of historical materialism "backwards", as it were, in time was important is evidenced in the now available *Ethnological Notebooks* (Krader 1974). Furthermore, these brilliantly introduced and annotated fragments show us that Marx was considerably more critical of his anthropological sources (Morgan, Phear, Maine, Lubbock) than was Engels, who used some of Marx's notes for his *Origin of the Family, Private Property and the State* (Marx and Engels 1970: 191-334).[5] We may conclude, then, that the *formen* can provide a critical basis for the analysis of precapitalist formations, without any violation of the method of historical materialism (Nicolaus 1973: *passim*).

But perhaps more importantly, Bonte also takes up a critical theme developed by Godelier (e.g. 1969, 1972, 1973), and that is: the transformation from pre-capitalist, "communal" (and "Germanic") modes of productions in classless social formations to those in which accumulation and exploitation dominate the relations of production represent "multiple forms of social historical evolution" (Bonte 1977). In this context, the Marxist critique of anthropology must be based upon "a *double relativism requirement* : 1) the recognition of the diversification of the paths of historical evolution and 2) the recognition of a plurality of structures capable of functioning as infrastructures" (Bonte 1975: 395, original emphasis).

Finally, a point that has often been made but needs constant repetition (cf. Bonte 1977), is that pastoral societies *do not* represent an earlier form of production and land-use than agricultural societies but are in fact later and more specialized adaptations of man to land (Rigby 1969b). By this I do not mean that ecological conditions are *necessarily* more critical in pastoral than agrricultural societies (cf. Goldschmidt 1965: 403-5), an issue to which I return later.

Both because of this, and the fact that I do not believe that the problematic of historical materialism posits the forces of production as the *only* driving force in historical transformations (see my quotation from Bonte above), I cannot agree with a pastoral Maasai colleague and friend when he juxtaposes the following statements:

> In order to produce, individuals even in the most primitive of . . . societies, have to enter into definite relations and connections with each other. They have to co-operate either freely or by compulsion--political or economic . . . Since these social relations entered into by the producers and the pattern of their participation in the whole act of production as well as exchange of the products of their labour are determined by the stage which the historical development of the social *productive forces* has reached at any given moment in time, it is in the internal development of the material means of production that we should seek to identify the lynch-pin of socio-economic transformation.

So far, so good; but he continues:

> Surely [a mode of life] as the pastoral Maasai have today . . . is as much of an anomaly . . . as the wretched conditions of slums to which exploitation forces the proleteriat to live in, in the great cities of the mass consumerist class societies of our time. The crucial difference between the two is that the principle contradiction in the pastoralist situation is between man and nature while in the latter case it is that between the working and exploiting classes. (Parkipuny 1975: 42)

Such curious lapses into Feuerbachian materialism in order to compare two altogether incomparable situations cannot provide a basis for a discussion of pastoralist transformation. They invite the oft-repeated (and quite useless) "hortatory" approaches to development, which proclaim the main obstacles to better life to be "poverty, ignorance, and disease".

I attempt in this chapter to demonstrate the "rationality" of a pastoral production (cf. Godelier 1972a, 1973), and hence its potential as a basis for socialist transformation. In this sense, I am repeating, upon the basis of another and better problematic, and with much more detailed analysis, a point I made some fifteen years ago (Rigby 1969b). Furthermore, contrary to the implications of the statement quoted above, at least a major part of the process of pastoralist production in Tanzania, and despite the inroads of commodity relations, still conforms to the concept of simple circulation (Marx, 1973 1957-8; 172 ff), as opposed to the situation in modes of production based upon antagonistic classes and exploitation; and this is because the herd is still largely conceived of as a means of production, and not as a product (see below).[6]

III

I begin with an examination of the issue of the relative emphases placed upon different means of production within the communal and "Germanic" (or domestic) modes of production, in this case livestock. During this discussion I also look, in some detail, at various forms of the appropriation of land for grazing and water in pastoral societies, ending with an analysis of the division of labour and the relations of production, within and between the basic production units. But, first, a word or two on definitional problems.

I have already referred to Alan Jacobs' pioneering and perceptive, albeit brief, comparative study of African pastoralists (Jacobs 1965b). His classification of "pure" versus "semi-pastoralists" fails partially because he does not emphasize sufficiently the relative weight given to livestock as a *means of production*, as opposed to product and other means of production (e.g. land) in the societies under consideration. Thus he suggests (1965b: 146) that "pastoralists consist of people who either (i) raise livestock for consumption; (ii) raise livestock mainly for trade or social exchange; or (iii) both". This classification depends primarily upon a notion of livestock in its *functions* as a *product*; it recognizes, but does not deal with, distinctions of dependence upon livestock as a means of production and reproduction of the community.

Nevertheless, Jacobs makes some critically important points which relate directly to the questions under consideration here, and his analysis provides an excellent starting point. In comparing various definitions of pastoralism, Jacobs notes that Kroeber (1948) ties pastoralism inseparably to nomadism (Jacobs 1965a: 145). Kroeber's error in this is still extremely widespread, as will be seen from the comparative studies that follow. Certainly, Ilparakuyo are not nomadic in any accurate sense of that term, and neither are other pastoral Maasai nor the Barbaig (cf. Jacobs 1965b: 176 and *passim*; Parkipuny 1975: 39, Klima 1964: 9-10, 1970: 18; for West African comparisons, see, for example, Stenning 1957, 1959; Dupire 1962). Despite the recurrence of the word "nomads" in the literature, most pastoral societies may be said to be primarily transhumant and only secondarily nomadic, and many cases of "spontaneous sedentarization" are reported (cf. Baxter 1975; Lewis 1975; Monod 1975; Salzman 1980; Dyson-Hudson 1980); thus nomadism is not a *necessary* condition of even "pure" pastoralism. One unfortunate consequence of the misapplication of the term is that pastoralists are thereby relegated to a "lower stage" of the development of productive forces, an error committed just as frequently by historical materialists as by bourgeois social scientists, and taken up avidly by the popular imagination.

Jacobs also compares the "pure" pastoralist Maasai with other pastoral and semi-pastoral societies, along a continuum ending with the semi-sedentary Jie of north-east Uganda, with regard to the magnitude of bridewealth prestations. He establishes that these *increase* in number with a relative decrease in the importance of the herd as a means of production. Thus, pastoral Maasai whose herds average 13-14 head of cattle per capita, give only four head of cattle and one sheep for bridewealth; the Jie, averaging herds of 3-4 head of cattle and 4 small stock per capita, give 50 head of cattle and 129 small stock as the average bridewealth.

Related to this, and somewhat paradoxically, Jacobs says (1965a: 149), "livestock appear to be important measures of wealth and social position *only* in those societies in which they are secondary sources of subsistence"; i.e. symbolically important, but not the primary means of production.

In this general context of bridewealth magnitude, status, and primary means of production, it may be necessary to make a distinction that is made by Klima for the Barbaig between "bridewealth" on the one hand, and what may be called "marriage cattle" on the other; the latter is also an important element in the *first* marriages of young men among Ilparakuyo and Maasai. Among the Barbaig, these "marriage cattle" are made up largely of "dowry" for the young couple to "set up house", and are economically the only important transfer of wealth at marriage (see below). In the case of pastoral Maasai, and also to some extent among Ilparakuyo, a young man betrothed to a girl (or even an elder in the same position) who is not yet old enough to be taken as a bride, may have to help his prospective father-in-law out of "financial difficulties" (*enyamali*) to the tune of 15-20 head of cattle "on indefinite terms" (Jacobs 1970: 33, but cf. 34). Jacobs adds, "Failure to do so may easily result in the father withdrawing his consent to the marriage . . ." This latter situation may, in fact, be at least partially the result of increasing commoditization of all cattle transactions, rather than a "pre-capitalist" form; but other factors are undoubtedly involved, since "perpetual debt" situations are common among pastoralists, and debts are inherited.[7]

At any rate, it is true of both Ilparakuyo and other pastoral Maasai that elders do not publicly "praise" their cattle, although *ilmurran* (young initiated men, sing. *olmurrani*) do have cattle songs (*isinkolioitin loo 'nkishu*) which include praise for one's beasts as well as one's own exploits. Among Ilparakuyo, only female cattle are sometimes given personal names; most beasts are known mainly by their colour, ear-marks (see below), and their places of origin.

Returning to the "classification" of pastoral and semi-pastoral societies, we may then make an alternative (if rough) distinction upon the basis of the "primary means of production". Thus, most pre-colonial Tanzanian social formations may be seen as based upon some variation of that communal mode of production which is characterized in transformation as the "Germanic" mode in the *Grundrisse* (Marx 1973: 476ff; cf. Bonte 1977), and which has also been termed the "domestic mode of production" (Sahlins 1972: Chapter 2, 3, and *passim*). I return later to discuss some aspects of this concept in more detail; suffice to say here that it opens strong links with the many excellent analyses of kinship systems functioning as relations of production in the domestic domain, explored in great detail within other problematics (e.g. Goody 1958; 1976; Stenning 1958).

Within this general category or mode of production, our matrix for the classification of societies on the basis of primary means of production may be as shown in Figure 3, below.

Figure 3
Means of Production: Basic Categories

Means of production	Settled agriculture (small stock)	Basic Categories* Agro-pastoral (cattle-herds)	"Pure pastoral"
Land	+	+	-
Labour	+	+	+
Livestock	-	+	+

* + = strong/primary
  - = weak/secondary

Note that this matrix is based *only* on the varying emphases given to the means of production, and it does not refer to products, exchange, or other "external" factors. Hence, although "pure" pastoralists in almost all cases consume a variety of agricultural products (cf. Jacobs 1965a), they do not make specific areas of land subject to individual, domestic, kin-group, or age-group rights; livestock and associated labour are thus not bounded by spatial factors; and so on. In terms of such a rough classification, the Ilparakuyo are "pure pastoralists". My own research confirms entirely Beidelman's succint statement:

> Baraguyu are purely pastoral people. But they differ from the Masai in being not only ready but forced to supplement pastoral product with grain and vegetables. Despite the many historical sources to the contrary, to my knowledge Baraguyu now practice no agriculture whatsoever although they consume agricultural produce obtained from others. They view any contact with a hoe as extremely disgusting. Their diet appears as a necessity, not choice; all Baraguyu maintain that a diet of flesh, blood, and milk is the ideal. (1960: 254)

Beidelman was writing of the situation 20 years ago; it is still *largely* true today, but there are exceptions, to which I return later. Beidelman goes on to quote what he rightly considers to be extremely questionable figures for Ilparakuyo livestock holdings in northern Kilosa District for 1957. Veterinary Department figures for the period gave an average of 3.03 head of cattle per capita, 0.37 small stock, and 0.09 donkeys. His own survey, however, of six homesteads, gives a more realistic figure of 8-13 head of cattle per person (adults and children), with no figures for small stock.

A recent sample survey (August 1977) of 23 households belonging to Ilparakuyo in west Bagamoyo District gave the figures set out in Table 1 (small stock figures are also available, but are not included here). They are compared with Jacobs' figures for Maasailand (1965a: 151), Kjaerby's figures for Barbaig (personal communication, and Spencer's for the Samburu (Isampurr) of northern Kenya.[8]

A number of interesting comparisons arise from these figures. For pastoral Maasai, Jacobs gives a figure of 13-14 head of cattle per capita (1970: 25), while Fosbrooke calculates that in the 1940s, there was a range of 25-50 head of cattle per adult male taxpayer, that is, per "cattle gate" in each *enkang'* settlement (see below). The Ilparakuyo figures yield an average of 8.1 cattle per person (adults and children; cf. Beidelman's figure of 8-13 head, above) 4.4 adult female cattle per capita, and an average of 93.9 head of cattle per household, ranging from 15 at the lowest to 381 at the highest. Ilparakuyo in west Bagamoyo average 50.5 head of cattle per adult male, a figure identical to Fosbrooke's upper limit for pastoral Maasai in 1948; but this identity is more likely to be based upon differences of definition. Among Samburu, the average figure for all estimates is 12 head of cattle per capita (Spencer 1973: 10). Several comparable figures for Barbaig emerge from Kjaerby's excellent material. From a total sample very similar in size to the Ilparakuyo one and to Jacobs' own Maasai figures, we find that among the Barbaig there are 5.3. head of cattle per capita, and 2.9 adult females per person, from a sample of 40 households averaging 9.5 persons per unit, as compared with 11.2 persons per household for the Ilparakuyo.

Jacobs (1965a) notes that, because of the great variations in milk yields of livestock due to factors such as the condition of the beast, the age of her calf, and the seasons of the year, if one adult pastoralist is to survive on the herd's major product (milk), 2-3 milch cows suffice in the wet season, 10-15 may be required in the dry season, and 20 or more during periods of drought. Given the proportion of milch cows in the average pastoralist herd and the proportion of total cattle in milk (Spencer gives 41.7% of *total* herd in milk at any one time for the Samburu), it is little wonder that most pastoralists have to supplement their diet with agricultural produce at one time or another, even if we include the intake of blood, fat and meat as products of the herd.

Ilparakuyo herds seem to indicate a significantly higher proportion of calves in the total herd, at the expense of oxen (bullocks), when compared to the pastoral Maasai and Barbaig. The relatively small size of the samples may account partially for this; but there are other elements involved. Not only does herd composition vary over seasons, but there are long-term fluctuations caused by drought and bovine disease which require policy decisions by the elders and *ilmurran* as to the future of each herd. Given the fact that there has been a fairly drastic reduction in Ilparakuyo herds during the past two to two and a half years, owing to East Coast fever, forced removal

Table 1
Comparative Livestock Holdings among East African Pastoralists

| Society | Cattle Holdings: | | | | | | People | | |
	adult females	bulls	oxen (bullocks)	calves female	calves male	Total	adults	children	total
Ilparakuyo	1,191	232	96	351	290	2,160	102	157	259
%	55%	11%	4%	16.3%	13.3%	100%	Av. persons per *enkang'*: 11.2		
				30%					
Pastoral Maasai[9]	57%	6%	14%	23%		100%	Av. cattle per *enkang'*: 95.9		
Pastoral Maasai[10]	60%	7%	11%	22%		100% (1,350)	Av. cattle per household: 50.5		
Barbaig[11]	1,107	161	288	127	186	2,020	378		378
%	55%	8%	14%	14.0%	9.0%	100%	Av. persons per household: 9.5		
				23%					
Samburu[12]	69.5%		30.5%						

to tsetse infected areas, and lack of access to suffcient veterinary supplies (see below), deliberate policy on the part of Ilparakuyo to achieve higher calving rates may also account for these differences. Ilparakuyo herds may grow rapidly over the next few years if conditions continue to improve, and the structure of the herd will consequently change. I discuss other factors by which Ilparakuyo are consciously attempting to replenish their herds in a later section on the division of labour. The Ilparakuyo and Barbaig figures, however, also seem to support Dahl and Hjort's generalization that losses of heifer calves are lower than for bull calves, and this is true also for Maasai herds. In the Ilparakuyo sample, 16.3% of the total herd is composed of female calves, while 13.3% are males; among Barbaig, the proportions are 14% and 9% (cf. Dahl and Hjort 1976: 37-8)

Also borne out from these comparisons is Jacob's generalization (1965b: 149) that bridewealth tends to be higher amongst those pastoralists for whom the cattle herd provides a lesser proportion of the total social product, with the odd exception of the Barbaig. Despite probable recent increase, we have seen that among pastoral Maasai, bridewealth is normally composed of only four head of cattle, one sheep, and some honey, with the rider that a prospective son-in-law may have to provide his future father-in-law with additional support before marriage (see above); there are also additional prestations of "marriage cattle" promised a new bride by her affines and co-wives (usually eight heifers and one bull, plus small stock) as well as wedding gifts given a young man at his first marriage (Jacobs 1970: 34, see also below). Among Samburu, bridewealth is also relatively low, usually six to eight head of cattle (Spencer 1965: 69-70).

Amongst Ilparakuyo, bridewealth prestations vary enormously, ranging from 27 head of cattle and Shs. 5,000 (about US$ 625 –about £430 Sterling at current rates), and additional gifts of honey, blankets etc. to 80 head of cattle and Shs. 10,000 (US $ 1,250 – about £860 Sterling at current rates) plus the additional prestations. These figures come from my own research in west Bagamoyo District; there may also be regional variations. Bridewealth prestations continue over long periods of time, creating virtually a system of perpetual debt. For the late 1950s, Beidelman gives a figure of 40 head of cattle, with honey and blankets, etc., and "some services" (1960: 275). This may indicate that among Ilparakuyo, as elsewhere, the average bridewealth is on the increase, within the wide variations from case to case.

Among the Barbaig, despite the relatively low level of cattle per capita,[13] bridewealth prestations are (and seem to be remaining) extremely low. Klima gives a figure of "one heifer and a barrel of honey" (Klima 1964: 10, 1970: 67-9). However, since Barbaig marriage is characterized by a relatively large "dowry", which forms the major part of what Klima calls "marriage cattle" (1970: 69-71), we are dealing with a radically different system of prestations, culturally mediated historical factors which distinguish them from other East African pastoralists (but cf. the interesting discussion by Lewis on bridewealth and dowry among the Somali; Lewis 1962: 21-2 and *passim*).

There are close comparisons amongst Ilparakuyo and pastoral Maasai in terms of the control of the major means of production, and the distribution of product; later, I pursue more complex comparisons with the Barbaig.

II

The division of labour in the domestic, or "Germanic", mode of production, is based on the initial conditions created by marriage. The basic principles upon which labour capacity is assessed are sex and age. I return to a discussion of these issues in more detail in the following section on the relations of production and labour capacity; first, however, it is necessary to analyse the access to, and control of, the means of production at greater depth.

Ilparakuyo, like other pastoral Maasai, do not conceive of land as "owned" by any group, category, community, or individual. This does not mean, however, that there are no concepts of "locality". As I have indicated in Chapter 3, they consider themselves as a discrete "section" (*oloho*) of the pastoral Maasai peoples, which involves a territorial concept. However, it is primarily because Ilparakuyo have their own "great prophets" (*Iloibonok kituaak*) that they distinguish themselves from the other pastoral Maasai, one of them is more important than the other, but does not interfere in the latter's sphere of interest.

Because Ilparakuyo live in relatively small clusters of homesteads (*inkang'itie*, sing. *enkang'*) amongst cultivating or agro-pastoralist, mainly Bantu-speaking, neighbours, stretching over a vast area from Upare in the north-east to Usangu in Mbeya District in the south, they consider each local cluster as constituting a sub-section of their territorial organization (also called *oloho*, pl. *ilohon*), within an overall dual division into ritual areas under each *oloiboni kitok*, or "major prophet". These *ilohon* have no definite boundaries for the Ilparakuyo, and serve merely to identify the locality in which one is currently living, or where one is currently visiting. However, ties of descent and affinity tend to be more numerous amongst those residents in one locality than between localities, and age-set activities are normally confined to local units, except for the large ceremonies transferring age-sets through the age-grade systems (see below). For purposes of litigation with non-Ilparakuyo, tax-paying, and so on, the current official administrative boundaries of "villages", "wards", "divisions", and "areas" (districts) are adhered to.

Ilparakuyo recognize that their chances of finding sufficient grazing, water, and a minimum of litigation with Bantu cultivators over cases such as herds raiding the latter's fields, are limited and, in fact, diminishing. It should also be recognized that current villagization policy is aggravating this situation (cf. Ndagala 1974). Futhermore, Ilparakuyo have precisely the same view as pastoral Maasai on the normal relationship of man to land, as adumbrated in my quotation from Parkipuny (1975: 27) above: that is, land, water, and grazing, with very few exceptions, are free to all men. But since Ilparakuyo are forced by circumstances, as we have seen, to rely heavily upon agricultural produce to augment their diet, they may on occasion "buy" rights over land cultivated by their Bantu neighbours; not rights in land as a means of production, but only an area as yielding a product necessary for consumption. Beidelman notes for Ilparakuyo in Kilosa during the late 1950s:

> Occasionally, a Baraguyu will speak of "buying a field." What he really means is that for a certain amount of cash, milk, or meat, he will obtain all of the crop produced by this field. Despite the Baraguyu's figure of speech, such a field belongs to the Bantu who works it [sic] and is not the Baraguyu's, nor will it ever be located near the Baraguyu's camp. (1960: 259).

This situation has altered somewhat in the case of certain Ilparakuyo homesteads in west Bagamoyo, particularly during the last three or so years of considerable loss of livestock (see below). Ilparakuyo homestead heads may actually claim rights of usufruct over agricultural plots on the same basis as their Bantu neighbour's; these are then cultivated with "paid" Bantu labour under the "owner's" supervision. This increases competition over land used for cultivation and land still available for grazing. In most cases in such circumstances, the pastoralist's fields will still be situated at some distance from his *enkang'*, in order to avoid problems with his herd. Nevertheless, the trend noted by Beidelman for the 1950s (cf. Ndagala 1974 *passim)* is increasing in intensity:

> The physical environment plus the competition for land with Bantu has led to a fairly widespread dispersion of camps. Camps are small, usually four or five houses [*inkajijik*] and usually one or two owners (and thus gates or [*inkishomitie*]). Population of a camp is about twenty or thirty, including children. Of course, one often finds camps with less than twenty inhabitants.[14] (1960: 259)

This relatively small size of *inkang'itie* as compared, for example, with those of other pastoral Maasai, leads to chronic problems of labour shortage for the daily care of Ilparakuyo herds; I return to this in more detail later. Here it is worthwhile noting that for the late 1950s, Jacobs gives an average of 4 to 8 families (stock-holding units) and an average of 30 to 60 persons per Maasai *enkang'* (1965a; 1970: 25), and even then there are labour shortage problems. Prior to villagization in the 1970s, Ndagala (1978: 142-4) gives an average of 2.5 families per Maasai *enkang'* with an average of 7 families in each household after "Operation Imparnati".[15]

Problems over diminishing grazing lands are common to all Tanzanian pastoralists, including pastoral Maasai and Barbaig. Indeed, it could be said that in this regard, the plight of pastoralists who occupy their own "exclusive" areas is greater than that of the Ilparakuyo, whose whole historical adjustment has been geared to expanding into small, relatively unoccupied areas. Rural development, resettlement, and villagization policies favour cultivators over "pure" pastoralists, as well as agricultural development over livestock development among semi-pastoralists (e.g. in Ugogo, Dodoma Region). Whatever these factors may eventually lead to, the pastoralists' attitudes towards land as an element in the overall means of production remains the same as it was in the past, thus allowing increasing encroachment by cultivators whose occupation implies permanency of usufruct rather than the temporary appropriation of areas of land characteristic of pastoral transhumance and migratory drift.[16]

Despite its relatively unacceptable evolutionary connotations and the essentially transitory nature postulated for it, Marx's "working hypothesis" of an "initial, naturally arisen spontaneous community [appearing] as first supposition" to production is remarkably prophetic, in an anthropological sense (Marx 1973: 472, 474):[17]

> Family, and family extended as a clan [*Stamm*: descent group] or through intermarriage between families [alliance] or combination of clans . . . Since we may assume that *pastoralism*, or more generally a migratory form of the mode of life, was the first form of the mode of existence, not that the clan settles in a specific site but that it grazes off what it finds – then the *clan community*, the natural community, appears not as a *result* of, but as a *presupposition for the communal appropriation* (temporary) and *utilization* of the land. (Original emphasis).

> At this point, Marx introduces the factor of a *culturally* relative historicity, a mediator, which deeply influences the specific formation the community takes, as an integral part of the objective conditions of production and reproduction:

> When they finally do settle down, the extent to which this original community is modified will depend upon various external climatic, geographical, physical, etc. conditions as well as their particular natural disposition – their clan character. This naturally arisen clan community, or, if one will, pastoral society, is the first presupposition – the community [*Gemeinschaftlichkeit*] of blood, *language, customs* [emphasis added] – for the *appropriation of the objective conditions of their life*, and of their life's reproducing and objectifying activity (activity as herdsmen . . . etc). (Original emphasis)

Turning to *one possible* transformation from such a "mode of existence",

Marx introduces the "Germanic" mode of production, a concept critically important to our present discussion (cf. Bonte 1974, 1977, 1981). Marx continues:

> The individual relates simply to the objective conditions of labour as being his; relates to them as the inorganic nature of his subjectivity, in which the latter realizes itself; the chief objective condition of labour does not itself appear as a *product* of labour, but is already there as nature . . . (1973: 485, original emphasis)

Not only are these passages extremely (and obviously) apposite to the analysis of pastoral societies and their transformation, of pastoral production and land as a factor of production; Marx also presages a number of *different possibilities* for the transformation of the communal and Germanic modes of production (cf. quotation from Bonte 1977 above). For example, I have elaborated in Chapter 3 some aspects of the age-set organization of Ilparakuyo as *functioning as relations of production*. Although in a slightly different context, in his discussion of the various forms of the elaboration of the division of labour, Marx considers transformations from "reciprocal" to "hierarchical" forms of the relations of production and exchange (but not *necessarily to class* relations). Thus: "The clan system in itself leads to higher and lower ancestral lineages [*Geschlechtern*], a distinction which is still further developed through intermixture with subjugated clans etc."[18] (Marx 1973: 474). The critical point here is that the German *Geschlecter* "may also refer to the sexes, linguistic groups, *generations*, etc. It is not entirely certain which of these distinctions Marx had foremost in mind " (Nicolaus, footnote to Marx 1973: 474)

With this "working hypothesis" providing, *mutatis mutandis*, a basic problematic to our discussion of the nature of pastoralist appropriation of land, implying grazing and water, we may now conclude this section of our discussion by noting one or two modifications in the concrete manifestations of such temporary appropriation. I have shown that exclusive rights to land, either communal or individual, are not entertained by pastoralists, leading to some contemporary problems of transformation. However, certain man-made "in-puts" designed to improve the conditions of the natural environment, those which may have been created by individuals or groups, may be subject to "rights of preference" which are passed on by inheritance, usually through members of a patrilineal clan (*enkishomi*, pl. *inkishomitie*); these rights again, however, do not carry the implication of exclusivity, but of primary control. Among Ilparakuyo, such rights relate, for example, to dry season wells sunk in river beds, with their associated furrows and drinking troughs; these may be controlled by particular *inkang'itie* or groups of homesteads. Among pastoral Maasai, the complex of deep wells at Naberera and Ngasumet are controlled by particular clans. But despite these rights of pre-eminence by certain kin and descent groups, two observations, must be made. Such rights are very rare and constitute the exceptions that prove the rule; even where they do exist, access by unrelated Ilparakuyo or Maasai cannot reasonably be denied. Fosbrooke expresses succinctly the position for south and central Tanzania Maasailand, although his use of the word "ownership" needs modification (see below):

> All the Naberera and other central Maasai wells are in clan ownership, as also are the springs around Losogonoi, Kibaya etc. The senior member of the clan resident on the water is in control, and, *in consultation* with the other local clansmen, *determines* the *order* of watering.

But most critically, he adds:

> The main practical application of this knowlege is that in effect the users of the water form a council for the settlement of disputes, under the "chairmanship" of the "owner" . . . A migrating Maasai may demand, and must be given, water at any well or spring when actually on the move, *drinking in priority* to any local cattle. (Fosbrooke 1948: 42, my emphasis; cf. Jacobs 1965a: 204).

It is entirely appropriate at this stage of our discussion to turn to a consideration of access to, and control of, the major means of production among Ilparakuyo, Maasai, and Barbaig.[19]

IV

In everyday discussion, Ilparakuyo refer to their herds (*incoo*, sing. *emboo*), which term denotes primarily cattle (*inkishu*, sing. *enkiteng'*) but also goats and sheep, and, at a stretch, donkeys, as "the herd of so-and-so", naming the head of a "family" or homestead. Contrary to the situation in Maasailand, Ilparakuyo homesteads (*inkang'itie*) are usually composed of some form or other of a patrilineal extended family, depending upon the stage in the developmental cycle it has reached. Mature and married sons often remain with their father (but more particularly, with their mother – see below), until the latter's death. Towards the end of the developmental cycle of the "average" domestic group, the residual herd still under the primary control of the father and elder of each family (*inkishu e 'boo*) is virtually finished, all the rest of the herd having been allocated to the various "houses" (*inkajijik*, sing. *enkaji*) of the polygynous extended family. It is rare for Ilparakuyo *inkang'itie* to have more than two or three gates (*inkishomitie*, sing. *enkishomi*) to the cattle byre, each one symbolizing an "independent" male family head and his herd (cf. the average of seven gates to each Maasai camp given by Jacobs, 1965a: 228). Even if an elder's sons are married *but still residing with their father*, they will usually retain only one gate.

However, in the case, for example, of the married sons of full brothers (or "gate-post" brothers: see below) only one of whom is still alive, the sons of the dead brother (or brothers) will establish their own gates if they are still residing with their classificatory father. When these sons have passed through *eunoto*, graduating from junior *ilmurran*-hood to senior *ilmurran*-hood: (cf. Beidelman 1965: 262-4; Jacobs 1958: 240-94), they soon move away to establish their own homestead or homesteads. Hence, each married man, other than married junior *ilmurran* ("warriors"), has his own gate. Beidelman notes for the late 1950s of Ilparakuyo in northern Kilosa:

> In those camps with two [or more] independent owners, i.e. two gates, almost any combination may be found: two sons of a dead father, two cousins, two friends, a man and his brother-in-law, etc. In the case of distant kin and friends, such stock associates tend to last only a short time [sic] and then disperse. Most associates divide amicably yet fairly frequently. Associates who are not father–son, are nearly always of the same age-group. (1960: 273)

All Ilparakuyo belong to one of a number of patrilineal, non-loacalized, clans, generally referred to by the same term as "gate" (*enkishomi*). All clans are grouped into two "moieties",[20] Iloorokiteng, "those of the black ox", and Iloodomong'i, "those of the red oxen". Each clan is sub-divided into two, or sometimes more, "sub-clans," usually referred to as *ilgilat* (sing. *olgilata*, from *agil*, "to break "; also refers to any "partition" or "room" of a house). Pastoral Maasai use this latter term for all segments of descent categories (Jacobs 1965a: 195ff), including those sub-divisions derived from matrifiliation and referred to as "gate-post" groups (*intaloishin*, sing. *entaloishi*). Ilparakuyo term these gate-post divisions *ilpaheta* (sing. *olpahe*: lit. "calf", "gate-post") and do not use the word *entaloishi*.

As with all such systems of the ideology of descent, usage differs according to the context of discussion and the relative structural positions of those involved. However, common to Ilparakuyo, other pastoral Maasai, and Barbaig, is the "extension" of descent categories to the cattle in each herd, by a system of "branding" cattle with distinctive ear markings (*ilponot* sing. *olponoto* for Ilparakuyo and Maasai). Jacobs associates these ear marks with what he calls "sub-clans", but these in turn are grouped by close similarities of ear markings within the dual "gate-post" divisions of each clan (Jacobs 1965b; 201).

Beidelman relates Ilparakuyo ear-marks to what he calls clans; my evidence indicates that sub-divisions of clans, i.e. "sub-clans," have distinguishing cattle ear-marks. For example, the Ilmosokoite clan (*enkishomi*), common in west Bagamoyo (cf. Beidelman 1960: 260), is sub-divided into three sub-clans (*ilgilat*), each with distinctive ear-marks which, however, bear close similarities to one another; these are Ilkashimani, Ilkonyokio, and Ildana-loo 'nkonyek.

Among Barbaig, the "clan" is also referred to by the term for "gate" (*desht*, cf. Wilson 1954: 39ff; Klima 1970: 39). Klima notes;

> While each animal carries three different brands – the father's clan, mother's clan, and father's mother's clan – a large number of animals within the family herd may not share the same brands, although they belong to the same owner.

This is inevitably the case for all pastoral herds.

But although each herd may be said to "belong" to one person, the head of either a polygynous or patrilineal extended polygynous family, all the animals in it are subject to a number of rights and duties, often overlapping, both in terms of control of them as a means of production as well as in terms of control over the herd's major products: milk, fat, blood, meat, and hides, for the basic purposes of social reproduction. The Ilparakuyo and Maasai adage, *Meeta enkiteng' olopeny* is true in both the above senses; for it implies literally that "a cow has no single owner", but also that the milk of a cow may be (and is) given to anyone (cf. Massek and Sidai 1974: 42).[21] Hence, when the English word "owner" is used to translate *olopeny*, a fundamental distinction in meaning must be made.

Typically, the English word "owner" conveys a relationship between man and "object" which is *exclusive* of all others, "non-owners", characteristic of the politio-jural institutions of capitalist society and mode of production (cf. the interesting discussion in Sahlins 1976: Chapter 4). The Ilparakuyo/Maasai concept, on the other hand, conveys what may be called an *inclusive* relationship between men and "objects", the family head presiding over a number of levels of rights in the "objects" concerned: livestock. This applies not only for kinship and descent categories and groups in Ilparakuyo and Maasai society, but to relationships within age-sets as well; a man, particularly when a junior *olmurrani*, "owns" literally nothing exclusively, *vis-à-vis* his age-mates, particularly those of the same sub-set. This applies with equal force to modern consumer units such as watches, radios and bicycles; an age-mate can take anything and keep it as long as he likes (cf. Chapters 2 and 3).

The first fundamental distinction in rights of access and control within the "family herd" is based upon the "gate-post" organization of the family. Each gate (*enkishomi*) among Ilparakuyo and Maasai is divided by the dual ordering of the matricentral units of each wife and her children into "those of the right hand gate-post" (*olpahe le'tatene*) and "those of the left hand gate-post" (*olpahe le'kedianye*, cf. Maasai *entaloishi*, pl. *intaloishin* Jacobs 1965a: 191-4, 1970:26).

The rate of polygyny among Ilparakuyo and Maasai elders is relatively high, a situation made possible by the fact that young men (*ilmurran*) find it difficult to get married, hence creating a large difference between the ages at which men (senior *ilmurran* or elders) get married to those of girls, who are normally married soon after puberty and initiation. Accurate figures for Ilparakuyo are not available, but from superficial personal observation, about 70% of elders (*ilmoruak* or *ilpayiani*) are polygynists at any one time. These are men of the present Ilkidotu age-set and above, who have gone through the *olng'eher* ceremony which transfers senior *ilmurran* to junior elders. However, a significant number of both senior and junior *ilmurran* are now getting married, often remaining with one wife until promotion to higher age-grades. Fosbrooke's figures for Tanzania Maasailand (1948: 44-5) indicate that 55.6% of "all adult men" (*including ilmurran*) were married, and that 40.7% of *all* married men were polygnists. But since even in the 1940s, a significant number of *ilmurran* (28%) were married,[22] it is not possible to compute the rate of polygny among elders.

Jacobs' samples for pastoral Maasai for the late 1950s, however, refer specifically to rates of polygyny among *elders* (1965a: 208, 1970: 30). These figures show that 65% of elders were polygnists (N=316), while from a smaller sample (N=109) he found that 61% of married elders had two wives; 27% had three wives; 5% had four wives; 4% had five wives; and 3% had six or more wives, one of whom had nine wives.

These figures for Ilparakuyo and Maasai, although based upon relatively small samples, indicate that the rate of polygny in these societies is considerably higher than for the "East African Cattle Area" as a whole, which show that of all married men, an average of only 24.7% are polygnists, the figure for "Sub-Saharan Africa" being 35% (Dorjahn 1959: 102).[23]

Hence, both ideally and actually, a majority of Ilparakuyo and Maasai men can hope to be polygnists at some stage in their lives, particularly if they survive to become mature and successful elders. The first wife's house (*enkaji*) is situated on the right-hand side of the husband's gate-post facing in, and is therefore the "founder" of the "right-hand gate-post category" (*opahe le'tatene*) within the family. The second wife will build her *enkaji'*, after a suitable period under the care of the senior wife, on the left; she becomes the "founder" of the "left-hand gate-post category," (*olpahe le'kedianye*). The third wife will be on the right, the fourth on the left, and so on (cf. Beidelman 1960: 270). This pattern may be altered only by certain factors in the procreative histories of some wives, and by the status of the *last* wife's position, which may be shifted from one gate-post group to the other for purposes of inheritance; a factor not directly of concern here.

Half-siblings of one gate-post category feel closer together, co-operate more, than with half-siblings of the "other side" and, theoretically, sons of one side may not inherit cattle allocated to the wives of the other side. Jacobs' statement for pastoral Maasai is true *pari passu* for the Ilparakuyo:

> If, for example, the first wife of a compound family of three households [*inka-jijik uni*] were to die without male issue, and the third wife had a son, then he would inherit the cattle allocated to the deceased first wife; sons of the second wife have no claim to these cattle, though they would, of course, become senior sons in respect of their father's residual herd [*inkishu e 'boo*]. Similarly, if, in the same example, the second wife died without male issue, her cattle would revert to her husband's residual herd, and if he died without using them to make another marriage, his full-brothers could, and frequently

> do, lay claim to these household cattle over the sons of the first and third wives. (1965b: 192-3)

This dual division of the family and its relation to control over livestock and their products is the first level of the critical operation of the principle of matrifiliation in inheritance and access to the means of production in Ilparakuyo and Maasai production units.

In the Barbaig social formation, the principle of dual classification is not emphasized to the extent demonstrable for Ilparakuyo and pastoral Maasai; matrifiliation, however, remains a crucial principle of organization, as we shall see. Among Barbaig clans, which are not localized, there appears to be an incipient hierarchy based upon an incipient, non-reciprocal duality of priestly and ritual clans on the one hand (*Daremgadyeg*), and what Klima calls "laical or secular clans" (*Homat'k*) on the other (Klima 1964: 10). This is associated further with a ritual chiefship, or paramountcy, of the owner "chief" (*ng'utamid*) of the patrilineally inherited "magic" or ritual fire (*gadyak't*). Dual categories do not seem to appear at a household level, but matrifocality in the control, distribution, and inheritance of livestock is perhaps even more emphasized among the Barbaig than among Ilparakuyo/Maasai, and is associated with the relatively high socio-economic and jural status of women in these societies.[24]

This is not the place to extend an analysis of the complex processes of bridewealth transfer and other marriage prestations in Ilparakuyo, Maasai, and Barbaig marriages, mentioned briefly above. But one or two particular points are apposite to the following discussion.

When a certain proportion of the prestations have been completed, the bride-to-be is escorted to her new home. Outside the cattle byre, she stops and refuses to go any further until she is promised gifts of livestock by her husband, his kinsmen, and the co-wives of her husband's *enkang'*. She does this several times, with a few steps between, until she has had physically pointed out to her eight or nine head of cattle, heifers and one bull, as well as certain small stock (cf. Jacobs 1970: 34). These will form the nucleus of her milking herd, and their increase will become the basis of her sons' inheritance. At the first marriage of a young man, this herd is normally attached to his mother's house (*enkaji*), where the young bride may reside until the birth of her first child; she is then allowed and assisted to build her own *enkaji*. Furthermore, although he may have given a large bridewealth (Ilparakuyo) or a small one, albeit with additional "loans" to his father-in-law (Maasai), a young man at first marriage receives a number of cattle as "wedding gifts" from his agnatic and matrilateral kin, as he has received beasts for his earlier development through the various age-set ceremonies and life-cycle rituals. Among pastoral Maasai, these "wedding" gifts may be up to 15 or 20 head of cattle, but examples of 40 or 50 have been reported (Jacobs: 1970: 34).

Llewelyn-Davies, in discussing female solidarity and fertility among the

Iloita section of pastoral Maasai, confirms this general pattern for marriage among them for the early 1970s, noting that the bride refuses to enter the *enkang'*

> until she has promised gifts of livestock (and therefore friendship) by some of the women . . . Those who should particularly give gifts are the bride's co-wives. But other women whose husbands' are related to the groom may also promise livestock [with the husbands' approval]. (Llewelyn-Davies 1978: 21)

She adds, however:

> When a man brings a new bride to his village, her arrival is marked by a ceremony which begins by dramatising the very reverse of female solidarity. The bride is met outside the entrance to the village [*enkang'*] by her fellow-villagers, women who are likely to be strangers to her. The women descend upon her, screaming threats and insults. Her appearance and character are abused, she is ugly, she is known to be a thief, and so on . . . She is not allowed through the gates of the village until she has broken down and wept.

All Ilparakuyo, Maasai, and Barbaig men pursue the goal of becoming eventually a respected elder, or a "notable" in the community (*olkarsis*, pl. *ilkarsisi*). This normally implies that a man not only presides over large herds, but also has a large kinship group, with a number of wives, children, sons and daughters-in-law, affines, and grandchildren. However, he must also have personal qualities which enable him to achieve such a position; wealth alone is not sufficient. Hence, although most "notables" are "wealthy" men, not all wealthy men are notables. Furthermore, as an elder pursues this goal of notability and "wealth" (*enkarsisisho*), his control over the primary means of production is progressively weakened and diluted, since wives, sons, affines, and matrilateral kinsmen increasingly claim their rights to, and control of, certain portions of the herd. Thus the so-called "owner" of a herd at no time has exclusive, individual control of the means of production nor over the product; what is more, in his pursuit of "notability," he is doing the very opposite of increasing his "wealth" as an individual by accumulating cattle, he is actually "accumulating" relationships. Not only do the members of his own family or *enkang'* progressively usurp his control, but also members of *other* families in other *inkang'itie* come to claim their rights as well as to fulfil their obligations.

However, we must not leave the discussion at the politico-juridicial level of the mode of production: namely, the exercise of rights and duties. I therefore draw attention now to two critical issues: 1) although *de jure* only men may "own" (i.e. exercise full control over) the primary means of production in pastoral societies, women play an *essential*, privotal role in the transfer of this control, by inheritance primarily transmitted from one generation to another through the mediation of matrifiliation; 2) when we analyse the actual process of production and consumption, all aspects of the relations of production, women have, *de jure* and *de facto,* virtually full control over the major objects of the productive process: milk, fat, hides and skins, as well as considerable control over the distribution of significant portions of other products, meat and blood.

These are obviously controversial assertions, and require analytical support; but it is the failure to make such distinctions that causes the considerable ambiguities and contradictions that occur in discussions of the position of women in pastoral social formations. What follows, therefore, is an exposition which is also an explicit critique of the commonly-held belief that in such societies, "women do all the work; men have all the rights". Such a conclusion can only arise out of a discussion of pastoral societies at the ideological level. Implicitly, then, the present analysis is also a critique of such statements as these: "Livestock *is owned* by individual men" [in Maasai society]; ". . . Women are bought and sold with stock as they put it"; and

> The maxim ['men care about cattle; women care about children'], harped upon in myth as well as conversation, implies a certain complementarity between men and women. But in fact, it devalues women's labour on the family herds and justifies men's control of all domestic animals, the basic means of production. (Llewelyn-Davies 1978: 7, 9, 3)

I have already demonstrated the fallacy of using without serious qualification the English words "own", "owner", in relation to control of, and access to, the means of production and product in pastoral societies – at least the ones under scrutiny here. Other authors are equally as ambiguous as Llewelyn-Davies in their assessment of male and female rights in livestock. For example, Klima states for the Barbaig (1964: 10)' "Cattle are the most valued property among the Barbaig and belong to both sexes." Yet by 1970, the same author is much more equivocal:

> Ownership of cattle is the perogative of males in Barabaig society, but the position of women in the network of stock relations is crucial. Although a women cannot own cattle outright, she does exercise some control over stock *given to her as gifts* on ritual occasions, and can be considered as a kind of holding unit from which in-payments of stock will eventually become out-payments to her children as they mature, marry, and later move away to establish families and homesteads of their own.

He then adds, "Each hut-group, composed of a mother and her children within a polygynous household is an *autonomous property-owning unit*" (Klima 1970: 41; my emphasis). Such ambiguities (and there are others) cannot be reconciled upon the level of the judical and ideological discussion which has given rise to them.

I propose to resolve these contradictions and dilemmas, commencing with an analysis of the division of labour, relations of production, and control of the production process in these pastoral societies, a) on the basis of sex and b) on the basis of age.

V

In the previous sections I have merely outlined the bases of polygyny, dual organization, and matrifocality in the production units of Ilparakuyo, Maasai, and Barbaig social formations. I now elaborate upon the principle of matrifocality, and hence matrifiliation, in these societies, as they operate in the process of production.

Among Ilparakuyo, the initial construction of the thorn fence (*esita*, pl. *isitan*) for the herd's cattle byre is the responsibility of men. Most of the work is done by senior *ilmurran*, aided by junior *ilmurran*, and supervised by the elder or elders of the family group. This division of labour, of course, varies a great deal according to the actual availability of personnel in any particular family group; elders often have to build their own byres with the aid of their junior *ilmurran* sons. Among pastoral Maasai, a similar division of labour is found, although the total group of families is usually much larger than among the Ilparakuyo, and hence the availability of labour less problematic (Jacobs 1965a: 218-19).

The construction of the individual houses (*inkajijik*) to be occupied by each married woman and her children is generally the responsibility of the married women of the group (*inkituaak*), aided by their husbands, sons, and the young girls nearing initiation and marriage (*intoyie*). In the past, *inkajijik* were built within the circle of the cattle byre; they are now usually constructed outside it, with additional fences for protection from the outside bush. Each house (*enkaji*) is the *property* of the married woman who builds and occupies it; it constitutes her private domain which cannot be tampered with by men or co-wives, on pain of being fined. The only concept of "property in land" – if it may be called such – entertained by Ilparakuyo, relates to abandoned homestead sites (*ilmuaateni*, sing. *olmuaate*) and these. belong *equally to men and women* (cf. Beidelman 1961a: 59).

Currently among Ilparakuyo, at lease those of West Bagamoyo District, men and women hire labour from amongst neighbouring Bantu cultivators to assist them in the construction of houses, but never for the preparation of the cattle byre itself (*emboo*, pl. *imbooitie*) and its fence (*esita*). The assistance required from non-Ilparakuyo in the construction of houses is at least partially the result of the increasing number of homestead-site movements imposed upon Ilparakuyo by current villagization and rural development policies. Thus, in addition to the historical reasons given by Beidelman for the change of building-styles among Ilparakuyo (1961a), from the Maasai style attributed to Ilparakuyo in the late 19th Century to those more like the structures of their Bantu neighbours, current policies are accelerating such changes; but the overall plan and control of the *enkang'* in terms of men and

and women remains the same.

Although the whole *enkang'*, or the autonomous (perhaps better, *partially* autonomous) patricentral polygnous families who may share one, can be considered as production units in terms of the welfare of the herds and decisions about transhumance, migration, and changes of residence, the *basic* unit in the actual process of production of the major social product is the *enkaji*, the matri-central unit of a married women and her children, in relation to her husband, who may have other obligations to other like units. The *enkaji* may also include at certain times young affines and their allocated herds, such as young daughters-in-law married to mature sons of the owner of the *enkaji* who have not as yet had children.

The internal organization of Ilparakuyo *inkajijik* varies a great deal, but they usually include two beds whose foot-ends face each other across the hearth, one for the owner of the house, her husband, and sometimes children, the other normally for her older children, visitors, or daughters-in-law. Between the owner's bed and the walls and corners that surround it are her storage places for the milk calabashes, gourds, and other personal possessions. Sometimes, particularly in the past, the calves of the house owner's allocated herd are tethered to posts inside the entrance passageway to the main room, during the night; and it is not infrequent to find the mother of a calf, tethered inside, blocking the whole entrance to the *enkaji* during the night. More frequently now, a calves' pen (*olale*, pl. *ilaleta*) is constructed within the cattle byre, where they are kept during the night.

The excellent description given by Jacobs of the integrity of the *enkaji*, both as a unit in the process of production and in the transfer of rights in the means of production in pastoral Maasai society, applies *mutatis mutandis* to the Ilparakuyo *enkaji* (cf. Beidelman 1960: 270-5). Because of the critical importance of this fact for our discussion, I quote Jacobs extensively:

> The principal activities of a house, and the household group that it represents [*enkaji*], are associated mainly with women. As houses are built and solely maintained by women, they are also regarded as their private property. There are, for example, strict conventions relating to entering a house, even for husbands, and no one enters without first being invited by the women owner, and never in her absence; spears, carried only by males, must always be left outside the house. Similarly, whereas males are concerned with the adult herd of livestock . . . it is women who look after the calves. These consist mainly of the progeny of the eight cows and a bull which husbands present to their wives when they bring them to their [*enkang'*] to set up a household . . . The decision to let calves graze with the main herd is made jointly by the husband and his wife. And among those families with sheep and goat holdings, it is generally the women who look after them . . . (1965a: 183)

Perhaps most importantly, women do all the milking, and *they control the distribution and consumption of milk*, the main product of the herd. As Jacobs notes for the Maasai, women "also have sole rights over the

the distribution of the milk that they draw". Women's activity in this productive process is not confined merely to the technical operation of the actual milking, but is enhanced by the special techniques of cleaning, sterilizing, smoking, and flavouring, as well as storing, the milk. Some women are known to be better at this than others, and for many young Ilparakuyo *ilmurran*, the milk from their mother's *enkaji* takes on a very special emotional and symbolic significance; a feeling which may be transferred to a "special wife" by older men. Thus one *olmurrani*, in the presence of some of his age-mates who concurred with his feelings, told me:

> Just after I had become a full *olmurrani*, and began going around with my age-mates and the young girls, I could not drink the milk from anyone's herd except my mother's. Other *ilmurran* could drink milk anywhere, but I would starve until I came home. Once, after a long period of wandering about and singing and dancing with the *intoyie*, I came home to find my mother was away and there was no milk in her calabashes. So I had to milk one of our cows myself; after drinking this I could then go to sleep. Now I can drink milk anywhere, but I still prefer that prepared by my mother.

This *olmurrani* had been married four years, and had just taken a second wife.

Jacobs' comments for the Maasai apply equally, once again, to the Ilparakuyo:

> Although there is no special prohibition nor shame attached to men milking cattle, this is typically performed by women of the household . . . Thus while husbands commonly indicate in which of their wives' houses they propose to sleep the night by saying, "I will come to drink milk with you tonight", custom dictates that males must wait in eating until milk is offered to them by females. The only exceptions to this rule are those of ceremonial occasion or the presence of a male guest, both of which permit males (sons as well as husbands) to ask, or even demand, of their household females (wives, mothers, sisters, or daughters) to provide milk. One of the most dishonourable acts which a husband can perform is to enter his wife's bedroom, where the milk calabashes are stored, in order to determine how much milk she has; for this not only involves an infringement of her *domestic right* to distribute milk as she sees fit, but it strikes at the very heart of the *mutual respect* [*enkanyit*] and *service* on which their economic unity as a household group must depend . . . (1965a: 183-4)

Llewelyn-Davies confirms this overall picture of a women's control of milk distribution and consumption for Iloita Maasai in the 1970s, noting that "She has milking rights over the females, and the right to sale or use of the hides of all stock [attached to her *enkaji*] which die or are slaughtered" (Llewelyn-Davies 1978: 8). She also emphasizes further the *control* a women has over the inheritance of access to the herd as a means of production when she adds, "*She alone is responsible for the allocation of specific animals* to [her sons], and she can *decide to give nothing* at all to a particular son" (my emphasis).

However, Llewelyn-Davies has a very different notion from that of Jacobs concerning the mutuality of respect (*enkanyit*) between husband and wife, maintaining that all legitimate sexual relations take place between unequals, *enkanit* thus losing all reciprocity; she adds that women say they are "never in charge (*aitore*) of the stock".[25] Again, an analysis which confuses the different levels of control of the means of production, and hence distorts the nature of the relations of productions and the productive process, leads Llewelyn-Davies to contradict her statement on the role of women in inheritance, quoted above, when she adds (1978: 9): "Women, then, are excluded from all important decisions relating to the welfare of the herds." How can all this be reconciled, particularly when we relate it to the Ilparakuyo material and the Maasai material quoted from Jacobs (above)? Certainly not by reference to an erroneous concept of "ownership".

To return to the importance and integrity of a married woman's *enkaji*, we may note that most Ilparakuyo men, however distinguished as elders they may be, never have a "house of their own". A man's waking hours are spent almost entirely outside the houses and even the *enkang'* itself. He sleeps in his mother's *enkaji*, or his wives' houses when he is married. While he is still an unmarried junior *olmurrani*, he may spend most of his time in other homesteads with his age-mates, sleeping in the houses they are able to use in their own homesteads. If any man is visiting, he may sleep in the house of one of his age-mates' wives or mother, or in the *enkaji* of one of his female affines or kinswomen. In one sense, therefore, all Ilparakuyo men are "strangers" in their own or any other's *enkang'*; thus they must maintain good relations characterized by mutual respect (*enkanyit*) with their female kin, spouses, or affines (but cf. Parkipuny 1975: 37).

This inviolability and integrity of a woman's *enkaji*, yet the absolute necessity for mutual interdependence of women and men, kin and affines, age-mates, elders and juniors, and rules of exogamy and incest, are further strengthened by jural, ritual, and emotional injunctions. As Jacobs states for the pastoral Maasai:

> The house is . . . an important *sanctuary* in the social life of the pastoral Masai. Not only is it a place where one returns to eat, sleep, rest, or entertain in private, but it is also within the house that children of a household are conceived, born, and largely brought up. And in order to help insure the continued security and fertility of the household as the basic *reproductive unit* of their society, the house is regarded as an inviolable area. My informants indicate, for example, that in the past, when Masai tribes were known to raid or war against one another, occupants of a house were never touched nor a house entered. Even today, one of the heaviest penalties for a breach of customary law is the ten head of cattle which must be paid by an aggressor who pursues

his victim into any house [*enkaji*] in order to fight, whether this be with words, fists, or swords. (1965a: 184-5)

As amongst Maasai, Ilparakuyo have utter contempt for a petty thief (*olapurroni*, pl. *ilapurrok*) who steals from any *enkaji*, while a cattle rustler (*olainyamoni*, pl. *ilainyamok*), when he steals from non-Ilparakuyo or Maasai, may be the subject of praise and heroic songs.

The ritual importance of the house, however, is limited. The hearth (*isoito le dukuya enkima*, lit. "the stones of the first fire") represents the male symbol, the male component, of the *enkaji* and the unity of the household as a group. Only men are allowed to use the fire-sticks to make the "first fire" in any *enkang'* among both Ilparakuyo and Maasai. Among Ilparakuyo, if a couple do not have children, or the only children of one wife have died and she cannot bear more, within a reasonable period, the women of the *enkang'* arrange a fertility ceremony and prepare honey beer (*enaiho*), an essential element in all Ilparakuyo rituals. The elders assemble in the wife's (or husband's mother's) *enkaji* and, saying blessings, "spray" the couple with a mixture of beer and saliva from their mouths while the latter sit together on a bed. This ceremony, called *inkamulak oo'nkituaak* (lit. "the saliva of the mature women") appears to be much more formalized and conducted in the "public domain" by pastoral Maasai women, for women, and takes place regularly every four years (Llewelyn-Davies 1978: 23-5ff). Finally, among Ilparakuyo, a crucially important "blessing" ceremony, performed the night before a youth is circumcised, takes place in his (or her) mother's *enkaji*. It is carried out by elders of the youth's father's-age-set, i.e. the house owner's husband's age-mates, although members of other age-sets (except junior *ilmurran*) may be present. The mother must be there for this ritual.

The significance of matrifiliation in the descent and inheritance system of the Barbaig is strongly emphasized by Wilson (1954: 36-9), as is the matrifocality in the process of pastoral production. Matrifiliation and affinal ties become the crucial points at which patrilineal descent and actual, continuing co-operation between homestead groups (*gheidik*, sing. *gheida*) are actually articulated in this society in which descent *groups* play a considerably more important part than they do among Ilparakuyo and Maasai. This is summed up by Wilson as follows:

[The] series of reciprocal obligations and observances between *gheidik* which are created by marriage is a basic element in the lineage principle in Barabaig society. The woman is the *focal point* and *her cattle are the overt symbol* of these relationships, just as she becomes the focal point in the segmentary principle within the agnatic lineage of her husband . . . (1954: 40)

Thus, even though descent ties are traced genealogically much deeper in Barbaig society than among Ilparakuyo and Maasai, the symbolic manifestations and the *practice* of the descent ideology being greater in the former, matrifiliation and matrifocality play a very similar role in all three societies. We have seen that the term for "clan" in Barbaig is also that for "gate" (*dosht*). Within this descent category, "maximal lineages" are identified by asking "from which room [i.e. woman of the *gheida* of the founding ancestor of the lineage] do you come?" (*Giban ga?*). A Barband answers this question

> with reference to the *son* of the ancestor of the *dosht* or to *that women whose son* is regarded as the founder of the lineage segment . . . Several names of lineage groups of this degree are actually found to be the names of women. (Wilson 1954: 37)

At the level of the process of production, the matricentral cells of a mother and her children are the basic units and, as we have seen, are also "autonomous property-owning units" (Klima 1970: 40). Wilson again locates the focal point of lineage continuity in the relations of production between the sexes at the homestead level, and he also emphasizes the control women have over the most important products of the herd: milk, hides, and certain portions of meat (Wilson 1954: 37). That Barbaig, despite the introduction of agriculture in certain areas, still view their herds as the major means of production is indicated by Klima:

> The Barbaig do not view their cattle as a living supply of beef, but if an animal dies of natural (or unnatural) causes they do not hestitate to use the meat. Anyone who would kill a cow or bull just for food would be the object of intense ridicule and derision if his deed were discovered and made widely known. (1970: 43)

To sum up so far, I hope I have now demonstrated that the division of labour on the basis of sex is fundamental in the relations of production and the process of production in Ilparakuyo, Maasai, and Barbaig society; and that although men "control" *de jure* and ideologically the basic means of production, women play a critical role *as a category* at all levels of the mode of production in the *transfer* of the rights of control and access to the means of production, from one generation to another, both *de jure* and *de facto*. In the latter sense, women have virtually total control of the primary objects of the productive process in its distribution and consumption, both elements in the relations of production. If any category of persons in Ilparakuyo, Maasai, and Barbaig social formations could be said to approximate in any way to having "individual ownership" of particular beasts in the herd, it is the young maturing sons of an elder, or their mothers; certainly it is not the "successful elder" (*olkarsis*) in the prime of his life. That the notable elders do not accumulate cattle but use them to *create* new social relationships. i.e. ensure the reproduction of the community as a whole by ensuring the reproduction of its constituent production units (domestic groups and their internal matricentral cells), surely implies the very opposite of the "fetishism of cattle" attributed to such societies by Bonte (1975: 386-9; 1977: 180-2, especially p.181). They are not mystifying real relationships by inverting the reality of commodities; they are re-creating the totality of the relations of production. I return to this again later.

Before concluding with an assessment of the implications of this study for modern development and social transformation in Tanzania, I must consider the issue of the division of labour on the basis of age organization; or, to put it more succinctly, how age-set and age-grade relations function as relations of production.

VI

In some pastoral societies, such as the Somali, the *field* of co-operation in the processes of production and control over the major means of production is extended beyond the basic production units upon the basis of the ideology of descent. Such an extension is necessary for the long-term reproduction of the community as a whole. I have shown that even among Ilparakuyo and pastoral Maasai, despite the relative lack of emphasis upon "putting the ideology of descent into practice", certain rights of access to "man-made or modified" improvements in the means of production and the productive forces (wells, water furrows, drinking troughs, etc.) are controlled primarily by descent or kinship groups. These groups, however, do not operate without being in combination with locally organized elements of the age-set structure to form "councils" or "meetings" (*inkinguenat*, sing. *enkiguena*)[26] whose primary function is to settle disputes arising from access to dry-seasons watering places (cf. Jacobs 1965b: 204 n). I have also shown that, as opposed to the highly developed age-set and age-grade organization of Ilparakuyo and Maasai, the Barbaig in similar contexts tend to extend the range of co-operation of the basis of descent rather than age-organization, although the latter exists in incipient form. This in turn is associated with considerable institutionalization of economic and politico-jural relations between the sexes. Despite the dominance of inter-sex and descent-group relations among Barbaig, they operate also within the context of generation-set organization which, however, in other situations is minimally stressed (Klima 1964: 17; Wilson 1953: 42).

A fundamental theoretical question needs to be posed at this point of the discussion. Given the similar development of productive forces, ecological circumstances, and a mode of production based upon livestock and labour as the primary elements of the productive process, why do Ilparakuyo and Maasai *choose* to extend co-operation beyond the basic units of production primarily upon the basis of age-set organization, subjugating the principle of descent to a secondary position, while other societies such as the Barbaig select to extend co-operation upon the ideology of descent as *praxis*?[27]

Within a different problematic from the present one, the same question has been posed in ecological terms and the answer left to haphazard contingency, typical of the notion of "discovery" in positivistic analytical reason:

> in the absence of clear boundaries, spatial groups are relatively unimportant [in pastoral societies] and another idiom must be found to unify the population. This must be flexible – able to bring together a large community for mutual defense, while allowing small units to operate independently when range conditions demand. Two mechanisms exist in Africa: segmentary lineages . . . and age-grades. The former, in its finest form, such as that of the Somali, can unify a large nation while preserving the independence of action of the individual household. The latter creates special institutional means for unifying a wide region for military action. (Goldschmidt 1965: 403-4)

We must therefore return to a more advanced stage of discussion of some of the theoretical issues raised in the first section of this chapter; that is, within the historical materialist problematic, what are the *cultural-historical* mediators which become *dominant elements*, at certain levels of the forces of production, in the organization of the social relations of production, in specific historical modes of production and social formations? This question may appear to constitute a denial of the problematic of historical materialism; it is only if one reduces this problematic to some form of vulgar economistic determinism.[28] In fact, Marx is seriously misunderstood in this context of discussion, since the question of mediators in the dialectical process is usually avoided by Marxists. What men produce, the *object* of production, and *how* they produce it, depends not only upon "the 'nature' of the means of subsistence they actually find in existence [in 'nature'] and have to reproduce", but also upon *conscious choice* within the context of cultural-historical conditions. Thus, Marx and Engels state:

> [A] mode of production must not be considered simply as being the reproduction of the physical existence of the individuals. Rather it is a *definite form of activity* of these individuals, a definite form of *expressing their life* [my emphasis], a definite *mode of life* on their part. (1976: 31-2, original emphasis)

In his penetrating critique of "the dialectic of nature" as proposed by Engels, and hence in defining the "domain of the dialectic", Sartre quotes Marx from *The Eighteenth Brumaire of Louis Bonaparte*, the full passage of which is the following:

> Men make their own history, but they do not make it just as they please . . . but under circumstances directly encountered, given and transmitted from the past. (Marx and Engels 1962: 247)

Sartre comments:

> If this statement is true, then both *determinism* and analytical reason must be categorically rejected as the method and law of human history. Dialectical rationality, the whole of which is contained in this sentence, must be seen as the permanent and dialectical unity of *freedom* and *necessity*. (1976: 35, my emphasis)

There are not only multiple forms of historical transformation, but also multiple forms of relations of production and forms of property at the same level of productive forces, *within* the overall determination of the economic instance. If this were not so, it would be inconceivable that both capitalist and socialist relations of production can exist as historical alternatives at the *same level* of productive forces. Godelier puts it this way:

> [A historical materialist and structuralist problematic] . . . enables us to trace and formulate in "operational" terms some of the problems that anthropology and history should explore more thoroughly if the past [and the present] of mankind is to be stripped of its mystery. [Among these are] . . . How does the heredity of functions and statuses arise in certain primitive societies? It should be noted that even in its simplest forms, primitive society has different statuses for men and women based on sexual division of labour; statuses which are made more complicated by a distinction between elders and juniors . . . How are these new types of social relations established outside kinship [domestic] relations? For example, are they age classes or voluntary, religious, political and economic associations? These relations can harmoniously merge with kinship organizations or stand in opposition to them . . . (1972b [1969]: 160)

Kinship and descent relations are essentially restricted (particularistic) relations, even if extended by complex ideologies of descent, alliance, and affinity. Age organizations (age-set and age-grade structures) are universalistic, thus they generalize and institutionalize a universal condition of man (cf. Eisenstadt 1956).

I have shown above that although all Ilparakuyo and Maasai belong to patrilineal clans, sub-clans, and other descent categories, genealogical reckoning seldom exceeds three generations in depth. Compensation for homicide (*inkishu o' loikop*, lit. "cattle of the murder/crime") calls for co-operation among clan members of one locality, relations of production and co-operation in the productive process upon descent groups as such. The description given by Jacobs for the Maasai "practice" of the ideology of descent applies *pari passu* to Ilparakuyo, with the rider (see above) that patrilineal polygynous extended *families* are far more important among the latter. Jacobs states:

> Except for heads of two- or three- generation lineages, there are no descent

155

group leaders, nor any specially constituted descent groups or courts to decide matters affecting their members as a whole. Although homicide calls for assistance and support from local members of a clan, any decision to act as a group in the matter is made by members meeting on an *ad hoc* basis, and it frequently happens that individual members will refuse to take part in the affair. Thus, in conceiving of descent groups as sibling divisions of the family cattle-gate, emphasis is placed upon individual rather than group relations. Descent groups are seen primarily as categories of kin rather than as corporate groups of kinsmen. And it is perhaps indicative of the lack of formal relations between groups *qua* descent groups that there exists no term in Masai to describe relations between descent groups *as groups*, all such relationships being referred to by terms denoting interpersonal kin relations. (1965a: 205)

In fact, Ilparakuyo and Maasai trace their own history primarily in terms of the age-set system, dating events from the circumcision periods of particular name age-sets, their transitional ceremonies through the age-grade structure, and their eventual extinction (see Chapter 4; Fosbrooke 1948: 11-12, 1956a; Jacobs 1968; Beidelman 1960: 262-7; Berntsen 1979a, 1979b, forthcoming). Elders do, however, have clan legends which relate the migrations of various groups and their inter-connections with other Maasai sections.

I have described in Chapter 3 certain aspects of Ilparakuyo age-set relationships functioning as relations of production within the wider social formation in which they find themselves. The age-set system of the pastoral Maasai has been extensively described and analysed (e.g. Fosbrooke 1948: 25-34, 1956a; Jacobs 1958, 1965a: 240-94; Huntingford 1969: 119-20). What must be noted for our present purposes is that the division of labour within each sex category, extending beyond the production units, is based largely upon age-set organization, and not upon kinship or affinal ties; although, of course, these latter play a subsidiary role.

Each age-set (*olporror*, pl. *ilporori*; *olaji*, pl. *ilajijik*) passes through three age-grades, the first two of which are sub-divided into "sub-grades" (Jacobs 1965a: 243). Uncircumcised youths (*ilayiok*, sing. *olayioni*) are not yet members of the system; they have no status in the public domain. It is they who provide the labour for most of the day-to-day herding duties during the wet and normal seasons, very young boys beginning with the task of tending young calves together with the flocks of sheep and goats. They do this near the homestead (*enkang'*) where certain grazing areas are specially preserved for this purpose. Older boys, from the age of about ten or eleven, begin to herd the mature cattle, often spending most of the day away from the homestead.

Since herding duties obviously vary with seasonal fluctuations as well as longer-term yearly changes in climactic conditions, as well as epidemics of bovine diseases, the young initiated men (*ilmurran*, or "junior warriors"), senior warriors, and even elders (*ilmoruak*) often have to undertake arduous dry-season herding activities, sometimes moving herds long distances in search of grazing and water in the pattern of seasonal transhumance and migration. Junior and senior *ilmurran* are also normally responsible for taking the herd for dipping or beasts to market, or for giving injections of serum to sick cattle.[29] As I show later, Ilparakuyo junior *ilmurran* are now increasingly responsible, either upon their own initiative or under the direction of elders, for other arduous, difficult, and sometimes dangerous tasks.

After circumcision (*emurata*; the entire ceremony is called *elatim*) and his first *olpul* meat-feast at which he presents a beast (before this he is still an *osipolioi*, pl. *isipolio*) a youth becomes an *olkiliai* (pl. *ilkiliani*, "fledgeling" warrior) and then finally a full *olmurrani*. However, each age-set of youths circumcised and initiated over an "open period" for circumcision of seven years is divided into sub-sets, normally three, which are grouped into "those of the right hand" and "those of the left hand" (*emurata e tatene* and *emurata e kedyanie*). The first sub-set is called *ilcang'enopiro* (sing. *olcan' enopiro*, lit. "the ostrich feathers"); the second is called *ilparing'otua* (sing. *olparing'otuani*, from *aipirri*, ("to run fast"); and the third sub-set is called the *ilkerimbuot* (sing. *olkerimbuoti*).[30]

The complex interrelationships among sub-sets of one full age-set, and the wide range of actual ages of the members of one set, sometimes influence strongly the "promotion" of individuals, and sets up through the age-grade structures, added to which is the *olpiron* ("fire-stick relationship") between alternate age-sets as totalities, the seniors acting as sponsors, the alternate juniors the "sponsored" (cf. Jacobs 1965a: 254ff; Fosbrooke 1948, 1956a; Beidelman 1968: 81). The senior sub-sets of junior *ilmurran* nearing their *eunoto* ceremony which promotes them to senior *ilmurran*, often behave like, and are often emotionally and jurally closer to, the current junior sub-sets of the senior *ilmurran*. Within each age-set (*olporror*), a senior sub-set exercises fairly strict disciplinary control of its junior sub-set or sub-sets, in relation to dress, dance, and behaviour in "public" situations. These distinctions die away gradually as elderhood is attained.

Ilparakuyo no longer build "warrior camps" (*imanyat*, sing. *emanyata*), although they did so in the past. Ilparakuyo elders say that many of the ritual and educational functions of these camps have now been transferred to the periodic "meat feasts" (*ilpuli*) which the junior *ilmurran*, particularly, organize periodically with the aid of their fathers and senior elders (cf. Chapter 3).

I now consider in historical perspective the position of junior *ilmurran* in the division of labour and the relations of production, the productive process, and notions of property. It is they who also "epitomize" Ilparakuyo (and Maasai) age-organization, as well as the commitment to a culture of great resilience and vitality; consequently, it is also the junior *ilmurran* who are under the greatest pressure from governmental agencies to "change their ways" and "modernize".

The literature on Ilparakuyo and pastoral Maasai abounds with references to their "aggressive and war-like nature", with special reference to the *ilmurran*; hence the translation of *ilmurran* (Anglicized as "moran") as "warriors". The nature of this "aggression" and the identity of the "aggressors" have been the subject of much recent debate. During this debate, much of the aggressive behaviour attributed to Maasai *ilmurran* in the historical sources has been shifted to the doorstep of the Ilparakuyo, the original allegation being ostensibly the result of mistaken identity during the 19th Century. Whatever the case may be, it is relevant to the present discussion to consider the *conclusions* drawn from these allegations by both colonial administrators and contemporary government officials of independent Tanzania. The argument runs as follows: since the functions of Ilparakuyo and Maasai *ilmurran* were basically aggression, warfare, and cattle-raiding in the past, they no longer have any purpose, any relevance to the division of labour and relations of production in modern independent Tanzania and the policies of rural development and socialist transformation. They must therefore be eliminated as a social category as they now merely roam about ("indecently dressed"), doing no work, and thus contributing nothing to the development of rural Tanzania.[31] My evidence from the Ilparakuyo indicates that both the historical premises and the contemporary conclusions drawn from them are seriously in error: I begin with the first.

The historical evidence upon the role of Maasai *ilmurran*, mainly from Kenya Maasailand but relevant also to Tanzania (e.g. Lawren 1968; King 1971; Tignor 1972; Waller 1976; Jacobs 1965a, 1968, 1975; Rigby forthcoming and *passim*) indicates that a) Maasai aggression in the 19th Century was caused mainly by European and Arab imperialist penetrations and administrative duplicity; b) territorial expansionism since the 19th Century has been mainly the prerogative of cultivating neighbours of Ilparakuyo and Maasai; and c) the conclusion drawn by Jacobs for the Maasai applies, once again, *pari passu* to Ilparakuyo:

> In short, although Masai are not to be absolved from raiding for cattle, it is important to see that their military organization was as much defensive as it was aggressive, and that as a pastoral society they were never more warlike than surrounding agricultural tribes.[32] (1965a: 153)

Unless, one may add, they were provoked by imperialist aggression.

Particulary during the 19th Century and until now, therefore, this defensive and protective role of the *ilmurran* and their pseudo-military organization was, and still is, critically important. First of all, cattle and other livestock are more easily stolen than land, and are prey to carnivorous predators – protection from these dangers is a twenty-four hour per day necessity. Furthermore, agriculture is a seasonal activity, much of the year being spent in technically unproductive work, as so many studies of so-called "rural under-employment" take pains to point out. Pastoralism, on the other hand, demands a year-round commitment of labour, leading to the chronic shortage of labour in all pastoral societies, as I have mentioned above. This is particularly so among Ilparakuyo and Barbaig as compared with pastoral Maasai, owing to the much smaller residential and co-operating units among the former. Finally, because of these factors, it is a *structural necessity* for such social formations, at their present level of productive forces and relations of production, to *maintain* a defensive organization, centred in the case of Ilparakuyo and Maasai upon the category of junior *ilmurran*. In one sense, this defence is not only against predators that endanger the herd, the means of production, but also against external (and often misconceived) efforts to destroy the ability of the community to reproduce itself. The theoretical grounds for this assertion are to be found, yet again, in the *Grundrisse*.

Although Marx is discussing other types of pre-capitalist formations (Ancient Romans, Greeks, Jews), he is discussing, within a broader framework, a communal mode of production, close to the transformation of "Germanic" mode. Given the rider that, as opposed to Marx's examples of the "ancient mode" which existed within the context of inegalitarian relations with other classes, Ilparakuyo, Maasai, and Barbaig are extremely egalitarian (at least in pre-colonial times: cf. Bonte 1975), the following formations from the *Grundrisse* are highly apposite. I have substituted "cattle" for land as the major means of production and property in the following passage:

> The survival of the commune is the reproduction of all its members as self-sustaining peasants, whose surplus time belongs precisely to the commune, the work of war etc. The property in one's own labour is *mediated* by property in the *condition* of labour – [herd of cattle], guaranteed in turn by the *existence* of the commune, and that in turn by surplus labour in the form of military services etc. by the commune members. It is not co-operation in wealth-producing labour by means of which the commune member reproduces himself, but rather communal labour for the communal interests (imaginary and real), for the upholding of the association inwardly and outwardly.[33] Property is . . . of the [Ilparakuyo/Maasai] variety; the private proprietor of [cattle] is such only as [Olparakuoni], but as an [Olparakuoni] he is a private proprietor of [cattle]. (Marx 1973: 476)

The fact that this "surplus labour" of Ilparakuyo *ilmurran*, and similar categories amongst Maasai and Barbaig, as organized categories of labour, are still critical for the reproduction of the community as a whole is illustrated by the three following examples. The first is taken from my own research among the Ilparakuyo.

I have shown above that among Ilparakuyo, as well as pastoral Maasai, an increasing proportion of junior *ilmurran* are getting married before their promotion to senior *ilmurran*-hood by passing through the *eunoto* ceremony. This in turn involves a more rapid devolution of responsibility for, and control of, the means of production, the herd, from elders to juniors. I have also noted that Ilparakuyo *ilmurran* are now made responsible for the purchase and administration of livestock disease-control medicines, sometimes under the direction of the elders. These in themselves are no small responsibilities; they involve marketing of livestock for the necessary cash, travel to the towns, and a search from chemist shop to chemist shop to locate the necessary serum (frequently a fruitless exercise), as well as the administration and control of large sums of money, often several thousand Tanzaninan shillings. But added to these are new and even heavier responsibilities laid upon the shoulders of *ilmurran*.

At several points in the preceding discussion, I have indicated that, owing to government policies favouring cultivators, the extension of parastatal ranching schemes, and a general lack of interest in the development of peasant pastoralists (particularly Ilparakuyo), as well as the inroads of trypanosomiasis, East-Coast fever, and the lack of veterinary supplies, Ilparakuyo herds have diminished considerably over the past few years. The work of rebuilding these herds has been delegated to junior and senior *ilmurran*, usually under the direction of the elders, but also upon their own initiative. This task is achieved in the following manner.

Cattle marketing facilities are now under the control of the Tanzania Livestock Marketing Company, but they lack the facilities to carry out all such functions. Company buyers therefore compete with others at official markets, an unsatisfactory procedure which often results in only a fraction of the herds taken to market being purchased. In order to rebuild their herds, Ilparakuyo elders and *ilmurran* have learned to circumvent this system to some extent. Ilparakuyo *ilmurran* now travel long distances by bus, lorry, or train from their home areas in Morogoro, Bagamoyo, Tanga, etc., to purchase cattle from other areas, mostly semi-pastoral or agro-pastoral (such as Dodoma). Since the overhead costs are high, they travel with large sums of money, and buy large numbers of cattle, frequently 500 or more. These cattle are then driven (with the aid of hired labour) or trucked to urban areas such as Morogoro, Dar es Salaam, Moshi, Tanga, where meat shortages are chronic. They are fattened in local grazings, then sold in bulk to private buyers, who retail them (at considerable profit) to small butcheries. Alternatively, Ilparakuyo may sell them direct to companies, state, and parastatal organizations which cannot get sufficient supplies of meat through the "normal" channels.

After several such trips, which are exhausting, often frustrating, and almost always dangerous either because of the large sums of cash carried around or the possibility of stock theft from the herds *en route*, a considerable profit may be realized.[34] This profit is then reconverted to carefully selected animals which are taken home to rebuild the herds and ensure the means of production necessary for the reproduction of the pastoral community.

It is clear, then, that the "surplus labour" provided by the social category of *ilmurran*, both junior and senior, is highly utilized in the contemporary

Ilparakuyo social formation for the reproduction of the community as a whole, and its continuing ability to survive against mounting odds, both physical and social. At the same time, *ilmurran* are still responsible for dry-season grazing activities, and the overall security of the community and the herd.

Thus, just as the elders control the major transactions which circulate livestock and women within the community in order to ensure the reproduction of the community as a whole, and not themselves as a class (cf. Terray 1972: 163-76), so too do Ilparakuyo *ilmurran still* provide an essential factor in the division of labour and social relations of production of the community at large, *beyond* the limited bounds of the matricentral and domestic units of production. These *ilmurran* are directly manipulating that sector of the herd set aside by the elders as its *necessarily commoditized* portion, in order to replenish the major part of the herd which remains as the primary means of production for the community. The main objective products of this major portion of the herd, milk, blood, etc., remain largely under the control of women in their preparation, distribution and consumption.[35]

My second example is also taken from the situation of Ilparakuyo of West Bagamoyo District. Despite the high densities of population in the area and the relative elimination of most herds of wild animals, the area has seen both the depredations of a herd of elephants (which affected mainly the cultivators) as well as a pair of lions. The latter killed a number of stock; one was eventually killed single-handed by an *olmurrani*. The ceremonies associated with such a feat of courage and daring were carried out by the Ilparakuyo community, although considerably reduced in time and scope.

The final example, which gained considerable attention in the national news media, concerns events which took place in June 1977. It was reported in the national press that members of the current junior *ilmurran* age-set of pastoral Maasai had apprehended smugglers on the Tanzania-Kenya border (which had been officially closed to all commercial or other transactions at the time). Members of the same age-set also recovered cattle stolen from a state ranch near the border by following the rustlers into Kenya and taking the cattle from them by force. The *ilmurran* then handed the cattle over to police at the border post of Namanga. The Maasai *ilmurran* were highly praised for these actions in the national press (*Daily News*, 30 June 1977) and their spirit of discipline and courage was remarked upon as being helpful to the national interest and socialist development in Tanzania (cf. Ndagala 1978: 52, 213-14).

VII

It now remains to conclude, in summary form, the implications of this analysis for pastoral production and socialist transformation among

Ilparakuyo, Maasai, and Barbaig of Tanzania.

1) Kinship, descent, and affinal relations, as well as age-organizations (in various forms), function as relations of production amongst all these groups of pastoralists, the former being emphasized in extending relations of co-operation beyond the basic producing units among Barbaig, the latter doing the same among Ilparakuyo and Maasai. This implies that, within the historical materialist problematic, at certain levels of the development of productive forces, the cultural-historical factor is crucial in defining the actual form of the relations of production and the productive process in societies in fundamentally the same ecological and economic circumstances, at the same level of productive forces. The theoretical grounds for articulating this factor are to be found that the notion of the *mediations* in the transformation of the processes of production and consumption within the dialectic of historical materialism as propounded by Marx in the *Grundrisse* and elsewhere. This is ultimately the critical element in the current debate on the articulation of historical materialist and structuralist problematics, and certain aspects of the phenomenological method.

2) The division of labour between the sexes in these pastoral societies must be understood by distinguishing levels of control in the basic means of production, the transfer of these rights from generation to generation, as well as by separating *de jure* from *de facto* rights, particularly in the concrete productive process and the most important products of this mode. These must further be seen against the background of the development cycle of the domestic groups whose reproduction provides the basis for the reproduction of the community at large.

3) The division of labour on the basis of age-set organization as functioning as relations of production for the reproduction of the community as a whole, and its relations with other communities and structures in wider social formations (Chapter 3 above), are still viable and essential elements in the overall division of labour, and must be taken into account in development strategies affecting these communities.

4) Articulation with commodity relations leads to a reconceptualization of the herd into its basic part (female cattle, heifers, productive animals) still viewed as the primary means of production, and a subsidiary part (oxen, steers, old animals) which is marketed as product. This reconceptualization has implications for livestock development on the basis of peasant production, and cannot be ignored in any discussion of socialist rural transformation, both for the better reproduction of agricultural rural communities, the urban areas, as well as the pastoralists themselves. The basis for development already exists in the contemporary relations of production and co-operation, on the basis of sex and age, both within and between existing production units.

5) if the pastoralists are coerced or too seriously encouraged to extend their productive activities to cultivation, this will a) cause an aggravation to the extant chronic shortage of labour; b) accelerate the growth of hired labour in agricultural production and hence the formation of a rural

proletariate even in non-plantation areas; c) cause a *reduction* in the status of women in pastoral societies by undermining their control over the production process, their strong position in relation to the means of production; and d) by entrenching agricultural commodity relations, place the major portion of production *entirely* in the hands of men.

6) In the light of the foregoing, immediate and total "sedentarization" of transhumant pastoralists should be avoided, semi-sedentarization taking its place: that is, "permanent villages" with reserved grazing for subsistence herds in the dry season could be set up, related to relatively unlimited movement of the main herd, within the pattern of transhumance, in search of grazing and water in that season and in bad years, returning to the permanent villages in the wet season.

7) This would release uncircumcised youths (*ilayiok* in Ilparakuyo and Maasai) from at least part of their daily herding duties, enabling them to attend school in the permanent villages. *Ilmurran*, junior and senior, would then undertake more of the day-to-day labour of pastoral management and responsibility which, as I have shown for Ilparakuyo, they are already doing with increasing intensity. Thus the *present trend* in the division of labour and pastoral production relations could be encouraged positively as a move towards socialist development, rather than the social category of *ilmurran* being destroyed upon the dubious grounds of its anachronistic character.

8) The strategy outlined in 6 and 7 above should be geared to a) better veterinary services to pastoral peasants than are available at present, with correspondingly less emphasis upon state ranching for the production of beef for export and consumption by the urban bourgeoisie and expatriates; b) *regional* specialization of production with better communications and marketing, so that pastoralists, while remaining pastoralists as they improve production, could obtain the agricultural products now necessary to supplement their diet, owing to decreasing resources of pasture, while agricultural peasants could obtain the necessary livestock products while improving upon agricultural production.

9) It is clear that many of the suggestions made in this conclusion are at variance with certain official policies, particularly in regard to the problems of settlement, the encouragement of pastoral production by *pastoral peasants*, and the development of existing relations of production in the division of labour, including the retention of the *ilmurran* category among Ilparakuyo and pastoral Maasai. But I hope the comparative analysis of pastoral production, presented here as a preliminary and tentative step towards deeper understanding of the specific types of transformation in pastoral societies, provides both theoretical direction and practical grounds for making some of these suggestions.

Notes

1. Written in May 1978.
2. In this connection, an immediate comparison comes to mind, one which might

      reward closer scrutiny: Owen Lattimore's work (1962, and *passim*) on the historical transformations of Mongolian pastoralists into the Mongolian People's Republic on the one hand, and Charles Frantz's survey of African pastoralists and national integration in Africa (1975) on the other.

3.   Sahlins uses McLellan's (1971) translation, which is substantially different from that of Nicholaus; this, however, does not materially alter his argument.

4.   Of course, a large number of issues remain unresolved. The necessity for further application of a historical materialist problematic with phenomenological theory has been extensively explored, for example, by Habermas (1971; cf. chapter 2 above). Such discussions have serious consequences for Marx's epistemology, as does the work of Sartre (particularly 1968, 1976).

5.   An interesting aside: in his answers to questions posed in the Victorian parlour game known as "Confessions", Marx states that his "favorite motto" was *"De omnibus dubitandum"*, "You must have doubts about everything"; this is somewhat reminiscent of Diderot, identified by Marx in the same game as his "favourite prose writer" (McLellan 1973: 457).

6.   Nicolaus sums up Marx's propositions as follows:

> [In the sphere of simple circulation] the relations among individuals . . . are those of liberty and equality, because the exchange of commodities is based, on the average, on the law of equivalence; the products exchanged are the embodiment of equal amounts of labour time. Liberty, because the partners in exchange presume and recognize each other as proprietors and none takes from the other by force. Entry and exit into exchange is freely chosen. Individual A and individual B are distinguishable only as buyer and seller; in an instant they exchange these roles, drop even this difference, and become a single kind of being. (1973: 17-18)

7.   Ndugu M.L. ole Parkipuny also notes (personal communication) the general rise in the number of livestock in bridewealth prestations in Tanzania Maasailand (but cf. Parkipuny 1975: 37-9).

8.   Ilparakuyo figures were obtained by Ndugu Toreto ole Koisenge and Ndugu Jonas Reuben Wanga under the auspices of the Jipemeyo Project and the direction of Kemal Mustafa, to whom I am most indebted.

9.   Based on District Veterinary Files, quoted in Jacobs 1965: 151; Parkipuny derives most of his figures directly from Jacobs (cf. Parkipuny 1975: 33-4).

10.   Jacobs' own sample count of 14 family households at Simanjiro, Tanzania, in 1957; this sample is similar in size to Ilparakuyo and Barbaig samples.

11.   Information kindly supplied by Ndugu Finn Kjaerby (personal communication, May 1978; cf. Kjaerby and Baynit 1979).

12.   The proportion of females in Samburu herds is based on an average of a number of estimates made in 1922, 1925, 1933, 1958-9, and 1962 (Spencer 1973: 10).

13   The figures for Barbaig in Table 1 are from Kjaerby's own recent research. However, elsewhere (Kjaerby 1976: 197) he gives figures derived from Veterinary statistics for 1969 as 2.5 head of cattle per capita in "Barabaig

Division", which is higher than the average for Mbulu District as a whole, given in the same figures; there are 16.5 head of cattle per Barbaig household from these figures, compared with his later figures which give 50.5 head per household (cf. Kjaerby and Baynit 1979).

14. It is likely that there is a great deal of local variation in camp size, related to ecological, economic, and political factors. It can be seen from the Table 1 that in west Bagamoyo District, the average number of persons per *enkang'* was 11.2. However, close kin and affines now build separate *inkang'itie* close together, rather than residing in one, as in the past; in some areas, reasons of security and co-operation may encourage people to build larger *inkang'itie*. Furthermore, the average size of homestead groups is probably diminishing, as with the pastoral Maasai and the Gogo (Parkipuny 1975; Ndagala 1978: 144; Rigby 1969a).

15. *Emparnat* (pl. *imparnati*) is the Maasai term for a "permanent settlement", associated in the past with the large groups of *inkang'itie* which clustered around the residences of important religious leaders and prophets (*iloibonok*, sing. *oloiboni*)

16. In the late 1950s and 1960s, however, encroachment of Ilarusa (Arusha) "agricultural Maasai" into pastoral Maasailand and pastures led to violence (Gulliver 1957, 1961, 1963).

17. I say "prophetic" in that Marx was working with extremely limited and in-accurate data on precapitalist formations at the time (cf. Krader 1974).

18. It has been suggested by Bonte (1975: 391-4) that the ritual experts or "pro-phets" of pastoral Maasai (*iloibonok*), owing to the penetration of com-modity relations and their monopoly over the *ultimate* sources (i.e. religious intervention) of fertility and security that guarantee the reproduction of the community, are *accumulating* cattle and wives, leading to "asymmetric" relations where the *iloibonok* are thus an incipient class, although "this is a *situation of transition* . . . We are not in a society of classes" (Bonte 1975: 394). His analysis is based upon the concept of "cattle fetishism" (Bonte 1974, 1975: 386-9, 1976: 180-2). However, since I consider cattle in these communities basically as a *means of production* (as does Bonte at various points of his analysis), and since the Marxist concept of fetishism is insepar-able from the notion of commodity, Bonte's analysis is unsatisfactory, *except in so far* as it relates to that *part of the herd* which is now relegated to the category of "commodities" under the present conditions (see final section of this chapter). Marx (1954: 77) states categorically: "This I call the fetishism which attaches itself to the products of labour, so soon as they are produced as commodities, and which is *therefore inseparable from the production of com-modities*" (my emphasis).

19. The issue of land for Barbaig is highly contentious and complex, requiring more attention than it can be given here. Suffice to say that their relegation to fixed boundaries, the encroachment of agro-pastoral groups such as Iraqw, and contemporary resettlement plans, have led to a good deal of conflict amongst neighbouring peoples (cf. Kjaerby 1967; 1979; Klima 1970: 18-25ff; Rigby 1976).

20. The term "moiety" is not strictly correct here, since at this level the social categories delineated are not exogamous. However, at lower levels of descent categories, the *principle* of dual organization influences the rules of exogamy (cf. Jacobs 1970, 1965b).

21. The noun *olopeny* (pl. *iloopeny*), translated so often as "owner", is based upon the same root as *openy* (pl. *oopeny*), an irregular form denoting a state, and meaning "alone", "by oneself (themselves)": see Tucker and Mpaayei 1955: 24, 205. Jacobs (1965a: 22) states' "Masai regard it as bad (*torono*), in the sense of anti-social, to live alone."

22. It is not clear from Fosbrooke's account whether his category of "warrior class" includes both junior and senior *ilmurran*, but judging from the rest of his discussion, it is likely that he does.

23. Spencer (1965: 14-15, 65, 289-90, 319-20) gives figures for rates of polygyny which confirm a high proportion of polygynous elders among Samburu, as does Llewelyn-Davies for pastoral Maasai in 1972 (1978: 16-17).

24. Space does not permit a comparative analysis of the contexts in which female solidarity is expressed in Ilparakuyo and Maasai societies (for example in the *enkishuroto* of the former; Llewelyn-Davies gives *olkishoroto*) and for Barbaig. But it appears that most pastoral and semi-pastoral societies in Tanzania do have occasions, always related in some manner to the herd, during which women assert themselves with aggressive and violent behaviour *vis-a`-vis* all men in general, fining particular men for alleged misdemeanours against their wives or other women (e.g. see Klima 1964; Llewelyn-Davies 1978; Rigby 1968a).

25. *Aitore* means literally "to command", "be in command", or "rule" and it has very specific *jural* connotations; it does not in any context apply to informal influence or *de facto* control. For example, in discussing the elder who has "most respect" in a pastoral Maasai *enkang'* (he who has *enkanyit naleng'*), Jacobs notes (1965a: 223) that such an elder need not "be the wealthiest nor the politically most important person" of their camp. He adds that Maasai

> speak of such persons as having "shade" (*oloip*), implying that, as people like to gather together in the shade of a tree to discuss matters of common interest, so too they like to gather around a man who has "much respect".

26. *Enkiguena* basically means "a meeting", within or between age-sets; in the latter case, the local unit of each age-set is represented by its spokesman (*ilaiguenak*, sing. *olaiguenani*), and such meetings are usually held for the settlement of disputes.

27. By this I am *not* transposing the discussion to the area of what Goody calls "minor disputes" in the study of kinship and marriage, such as those between "so-called 'descent' and 'alliance' theorists, extensionists and categorists" (Goody 1976: 2, 135n). I am posing an altogether different and more fundamental question.

28. Cf. Sahlins's (1976: 4-18) discussion of Worsley's (1956) critique of Fortes (1945, 1949) and Fortes' reply (1969: 220ff)

29. Ilparakuyo, like other pastoral Maasai, are strongly oriented towards the utilization of modern methods of disease control in their herds. Since serum is frequently not available from Veterinary Department sources (most of this going to state ranches), Ilparakuyo spend vast sums of money purchasing livestock medicines from commercial chemists in Dar es Salaam and

other urban centres.

30.   The fourth sub-set, *iltareto*, mentioned by Fosbrooke as occuring only in the "right hand" group, is not known among Ilparakuyo.

31.   Ndagala (1978: 212) notes, "Government authorities have come out openly against the period of warriorhood for various reasons, among them 'the warriors' shameful attire' and the 'warriors' excessive laziness'. "Even Hatfield, sociologist with the Maasai Range Project, refers to the "redundancy" of the *ilmurran*, presumably referring mainly to junior *ilmurran*. If this is so for pastoral Maasai, it is certainly not so for Ilparakuyo, as I demonstrate below.

32.   See Chapter 4, Beidelman 1960, Ndagala 1974, for Ilparakuyo; cf. Ndagala 1978 for Maasai; Kjaerby 1976, Rigby 1976 for Barbaig.

33.   This mention of "imaginary and real" reintroduces the cultural-historical factor as a mediator also in the concrete form in which "communal labour for the communal interests" is expressed in particular social formations. Cf. Klima's formulation, within a "cultural ecology" concept, for Barbaig (Klima 1970: 5): "a society's cultural repertoire consists of learned problem solutions which give the members both *real* and *illusory* control over events occurring in their social and physical environments".

34.   I have a good deal of data on this system; for obvious reasons, I cannot be more explicit at this stage.

35.   Talking of Ilparakuyo in the late 1950s, Beidelman (1960: 258) states that "Baraguyu are deeply oriented to a cash market, far more than they themselves realize. Local cattle auctions have replaced warfare as a means of economic adjustment between Baraguyu and Bantu." If this was the case then, at least now they are fully aware of the situation, to the extent of manipulating it consciously towards ensuring their reproduction as a community.

7. Conclusion: Some Theoretical Implications of Pastoral Development Strategies

"Erisio enkiteng' nabo elukunya o'lee"
"One cow is as good as a man" – if a person cares for his cattle, he and the community will prosper.

Rather than attempting to "evaluate" the consequences and achievements of "livestock" sector interventions in semi-arid regions" in any comprehensive sense, a task which has been admirably addressed in a number of recent discussions and publications (e.g. Ferguson 1979; Jacobs 1978; Hoben 1979; Horowitz 1979; AIDPEP 1980), my concern is a much more reflexive one of exploring not only the "principal social, economic, environmental, and other assumptions that implicitly or explicitly underlie these interventions" (AIDPEP 1980: 1), but also to examine the very nature of the research process itself, its theoretical problematics, and its relevance to the historical processes manifested in specific pastoral social formations. Brief examples of the kind of thing I mean are represented by Dahl and Hjort's and Salzman's recent discussions of the concepts "pastoralism" and "nomadism" (Dahl and Hjort 1980; Salzman 1980). Basic to my argument is a central element in the problematic of historical materialism: that there is a dialectical relation between theory and praxis in any social science that has any historical significance; or, in other words, if there are to be any "research *priorities*" at all in pastoral studies.

II

The present discussion is limited to the pastoral social formations of eastern Africa. There are both theoretical and practical reasons for this, some of which are further elaborated in later sections of this chapter. The preliminary point to be noted here is that historically these pastoral formations have not been part of, or linked to, pre-capitalist state structures (with the exception of the pastoral elements of the inter-lacustrine states, which form a special case and are not subject to the generalizations advanced here).

168

Although all of these social formations have had relations of one kind or another of interdependence with non-pastoral neighbouring peoples, they have an historical specificity that distinguishes them from many of the pastoral societies of west and north Africa, the Middle East, and Asia (cf. Lefébure 1979; Chapters 5 and 6). This is not an argument for "historical particularism" which, as Salzman argues (1980: 4), may exclude theoretical formulations; in fact, both Salzman's concern over the "materialist dilemma" as well as Asad's otherwise correct application of the mode of production concept (1978) are inadequate, a point to which I return later. The issue here is the nature of the historical specificity of these East African pastoral formations and the consequences of this specificity for the mode of production concept and the "development strategies" which have intervened to transform them, and vice versa.

The second central issue encompasses the following element. This historical reality of these East African pastoral formations involves: a) their pre-colonial transformations in relation to their non-pastoral neighbours; b) their articulation with peripheral capitalism in the colonial state; and c) their continuing and increasing articulation with "unique" forms of capitalist exploitation through the national state structures of East Africa. One manifestation of the differential penetration of peripheral capitalism into pastoral as opposed to agro-pastoral or predominantly cultivating communities is the loss of pastures and water resources to the encroachment of government-sponsored cultivator (and other, such as "wildlife" and tourist) activities, and this is still a burning issue.[1] In turn this has resulted in a tendency almost everywhere towards increasing interdependence between pastoral formations and their cultivating neighbours, with or without a trend towards the incorporation of at least minimal agricultural production by formerly "purely" pastoral formations such as the Barbaig, Ilparakuyo, pastoral Maasai, and Borana (Chapters 1, 3, 6 above; cf. Kjaerby 1979; Beidelman 1960; Parkipuny 1975; ole Saibull 1974; Ndagala 1974; 1978; Dahl 1979).

The implications of this latter trend, which has been (and still is) encouraged or actively forced upon some pastoral formations during both colonial and independence periods, are particularly manifested in changes in return on labour commitment, a major problem examined in detail for the Barbaig by Kjaerby in a seminal paper (1979: 96-104, and *passim*; see below). Two major problems which require detailed and intensive research in probably all pastoral areas arise from Kjaerby's findings for the Barbaig.

As research from other areas also shows, pastoral production requires a much heavier commitment of labour on a 365-day per year basis than does cultivation. But even with this much higher level of labour commitment and its consequent implications for development strategies (for example in education), Kjaerby's work clearly indicates that, even when adjusted for drought and normal years in these pastoral areas, "the productivity of labour in cattle production is generally higher than for maize production". Kjaerby rightly concludes:

> The general superiority of labour productivity in cattle production over that in maize production is basically related to environmental and climatic conditions which are more suitable for cattle production ... In contrast to agricultural societies, where the labour power of school-aged children is more marginal and temporary to agricultural activities, children in pastoral societies are heavily and continuously engaged in herding, day in and day out, and this explains the reluctance of pastoralists to send their children to school. It thus has to be made clear that this reluctance is not due to conservatism or ignorance as maintained by some government officials, but due to the problem of having to carry out a lot of labour tasks. (1979: 103-4)

This statement could apply without alteration to the Ilparakuyo situation where elders and *ilmurran* (young initiated men, "junior warriors") are taking an increasing load of day-to-day herding so that young boys (*ilaiyok*) can go to school, and I suspect that this situation occurs throughout the pastoral areas of East Africa. There is an urgent need to understand its full and long-term consequences.

But the problem does present a contradiction which is quite apparent to the pastoralists themselves. Ilparakuyo and Barbaig are fully aware that labour returns are much higher on pastoral than on agricultural activities, despite the fact that many Ilparakuyo live in areas relatively well suited to cultivation. As Kjaerby succinctly notes for Barbaig;

> From the point of view of pastoral land-use we have a contradictory situation. Land alienation [and for Ilparakuyo we may add villagization] and alien agro-pastoral encroachment has led to an increase in stocking densities. The Barbaig are fully aware of the problem but, willingly or unwillingly, contribute to this trend by adopting cultivation. The historical conditions influencing national agricultural policies have imposed an untenable situation upon the Barbaig [and, we may add, Ilparakuyo, pastoral Maasai, and others]. They are forced to undermine the environmental basis for their preferred way of life. (1980: 46)

The Ilparakuyo differ from the Barbaig in that most of the labour involved in their maize and food-crop production is supplied by their cultivator neighbours, in return for cash or pastoral products, usually both, with consequently increasing interdependence between the two interlocked formations (Chapters 3 and 6, above). At any rate, a major question to be answered for each pastoral area undergoing these pressures and trends, and given the facts outlined above relating to the productivity of labour, then, is: why do pastoralists begin to cultivate, or aid and abet, the encroachment of cultivation upon their own environmental base?

This problem, however, has much deeper theoretical implications than appear at first sight and which need to be explored. But before we can do this, I must return to the question of the nature of pastoralist production in relation to the concept of modes of production and these historically specific social formations.

III

I commence by reaffirming Asad's position (1979: 425) that theoretical development cannot take place without "the adoption of a problematic based on a coherent concept of mode of production". But Salzman's worry over Asad's formulation is very real, for the latter, while rightly eschewing a "pastoral mode of production", fails to develop two aspects of the argument essential to the historical materialist problematic, thus leaving himself open to what Salzman identifies as the "materialist dilemma". We may uncover these two aspects by examining this false dilemma.

The development of the mode of production concept in general, and in relation to East African pastoral formations in particular, does not depend upon a choice

> between a reductionist position which does not seem to be able to work in practice and a permissive position [attributed by Salzman to Godelier (1977)] in which mode of production accommodates so much that it means little more than "way of life". (Salzman 1980: 4)

For while a mode of production is a unique articulation of the forces and relations of production, it is *also* a unique articulation of the economic, juridico-political, and ideological instances of that social formation. These two forms of articulation are indissolubly linked in any particular mode of production, and one cannot be discussed without the other. Thus the question of a "choice" between a "hard" position in which "social organization, kinship, political structure, ideology, and other idea systems are determined superstructures" (Salzman 1980: 4), on the one hand, and a "soft" position in which all these represent a random hodgepodge of a "way of life" on the other does not arise. The concept of mode of production enables us to theorize precisely about the role of each of these instances in any social formation in relation to their dominant or non-dominant position within it, and the precise nature of their articulation with each other. I will illustrate this in relation to East African pastoral formations as a way of returning to our initial concerns.

It is generally recognized in historical materialist analysis that it is only in the capitalist mode of production that the economic instance determines its own dominance. In all other known pre-capitalist modes of production, the economic instance determines the dominance of either the juridico-political or ideological (or both) instances. In the Germanic mode of production,[2] which admirably characterizes the basic articulation of forces and relations of production in East African pastoral (as well as agricultural) social formations (cf. the work of Bonte and myself, *passim*), the ideological instance is dominant. But it is at this point that we must turn to the nature of theorization about a mode of production.

A mode of production is a theoretical construct which *does* imply generalization, as Salzman asserts (1980: 4), but any theory of mode of production cannot proceed without reference to the concrete historical social formations in which it occurs, whatever the opinions of Hindess and Hirst (1975) to the contrary. The successful application of the concept "Germanic mode of production" to East African pastoral formations (as well as to their cultivating neighbours) thus entails specifying the real nature of the dominance of the ideological instance in them.

Both descent and kinship organizations and age-set systems emanate from the ideological domain, representing arbitrary categorizations of relations referring to biologically assumed characteristics and functioning, on occasion, as relations of production. I have suggested in Chapter 6 that there is a correlation between the relative dominance of one or other of these principles of organization and the relative emphasis upon pastoral versus agricultural activities. There is no need to repeat those arguments here. But the specific nature of the age-set organization as ideologically dominant and as functioning as relations of production in such pastoral formations as that of the Ilparakuyo is further elaborated in other ideological constructs relating to the nature of *pastoral appropriation of the environment*, as opposed to the agro-pastoral or agricultural formations within the Germanic mode of production. This needs further elaboration, and this can best be done by a comparison between the pastoral and agricultural instances of the Germanic mode of production.

Lefébure (1979) has shown clearly the crucial role of descent ideology in the reproduction of social formations with the Germanic mode of production. I have extended this argument to the role of age-set organizations in specific East African pastoral formations, in comparison with those in which descent ideology is dominant (Chapters 3 and 6). But one crucial element has been missing from these earlier formulations, and this concerns the nature of pastoral appropriation of the environment and the central role of ideology in this most basic of "economic" processes.

Most of the eastern African cultivator communities represent the Germanic mode of production in which the domestic group is the major unit of production and reproduction, both social and biological, linked in wider community relations of production by some form of lineal descent ideology, kinship, and affinal organization. Appropriation of the major means of production (land) is ideologically based upon "communal" tenure of areas in which descent group members and their associated kinship and affinal links establish rights of usufruct. But the exercise of the latter rights, however "temporary", based upon the domestic group, its head, and the matricentral units of married women within it, represents a *direct and exclusive* appropriation of land, and legal mechanisms exist in the juridico-political domain in order to maintain such "rights of exclusion". In these agricultural formations, then, men objectify "nature" (land) in two ways: ideologically as "communal" property, but in the actual process of appropriation as an exclusive possession, albeit temporary and subject to a number of community strictures. In a materialist sense, the core notion of a proprietory right in nature is established and maintained through the right of exclusion

(Marx 1973: 1857-8). Man is "subject", nature is "object". The apparent but not serious contradiction in this form of the appropriation of nature is resolved by ideological elaborations upon the mystical relationship between lineal ancestors and areas or objects in the physical environment.

In East African pastoral formations, on the other hand, which again represent the Germanic mode of production in that the domestic group is again the major unit of production and reproduction (cf. Bonte: *passim*), the major means of production are the herds, not the land, although there are elements of differential control over certain natural or man-made resources (such as wells) by descent groups. This "control" is never exclusive. Community relations of production among, for example, Ilparakuyo and pastoral Maasai, are based upon age-set as well as kinship relationships.

But the main point here is that, whatever the nature of control over the herd and its products (and there is some theoretical controversy on this question), the control the domestic group has in the herd as the major means of production is *not* a proprietory right in "nature", as in land, but in a *product of social labour itself* in the context of a generally accessible nature. Thus nature is not apprehended as "object" in which man as "subject" establishes rights of exclusion. This basic economic fact is again elaborated in these social formations in terms of the identification of land and its flora and fauna with a generalized "gift from God" (*Nkai* for Ilparakuyo and pastoral Maasai) and an ideological stricture upon digging it up (and hence "destroying" it) or killing the fauna that occupy it (as in hunting, cf. Galaty: *passim*).

Here, then, are a number of issues of major theoretical and practical significance. Although both cultivator and pastoralist formations in eastern Africa represent, in their "pre-contact" elements, the Germanic mode of production, the differences in the major means of production result in distinctive manifestations of this mode of production in historically specific types of social formation with distinctive dominant ideologies, as well as distinctive emphases upon organizational features such as age-sets and descent groups.

IV

It is quite clear from this that the historical uniqueness of the East African pastoral formations is radically affected in a most fundamental sense by any trend towards any form of cultivation, although this does not represent a transformation of the mode of production. Not only is there a shift in emphasis from one means of production to another (the herd to the land, the factor of labour being constant but differing in productivity), but there is also a drastic change in the form of objectification and appropriation of nature and its dominant ideological underpinnings. This in turn involves a revaluation of the constitution of the "subject" and the objectification of the "other", a fact which threatens the very foundations of the social formation itself and the ideological conditions of its reproduction. Hence the reluctance of these pastoral social formations to adopt cultivation, despite the mounting pressures at all levels for them to do so, and their consequent search for other methods of "dealing with" the encroachment of commoditization and the penetration of peripheral capitalism. This latter point needs some further explication, and for this I turn briefly to my own research among the Ilparakuyo of Tanzania.

I have already noted that Ilparakuyo, like all other pastoralists, have long been faced with a diminishing resource base of suitable grazing and water facilities. As a result, herd size has decreased, and there is a consequent increase in dependence upon agricultural products. This has been accelerated in recent years by such government policies as villagization. In the Ilparakuyo area of west Bagamoyo District in which I work, the "herders" village (*kijiji cha wafugaji*) allocated to the villagization of the whole Ilparakuyo community in the area is only 90,000 acres, much of it still tsetse infested, although clearing is continuing.

There have been several responses to these increasingly severe conditions by the Ilparakuyo. Some homestead groups and clusters (*ikang'itie*) have opted for the age-old solution of movement out of the congested areas to new rangelands where herd size can be increased again and a largely pastoral mode of existence be re-established. Such areas still exist in parts of east-central and southern Tanzania such as in the Morogoro and Mbeya regions, and my recent visit has verified the continuation of such moves. However, this is obviously a short-term solution.

Others have increased their interdependence with their immediate cultivating nieghbours by exchanging pastoral products or cash from pastoral products for labour in the cultivation of crops, or the direct purchase of grain from them. Still others, in combination or without the other "solutions", have entered into largely "illegal" trade in beef cattle and veterinary medicines, both of these activities reinforcing the crucial role of the junior (and senior) "warriors" (*ilmurran*) in the social reproduction of their society (Chapter 6), through the rebuilding of the homestead herd. All of these represent attempts to deal with peripheral capitalism without capitulation to the relatively poorer status of cultivators or being swamped by commoditization with its end not only of "peasantization" of the pastoralist but also of his ultimate "proletarianization" and "marginalization" and the formation of classes in previously classless social formations (cf. Dahl 1979: 254-65; Bradburd 1981).

For the time being, some of these are "solutions" for Ilparakuyo, leaving intact the ideological conditions for the reproduction of their pastoral social formation. But even if cultivators and not themselves are actually digging the soil and cultivating "their" fields of maize and other crops, Ilparakuyo are being inevitably drawn into forms of objectification of their environment which compete with their cultivating neighbours and which ultimately deny and destroy their own mode of existence.

V

In conclusion, it would seem imperative that research be concentrated upon some of the processes briefly identified here; but at the same time our theoretical position must constantly be modified and strengthened if the real depth of their consequences are to be understood, and, perhaps, averted. From the evidence increasingly available, to avert the dissolution of the very foundations of these East African pastoral formations would be of benefit not only to them and the nation-states of which they are a part, but also ultimately to the benefit of mankind as a whole. Any attempt to achieve this entails a constant revision of the theoretical problematics that guide research in the light of the evidence revealed in the processes of historical transformation taking place, some as a result of policy interventions which have occurred and are occuring in these formations themselves.

These tasks may be encompassed under the following research areas: 1) differentiation in terms of labour allocation, the ways in which pastoral formations 'handle'' the encroachment of commoditization and peripheral capitalism, etc.; 2) the relations between changes in the major means of production and class formation, and the continuing ability of some production units to commit themselves to the pastoral mode of existence; and 3) the functional transformation of such structures as age-sets and descent groups as a critical aspect of the overall transformation of the relations of production in the continuing attempts by pastoralists to order their increasing involvement with historical processes engendered by forces outside their direct control.

Notes

1. A contemporary example of immediate importance is the resurgence of the debate on the exclusion of the pastoral Maasai from the Ngorongoro crater in Tanzania, in which almost all the demonstrated facts of pastoral production and appropriation of the environment have been inverted to justify the position taken by agencies of "development" in the area.
2. I am somewhat puzzled by Salzman's dismissal of the concept of the Germanic mode of production as "anachronistic", as he gives no reasons for his epithet, nor any critique of its extensive use in the analysis of pastoral social formations. Perhaps one may dismiss in similar fashion such "anachronistic" ideas as that of "kinship system" and "political organization"?

Bibliography

Alavi, Hamza, 1974: "Peasant Classes and Primordial Loyalties", *Journal of Peasant Studies*, 1, pp.23-62.

Althusser, Louis, 1969: *For Marx*, London: Allen Lane (New Left Books, 1977).

————— 1970: "The Errors of Classical Economics: an Outline for a Concept of Historical Time", in Althusser, Louis and Etienne Balibar: *Reading Capital*, London: New Left Books.

————— 1971: "Ideology and Ideological State Apparatuses: Notes Towards an Investigation", in Althusser, Louis: *Lenin and Philosophy and Other Essays*, London: New Left Books.

Amin, Samir, 1976: *Unequal Development*, New York: Monthly Review.

————— 1980: *Class and Nation, Historically and in the Current Crisis*, New York: Monthly Review.

Anacleti, A.O. (ed), 1980: *Jipemoyo 2, 1980*, Uppsala: Scandinavian Institute of African Studies for Ministry of National Culture and Youth, Dar es Salaam, and the Academy of Finland.

Aron, Raymond, 1957: *German Sociology*, Glencoe: The Free Press.

Asad, Talal, 1978: "Equality in Nomadic Systems: Notes Towards the Dissolution of an Anthropological Category". *Critique of Anthropology*, 3, pp.57-65. Reprinted in Équipe écologie et anthropologie des sociétés pastorales (eds): *Pastoral Production and Society*, Cambridge: Cambridge University Press.

Augé, Marc, 1982: *The Anthropological Circle: Symbol, Function, History*, Cambridge: Cambridge University Press.

Barth, Fredrik, 1964: "Capital, Investment and the Social Structure of a Pastoral Nomad Group in South Persia", in Firth, R. and B.S. Yamey (eds): *Capital, Saving, and Credit in Peasant Societies*, London: George Allen and Unwin. Reprinted in LeClair, E.E. and H.K. Schneider (eds): *Economic Anthropology*, New York: Holt, Rinehart, and Winston.

Bastide, Roger, 1971: *Anthropologie appliquée*, Paris: Payot, translated as *Applied Anthropology* by Alice L. Morton, London: Croom Helm, 1973.

Bateson, Gregory, 1958 [1936]: *Naven*, Stanford: Stanford University Press.

————— 1973: *Steps to an Ecology of Mind*, London: Paladin.

Baumann, O., 1894: *Durch Massailand zur Nilquelle*, Berlin: Reimer.

Baxter, P.T.W., 1972: "Absence Makes the Heart Grow Fonder: Some Suggestions why Witchcraft Accusations are Rare among East African Pastoralists", in Gluckman, M. (ed): *The Allocation of Responsibility*, Manchester: Manchester University Press.

————— 1975: "Some Consequences of Sedentarization for Social Relationships", in Monod, T. (ed): *Pastoralism in Tropical Africa*, London: Oxford University Press for International African Institute.

Baxter, P.T.W. and Almagor, Uri (eds) 1978: *Age, Generation and Time*, New York: St. Martins's.

Beckwith, C. and ole Saitoti, T., 1980: *Maasai*, New York, Abrams.

Beidelman, T.O., 1960: "The Baraguyu", *Tanganyika Notes and Records*, 55, pp.245-78.

———— 1961a: "Notes on Baraguyu Housetypes and Economy", *Tanganyika Notes and Records*, 57, pp.56-66.

———— 1961b: "Beer Drinking and Cattle Theft in Ukaguru", *American Anthropologist*, 53, pp.534-49.

———— 1962a: "A Demographic Map of the Baraguyu", *Tanganyika Notes and Records*, 58/59, pp.8-10.

———— 1962b: "A History of Ukaguru", *Tanganyika Notes and Records*, 58/59, pp.11-39.

———— 1963: Kaguru Time Reckoning: an Aspect of the Cosmology of an East African People", *Southwestern Journal of Anthropology*, 19, pp.9-20.

———— 1965a: "Some Baraguyu Cattle Songs", *Journal of African Languages*, 4, pp.1-18.

———— 1965b: "A Masai Text", *Man*, 65, p.191.

———— 1968: "Some Hypotheses Regarding Nilo-Hamitic Symbolism and Social Structure", *Anthropological Quarterly*, 41, pp.78-89.

———— 1980: "Women and Men in Two East African Societies", in Karp, Ivan and Charles Bird (eds): *Explorations in African Systems of Thought*, Bloomington: Indiana University Press.

Bell, Daniel, 1960: *The End of Ideology: on the Exhaustion of Political Ideas in the Fifties*, New York: The Free Press.

Berger, P. and Luckmann, Thomas, 1971: *The Social Construction of Reality*, Harmondsworth: Penguin.

Bernstein, Basil, 1965: "A Socio-Linguistic Approach to Social Learning", in Gould, J. (ed): *Penguin Survey of the Social Sciences, 1965*, Harmondsworth: Penguin.

Bernstein, Richard J., 1971: *Praxis and Action*, Philadelphia: University of Pennsylvania Press.

Berntsen, John L., 1979a: "Maasai Age-sets and Prophetic Leadership", *Africa*, 49, pp. 134-46.

———— 1979b: "Pastoralism, Raiding, and Prophets: Maasailand in the Nineteenth Century", Ph.D. dissertation, University of Wisconsin.

———— Forthcoming: "The Enemy is Us: Eponymy in the Historiography of the Maasai."

Bétaille, Andre, 1978: "Ideologies: Commitment and Partisanship", *L'Homme*, 18, pp.47-67.

Bloch, Maurice (ed) 1975: *Marxist Analyses and Social Anthropology*, ASA Studies, 3, London: Malaby.

Boakes, R.A. and Halliday, M.S., 1970: "The Skinnerean Analysis of Behaviour", in Borger, R. and F. Cioffi (eds): *Explanation in Behavioural Sciences*, Cambridge: Cambridge University Press.

Bohannan, Paul, 1953: "Concepts of Time among the Tiv of Nigeria", *Southwestern Journal of Anthropology*, 9, pp.251-62. Reprinted in Middleton, J. (ed): *Myth and Cosmos*, New York: Natural History Press.

Bonte, Pierre, 1973: "Études sur les Sociétés de Pasteurs Nomades", *Cahiers du CERM* (Paris), No.109, pp.6-32.

———— 1974: "Études sur les Sociétés de Pasteurs Nomades, 2: Organisation économique et sociale des pasteurs d'Afrique Orentale", *Cahiers du CERM* (Paris), No. 110, pp.1-95.

———— 1975: "Cattle for God: an Attempt at a Marxist Analysis of the Religion of East African Herdsmen", *Social Compass*, 22, pp.381-96.

———— 1977: "Non-stratified Social Formations among Pastoral Nomads", in Friedman, J. and M. Rowlands (eds): *The Evolution of Social Systems*, London: Duckworth.

———— 1981: "Marxist Theory and Anthropological Analysis: the Study of Nomadic Pastoralist Societies", in J. Kahn and J.P. Llobera (eds): *The Anthropology of Pre-capitalist Societies*, London: Macmillan.

Boon, James A., 1972: *From Symbolism to Structuralism*, Oxford: Blackwell.

Bourdieu, Pierre, 1963: "The Attitude of the Algerian Peasant towards Time", in Pitt-Rivers, J. (ed): *Mediterranean Countrymen*, Paris: Mouton.

———— 1977: *Outline of a Theory of Practice*, Cambridge: Cambridge University Press.

Bourgeot, André, 1981: "Nomadic Pastoral Society and the Market: the Penetration of the Sahel by Commercial Relations", in J.G. Galaty and P.C. Salzman (eds): *Change and Development in Pastoral Societies*, Leiden: E.J. Brill.

Bradburd, Daniel A., 1981: "*When Nomads Settle*: a Critical Comment on a Critical Problem", *Nomadic Peoples*, 8, pp.35-9.

Bridges, R.C., 1968: "Introduction" to Krapf, J.L. (1880): *Travels, Researches, and Missionary Labours During Eighteen Years Residence in Eastern Africa*, 2nd ed. London: Frank Cass.

Bryceson, Deborah F. and Mbilinyi, Marjorie, 1980: "The Changing Role of Tanzanian Women in Production", in Anacleti, A.O. (ed): *Jipemoyo* 2, 1980, Uppsala: Scandinavian Institute of African Studies, for Ministry of National Culture and Youth, Dar es Salaam, and The Academy of Finland.

Burton, Richard F., 1872: *Zanzibar: City, Island and Coast*, 2 vols. London: Tinsley Bros.

Buxton, Jean C., 1963: *Chiefs and Strangers: a Study of Political Assimilation among the Mandari*, Oxford: Clarendon.

Caws, Peter, 1968: "What is Structuralism?" *Partisan Review*, 35, pp.75-91.

Chomsky, Noam, 1959: "Review" of Skinner, B.F. (1957): *Verbal Behaviour*, in *Language*, 35, pp.26-58.

———— 1967: "The Formal Nature of Language", in Lenneberg, E.H. (ed): *Biological Foundations of Language*, New York: Wiley.

Cicourel, A.V., 1973: *Cognitive Sociology*, Harmondsworth: Penguin.

Clammer, John (ed) 1978: *The New Economic Anthropology*, New York: St. Martin's.

Colletti, Lucio, 1972: *From Rousseau to Lenin: Studies in Ideology and Society*, New York: Monthly Review.

Comité Information Sahel, 1974: *Qui se nourrit de la famine en Afrique? Le dossier politique de la famine au Sahel*, Paris.

Dahl, Gudrun, 1979: *Suffering Grass: Subsistence and Society of Waso Borana*, Stockholm: Stockholm Studies in Anthropology, No.9.

Dahl, Gudrun and Hjort, Anders, 1976: *Having Herds: Pastoral Herd Growth and Household Economy*, Stockholm: Stockholm Studies in Social Anthropology, No.2.

———— 1980: "Some Thoughts on the Anthropological Study of Pastoralism", *Nomadic Peoples*, 5, pp.11-15.

Diamond, Stanley, 1974: *In Search of the Primitive*, New Brunswick, N.J.: Transaction Books.

Douglas, Mary, 1966: *Purity and Danger: an Analysis of Concepts of Pollution and Taboo*, London: Routledge and Kegan Paul.

Dorjahn, Vernon, 1959: "The Factor of Polygyny in African Demography", in Bascom, W.R. and M.J. Herskovits (eds): *Continuity and Change in African Cultures*, Chicago: Chicago University Press.

Dunayevskaya, Raya, 1973: *Philosophy and Revolution*, New York: Dell.

Dupire, Marguerite, 1962: *Peuls Nomades: Etude descriptive des Wodaabe du Sahel nigérien*, Paris: Institute d'Ethnologie.

Dyson-Hudson, Neville, 1962: "Factors Inhibiting Change in an African Pastoral Society: The Karimojong of Northeast Uganda", *Transactions of the New York Academy of Science*, 11, pp.771-801.

——————— 1966: *Karimojong Politics*, Oxford: Clarendon.

Easthope, G., 1974: *A History of Social Research Methods*, London: Longmans.

Eisenstadt, S.N., 1956: *From Generation to Generation*, London: Collier Macmillan.

Engels, Frederick, 1940 [1878]: *Dialectics of Nature*, New York: International Publishers.

——————— 1975 [1894]: *Anti-Dühring*, Moscow: Progress Publishers.

——————— 1957 [1894-5]: "On the History of Early Christianity", K. Marx and F. Engels: *On Religion*, Moscow: Foreign Languages Publishing House. Reprinted New York: Schocken Books (1964).

Evans-Pritchard, E.E., 1937: *Witchcraft, Oracles and Magic Among the Azande*, Oxford: Clarendon.

——————— 1939: "Nuer Time Reckoning", *Africa*, 12, pp.189-216.

——————— 1940: *The Nuer*, Oxford: Clarendon.

——————— 1965: *Theories of Primitive Religion*, Oxford: Clarendon.

Ferguson, D.S., 1979: "A Conceptual Framework for the Evaluation of Livestock Production Projects and Programs in Sub-Saharan West Africa", Ann Arbor: Michigan University Center for Research in Economic Development (mimeo).

Feuchtwang, Stephan, 1975: "Investigating Religion", in Bloch, M. (ed): *Marxist Analyses and Social Anthropology*, ASA Studies No.2, London: Malaby.

Firth, Raymond (ed), 1967: *Themes in Economic Anthropology*, ASA Monographs No.6, London: Tavistock.

Fischer, Gustave A., 1885: *Das Masai-land: Bericht über die in Auftrage der Geographischen Gesellschaft in Hamburg Ausgeführte Reise von Pangani*, Hamburg: L. Friedericksen.

Fisher, H., 1973: "Conversion Reconsidered: Some Historical Aspects of Religious Conversion in Black Africa", *Africa*, 43, pp.27-40.

Fortes, Meyer, 1945: *The Dynamics of Clanship among the Tallensi*, London: Oxford University Press.

——————— 1949a: *The Web of Kinship among the Tallensi*, London: Oxford University Press.

——————— 1949b: "Time and Social Structure: an Ashanti Case Study", in Fortes, M. (ed): *Social Structure: Studies Presented to A.R. Radcliffe-Brown*, Oxford: Clarendon. Reprinted New York: Russell and Russell (1963).

——————— 1958: "Introduction" in Goody, J. (ed): *The Developmental Cycle in Domestic Groups*, Cambridge Papers in Social Anthropology No.1, Cambridge: Cambridge University Press.

——— 1969: *Kinship and the Social Order*, London: Routledge and Kegan Paul.

Fosbrooke, Henry A., 1948: "An Administrative Survey of the Masai Social System", *Tanganyika Notes and Records*, 26, pp.1-50.

——— 1956a: "The Masai Age-Group System as a Guide to Tribal Chronology". *African Studies*, 15, pp.188-206.

——— 1956b: "Introduction and Annotations" in Lemenye, Justin (1956): The Life of Justin: an African Autobiography", *Tanganyika Notes and Records*, 41/42, pp.31-57, 19-30.

Foster-Carter, Aidan, 1978a: "The Modes of Production Controversy", *New Left Review*, 107, pp.47-77.

——— 1978b: "Can we Articulate 'Articulation'?" in Clammer, John (ed): *The New Economic Anthropology*, New York: St. Martin's.

Frantz, Charles, 1975: *Pastoral Societies, Stratification, and National Integration in Africa*, Uppsala: Scandinavian Institute for African Studies Research Report No.30.

Fratkin, Elliott, 1974: "Why Elephant is an Old Woman: Animal Symbolism in Samburu", *Mila*, 2, pp.23-37. (Institute of African Studies, Nairobi University.)

Friedman, Jonathan, 1975: "Tribes, States, and Transformations", in Bloch, M. (ed): *Marxist Analyses and Social Anthropology*, ASA Studies No.2, London: Malaby.

Galaty, John, 1977: "The Pastoral Image: The Dialectic of Maasai Identity", Ph.D. dissertation, University of Chicago.

——— 1978: "Pollution and Pastoral Anti-Praxis: the Issue of Maasai Inequality", (manuscript).

——— 1982: "Being 'Maasai'; Being 'People of Cattle': Ethnic Shifters in East Africa", *American Ethnologist*, 9, pp.1-20.

Galaty, John G. and Salzman, Philip C. (eds), 1981: *Change and Development in Pastoral Societies*, International Studies in Sociology and Social Anthropology, Vol.XXXIII, Leiden: E.J. Brill.

Garaudy, Roger, 1970: *Marxism in the Twentieth Century,* London: Collins.

Geertz, Clifford, 1973: *The Interpretation of Cultures*, New York: Basic Books.

Gellner, Ernest, 1978: "Notes Towards a Theory of Ideology", *L'Homme*, 18, pp.69-82.

Glucksmann, M., 1974: *Structuralist Analysis in Contemporary Social Thought: a Comparative Analysis of the Theories of Claude Lévi-Strauss and Louis Althusser*, London: Routledge and Kegan Paul.

Godelier, Maurice, 1966: "Système, Structure, et Contradiction dans le *Capital*", *Les Temps Modernes*, 246, trans. Ben Brewster, and reprinted in Blackburn, R. (ed): *Ideology in Social Science*, London: Fontana/Collins.

——— 1972a: *Rationality and Irrationality in Economics*, London: New Left Books.

——— 1972b [1969]: "The Thought of Marx and Engels Today and Tomorrow's Research", *International Journal of Sociology*, 2, pp.133-77.

——— 1972c [1966]: "Comments on the Concepts of Structure and Contradiction", *International Journal of Sociology*, 2, pp.178-88.

——— 1972d: "Structure and Contradiction in *Capital*", in Blackburn, Robin (ed): *Ideology in Social Science: Readings in Critical Social Theory*, London: Fontana/Collins.

——— 1977: *Perspectives in Marxist Anthropology*, Cambridge Studies in Social Anthropology No.18, Cambridge: Cambridge University Press.

Goldmann, Lucien, 1964: *The Hidden God*, London: Routledge and Kegan Paul.

Goldschmidt, Walter, 1965: "Theory and Strategy in the Study of Cultural Adaptability", *American Anthropologist*, 67, pp. 402-8.

Goodfriend, Douglas E., 1978: "Plus ça change; Plus c'est la même chose: the Dilemma of the French Structural Marxists", *Dialectical Anthropology*, 3, pp.105-27.

Goody, Jack, 1976: *Production and Reproduction: a Comparative Analysis of the Domestic Domain*, Cambridge: Cambridge University Press.

Goody, Jack (ed) 1958: *The Developmental Cycle in Domestic Groups*, Cambridge Papers in Social Anthropology No.1, Cambridge: Cambridge University Press.

Gramly, R.M., 1975: "Meat-feasting Sites and Cattle Brands: Patterns of Rockshelter Utilization in East Africa", *Azania*, 10, pp.107-21.

Groves, C.P., 1954: *The Planting of Christianity in Africa*, 4 vols., London: Lutterworth Press.

Gulliver, P.H., 1955: *The Family Herds*, London: Routledge and Kegan Paul.

—————— 1957: "A History of Relations Between Arusha and Masai", Kampala: East African Institute of Social Research Conference Proceedings, Makerere University (mimeo).

—————— 1961a: "Structural Dichotomy and Jural Processes among the Arusha of Northern Tanganyika", *Africa*, 31, pp.19-35.

—————— 1961b: "Land Shortage, Social Change, and Social Conflict in East Africa", *Journal of Conflict Resolution*, 5, pp.16-26.

—————— 1963: *Social Control in an African Society*, London: Routledge and Kegan Paul.

—————— 1969: "The Conservative Commitment in Northern Tanzania: the Arusha and Masai", in Gulliver, P.H. (ed): *Tradition and Transition in East Africa*, London: Routledge and Kegan Paul.

Habermas, Jürgen, 1970a [1966]: "Knowledge and Interest", in Emmett, D. and MacIntyre, A. (eds): *Sociological Theory and Philosophical Analysis*, London: Macmillan.

—————— 1970b: "Toward a Theory of Communicative Competence", in Dreitzel, H.P. (ed): *Recent Sociology No.2*, London: Macmillan.

—————— 1971: *Knowledge and Human Interest*, Boston: Beacon Press.

Hall, Edward T., 1959: *The Silent Language*, New York: Fawcett.

Hallowell, A.I., 1937: "Temporal Orientations in Western Civilization and in a Pre-literate Society", *American Anthropologist*, 39, pp.647-70.

Hannington, J., 1886: *The Last Journals of Bishop Hannington*, Dawson, E.C. (ed): London: Seeley and Company.

Harris, Marvin, 1968: *The Rise of Anthropological Theory*, New York: Thomas Crowell.

—————— 1979: *Cultural Materialism: the Struggle for a Science of Culture*, New York: Random House.

Harvey, Mark, 1972: "Sociological Theory: the Production of a Bourgeois Ideology", in Pateman, T. (ed): *Counter Course*, Harmondsworth: Penguin.

Hayes, E.N. and Hayes, T. (eds), 1970: *Claude Lévi-Strauss: the Anthropologist as Hero*, Cambridge, Mass.: Massachusetts Institute of Technology Press.

Hedlund, Hans, 1979: "Contradictions in the Peripheralization of a Pastoral Society: the Maasai", *Review of African Political Economy*, 15/16, pp.15-34.

Hegel, G.F., 1900: *Philosophy of History*, New York: The Colonial Press.

Henderson, W.O., 1965: "German East Africa, 1884-1918", in Harlow, V.,

Chilver, E.M. and Smith, A. (eds): *History of East Africa*, Vol.11., Oxford: Clarendon.

Hindess, Barry, 1973: *The Use of Official Statistics in Sociology*, London: Macmillan.

Hindess, Barry and Hirst, Paul Q., 1975: *Pre-capitalist Modes of Production*, London: Routledge and Kegan Paul.

————— 1977: *Mode of Production and Social Formation*, London: Macmillan.

Hoben, Alan, 1976: "Social Soundness of the Maasai Livestock and Range Management Project", Washington DC: Agency for International Development.

————— 1979: "Lessons from a Critical Examination of Livestock Projects in Africa", Washington DC: Agency for International Development, Program Evaluation Paper No.26.

Horowitz, M.M., 1979: "The Sociology of Pastoralism and African Livestock Projects", Washington DC: Agency for International Development, Program Evaluation Discussion Paper 6.

Hoffman, John, 1975: *Marxism and the Theory of Praxis*, London: Lawrence and Wishart.

Hollis, A.C., 1905: *The Masai: their Language and Folklore*, Oxford: Clarendon, reprinted by Negro Universities Press, Westpoint, Conn. (1970).

————— 1910: "A Note of the Masai System of Relationship and Other Matters", *Journal of Royal Anthropological Institute*, 30, pp.473-82.

Horton, Robin, 1967: "African Traditional Thought and Western Science", *Africa*, 37, 1/2, pp.50-71, 155-87.

————— 1971: "African Conversion", *Africa*, 41, pp.85-108.

————— 1975: "On the Rationality of Conversion", *Africa*, 45, 3/4, pp.219-35, 373-99.

Hotchkiss, Willis R., 1937: *Then and Now in Kenya Colony*, New York: Flemming H. Revell.

Hountondji, Paulin, 1976: *Sur la 'philosophie' africaine*, Paris: Maspero, English trans: *African Philosophy: Myth and Reality*, London: Hutchinson (1983).

Hughes, H.S., 1968: *The Obstructed Path*, New York: Harper and Row.

Huntingford, G.W.B., 1969 [1953]: *The Southern Nilo-Hamites*, London: International African Institute.

Huxley, Elspeth, 1935 [1953]: *White Man's Country*, 2 vols. London: Chatto and Windus.

Hyppolite, Jean, 1969: *Studies on Marx and Hegel*, New York: Basic Books.

Irons, W. and Dyson-Hudson, N. (eds) 1972: *Perspectives on Nomadism*, Leiden: Brill.

Jacobs, Alan. H., 1958: "Masai Age-groups and Some Functional Tasks", East African Institute of Social Research Conference Proceedings, Makerere University (mimeo).

————— 1965a: "The Traditional Political Organization of the Pastoral Masai", D.Phil. thesis, Nuffield College, Oxford.

————— 1965b: "African Pastoralists: some General Remarks", *Anthropological Quarterly*, 38, pp.144-54.

————— 1968a: A Chronology of Pastoral Maasai", in Ogot, B.A. (ed): *Hadith I*, Nairobi: East African Publishing House.

————— 1968b: "The Irrigation, Agricultural Maasai of Pagasi", Proceedings of the Annual East African Social Science Conference, Dar es Salaam (mimeo).

————— 1970: "Maasai Marriage and Bridewealth", *Mila*, 1, pp. 25-36. (Institute of African Studies, Nairobi University.)

————— 1975: "Maasai Pastoralism in Historical Perspective", in Monod, T. (ed): *Pastoralism in Tropical Africa*, London: Oxford University Press for International African Institute.

————— 1978: "Development in Tanzania Maasailand: the Perspective over Twenty Years, 1957-1977". Report prepared for USAID Mission in Tanzania: Washington DC: Agency for International Development.

————— 1979: "Maasai Inter-tribal Relations: Belligerent Herdsmen or Peaceable Pastoralists?" in Fukui, K. and Turton, D. (eds): *Warfare among East African Cattle Herders*, Senri Ethnological Studies 3, Osaka: National Museum of Ethnology.

————— 1980: "Pastoral Development in Tanzania Maasailand", paper presented at the 23rd Annual Meeting of the African Studies Association, Philadelphia, 15-19 October 1980.

Johnston, H.H., 1886: *The Kilima-Njaro Expedition*, London: Kegan Paul, Trench.

Kahn, Joel S. and Llobera, Josep R. (eds) 1981: *The Anthropology of Precapitalist Societies*, London: Macmillan.

King, Kenneth, 1971a: "A Biography of Molonket Olokirinya ole Sempele", in K. King and Ahmed Salim (eds): *Kenya Historical Biographies*, Nairobi: East African Publishing House.

————— 1971b: *Pan-Africanism and Education*, Oxford: Clarendon.

————— 1971c: "The Kenyan Maasai and the Protest Phenomenon, 1900–1960", *Journal of African History*, 12, pp.117-37.

Kipury, Naomi, 1978: "Engagement and Marriage among the Maasai", *Kenya Past and Present*, 9, pp.38-42.

Kjaerby, Finn, 1976: "Agrarian and Economic Change in Northern Tanzania", M.A. dissertation, University of Copenhagen.

————— 1979: (With William Baynit); *The Development of Agro-Pastoralism among the Barbaig in Hanang District*, Dar es Salaam: Bureau of Resource Assessment and Land Use Planning, Research Paper No. 56, University of Dar es Salaam.

Klima, G.J., 1964: "Jural Relations between the Sexes among the Barabaig", *Africa*, 34, pp.9 20.

————— 1970: *The Barabaig: East African Cattle Herdsmen*, New York: Holt, Rinehart and Winston.

Koestler, Arthur, 1967: *The Ghost in the Machine*, London: Pan Books.

Kokwaro, J.O., 1976: *Medicinal Plants of East Africa*, Nairobi: East African Literature Bureau.

Krader, Lawrence, 1974a: "Beyond Structuralism: the Dialectics of the Diachronic and Synchronic Methods in the Human Sciences", in Ino Rossi (ed): *The Unconscious in Culture*, New York: Dutton.

————— 1974b: "Introduction", transcript. and ed. Marx, Karl: *The Ethnological Notebooks of Karl Marx*, Assen: Van Gorcum.

Krapf, J.L., 1854: *Vocabulary of the Enkutuk Eloikop*, Tübingen: Fues.

————— 1968 [1860]: *Travels, Researches, and Missionary Labours During Eighteen Years of Residence in Eastern Africa*, 2nd ed. London: Frank Cass.

Kroeber, A.L., 1948: *Anthropology*, New York: Knopf.

Kulet, Henry R. ole, 1972: *To Become a Man*, Nairobi: Longman.

Kuper, Adam, 1973: *Anthropologists and Anthropology: The British School,*

1922-1972, London: Allen Lane.

Lamphear, J., 1976: *The Traditional History of the Jie of Uganda*, London: Oxford University Press.

Lattimore, Owen, 1962: *Nomads and Commissars*, New York: Oxford University Press.

Last, J., 1882: "A Journey into Unguru Country from Mamboia, East Central Africa", *Proceedings of the Royal Geographical Society*, IV.

——— 1883a: "A Visit to the Masai People Living Beyond the Borders of the Nguru Country", *Proceedings of the Royal Geographical Society*, V.

——— 1883b: "A Visit to the Wa-Itumba Iron-workers and the Mangaheri near Mamboia in East Central Africa", *Proceedings of the Royal Geographical Society*, V.

——— 1885: *Polyglotta Africana Orientalis*, London: SPCK.

Lawren, W.L., 1968: "Masai and Kikuyu: an Historical Analysis of Culture Transmission", *Journal of African History*, 9, pp.571-83.

Leach, Edmund, 1954: *Political Systems of Highland Burma*, London: Bell.

——— 1961: *Rethinking Anthropology*, London: Athlone.

Leach, Edmund, (ed) 1968: *Dialectic in Practical Religion*, Cambridge Papers in Social Anthropology No.5, Cambridge: Cambridge University Press.

Lefébure, Claude, 1979: "Introduction: the Specificity of Nomadic Pastoral Societies", in Équipe écologie et anthropologie des sociétés pastorales (eds): *Pastoral Production and Society*, Cambridge: Cambridge University Press.

Lefebvre, Henri, 1968: *The Sociology of Marx*, Harmondsworth: Penguin.

Lemenye, Justin, 1956: "The Life of Justin: an African Autobiography", Fosbrooke, H.A. trans. ed, and ann. *Tanganyika Notes and Records*, 41/42, pp.31-57, 19-30.

Lenin, Vladimir I., 1972 [1908]: *Materialism and Empirio-Criticism*, Moscow: Progress Publishers.

Lévi-Strauss, Claude, 1949: *Les structures élémentaires de la parenté*, Paris: Presses universitaires de France.

——— 1962: *La pensée sauvage*, Paris: Plon.

——— 1963: *Structural Anthropology*, New York: Basic Books.

——— 1966: *The Savage Mind*, London: Weidenfeld and Nicholson.

——— 1967: *The Scope of Anthropology*, London: Jonathan Cape.

——— 1969: *The Elementary Structures of Kinship*, trans. Bell, J.H. and J.R. von Sturmer; ed Rodney Needham, London: Eyre and Spottiswoode.

Lévy-Bruhl, Lucien, 1910: *Les fonctions mentales dans les sociétés inférieurs*, Paris: Alcan.

——— 1923: *Primitive Mentality*, Boston: Beacon Press.

——— 1938: *L'Expérience mystique et les symboles chez les primitifs*, Paris: Alcan.

Lewis, I.M., 1962: *Marriage and the Family in Northern Somaliland*, Kampala: East African Institute for Social Research Study No.15.

——— 1968: "Spirit Possession and Deprivation Cults", *Man* (NS), 1, pp.307-27.

——— 1969: "Spirit Possession in Northern Somaliland", in Beattie, J.M. and J. Middleton (eds): *Spirit Mediumship and Society in Africa*, London: Routledge and Kegan Paul.

——— 1970: *Ecstatic Religion*, Harmondsworth: Penguin.

——— 1975: "The Dynamics of Nomadism: Prospects for Sedentarization", in Monod, T. (ed): *Pastoralism in Tropical Africa*, London: Oxford University Press for International African Institute.

Lewis, Philip E., 1966: "Merleau-Ponty and the Phenomenology of Language", *Yale French Studies*, 36/37, pp.19-40.

Leys, Norman, 1926 [1924]: *Kenya*, London: Hogarth Press.

Lindblom, Gerhard, 1920: *The Akamba*, Uppsala: Appelbergs.

Llewelyn-Davies, Melissa, 1979: "Two Concepts of Solidarity among Pastoral Maasai Women", in Caplan, P. and J.M. Bujra (eds): *Women United, Women Divided*, Bloomington: Indiana University Press.

————— Forthcoming: "Women, Warriors, and Patriarchs".

Lipset, S.M., 1960: *Political Man: the Social Bases of Politics*, Garden City, New York: Doubleday.

Lyons, John, 1970: *Chomsky*, London: Fontana/Collins.

Mafeje, Archie, 1976: "The Problem of Anthropology in Historical Perspective: an Inquiry into the Growth of the Social Sciences", *Canadian Journal of African Studies*, 10, pp.307-33.

Manners, Robert K., 1967: "The Kipsigis of Kenya: Culture Change in a 'Model' East African Tribe", in Steward, J. (ed): *Contemporary Change in Traditional Societies*, Vol.1, Urbana: University of Illinois Press.

Marx, Karl, 1954 [1867]: *Capital*, Vol.1, Moscow: Progress Publishers.

————— 1962: *The Eighteenth Brumaire of Louis Bonaparte*, in Marx, K. and F. Engels: Selected Works, Vol. 1, Moscow: Foreign Languages Publishing House.

————— 1973 [1857-1858]: *Grundrisse: Foundations of the Critique of Polical Economy*, Harmondsworth: Penguin.

————— 1975 [1843-1844]: *Early Writings*, Harmondsworth: Penguin.

Marx, K. and Engels, Frederick, 1964: *On Religion*, Moscow: Foreign Languages Publishing House. Reprinted New York: Schocken Books.

————— 1970: *Selected Works*, Vol.3, Moscow: Progress Publishers.

————— 1976 [1846]: *The German Ideology*, in K. Marx and F. Engels, *Collected Works*, Vol.5, pp.19-539. Moscow: Progress Publishers.

Massek, A. Ol'oloisolo and Sidai, J.O., 1974: *Eng'eno oo 'lMaasai: Wisdom of Maasai*, Nairobi: Transafrica Publishers.

Mauss, Marcel, 1923: "Comments on an Address by Lucien Lévy-Bruhl on 'La Mentalité primitive'," *Bulletin de la Société francaise de philosophie*, 18, pp.24-8.

Mbiti, John S., 1969: *African Religions and Philosophy*, London: Heinemann.

McKeon, Michael, 1981: "The 'Marxism' of Claude Lévi-Strauss", *Dialectical Anthropology*, 6, pp.123-50.

McLellan, David, 1971: *Marx's Grundrisse*, London: Macmillan.

————— 1972: "The *Grundrisse* in the Context of Marx's Works as a Whole", in Walton, P. and S. Hall (eds): *Situating Marx*, London: Human Context Books.

————— 1973: *Karl Marx: His Life and Thought*, London: Macmillan.

Mead, Margaret (ed) 1955: *Cultural Patterns and Technical Change*, New York: Mentor for UNESCO.

Melotti, Umberto, 1977: *Marx and the Third World*, London: Macmillan.

Mennel, Stephen, 1974: *Sociological Theory: Uses and Unities*, London: Nelson.

Merker, M., 1910: *Die Masai*, Berlin: Reimer. Reprinted by Johnson Reprint Corporation, New York (1968).

Mol, Fr. Frans, 1978: *Maa: a Dictionary of the Maasai Language and Folklore*,

Nairobi: Marketing and Publishing Limited.

Monod, Jacques, 1972: *Change and Necessity*, London: Collins.

Monod, Thoedore, 1975: "Introduction" in Monod, T. (ed): *Pastoralism in Tropical Africa*, London: Oxford University Press for International African Institute.

Morgan, Lewis H., 1870: *Systems of Consanguinity and Affinity of the Human Family*, Smithsonian Contributions to Knowledge, 17, pp.4-602.

———— 1877: *Ancient Society*, New York: Henry Holt.

Morton-Williams, Peter, 1968: "The Fulani Penetration into Nupe and Yoruba in the Nineteenth Century", in Lewis, I.M. (ed): *History and Social Anthropology*, London: Tavistock.

Moser, Heinz, 1981: "The Participatory Research Approach on Village Level: Theoretical and Practical Implications", in Paakkanen, L. (ed): *Jipemoyo 4*, 1981. Helsinki: Institute of Development Studies, University of Helsinki for Ministry of National Culture and Youth, Dar es Salaam, and the Academy of Finland.

Moskvichov, L.N. 1974: *The End of Ideology Theory: Illusions and Reality*, Moscow: Progress Publishers.

Mpaayei, J. Tompo ole, 1954: *Inkuti Pukunot oo 'Lmaasai*, London: Oxford University Press.

Mueller, Claus, 1970: "Notes on the Repression of Communicative Behaviour", in Dreitzel, H.P. (ed): *Recent Sociology* No.2, London: Collier-Macmillan.

Muriuki, Godfrey, 1974: *A History of Kikuyu, 1500-1900*, Nairobi: Longman.

Mustafa, Kemal, 1977: "Notes Towards the Construction of a Materialist Phenomenology for Socialist Development Research on the Jipemoyo Project", in Swantz, M-L. (ed): *Jipemoyo 1*, 1977. Uppsala: Scandinavian Institute of African Studies, for Ministry of National Culture and Youth, Dar es Salaam and the Academy of Finland.

Ndagala, Daniel, 1974: "Social and Economic Change among the Pastoral Wakwavi and its Impact on Rural Development", M.A. dissertation, University of Dar es Salaam.

———— 1978: "Ujamaa and Pastoral Communities in Tanzania: a Case Study of the Maasai", Ph.D. thesis, University of Dar es Salaam.

Ndeti, Kivuto, 1972: *Elements of Akamba Life*, Nairobi: East African Publishing House.

Needham, Rodney, 1972: *Belief, Language, and Experience*, Oxford: Blackwell.

Nicholaus, Martin, 1973: "Foreword" to Marx, K. (1857-8): *Grundrisse*, Harmondsworth: Penguin.

Nyerere, Julius K., 1968: *Ujamaa: Essays on Socialism*, Dar es Salaam/New York: Oxford University Press.

Oliver, Roland 1952: *The Missionary Factor in East Africa*, London: Longman.

O'Neill, John, 1972: *Sociology as a Skin Trade*, London: Heinemann.

Paakkanen, Liisa (ed) 1981: *Jipemoyo 4*, 1981, Helsinki: Institute of Development Studies, University of Helsinki, for Ministry of National Culture and Youth, Dar es Salaam, and the Academy of Finland.

Parkipuny, M.L. ole, 1975: "Maasai Predicament Beyond Pastoralism: a Case Study in the Socio-Economic Transformation of Pastoralism", M.A. dissertation, University of Dar es Salaam.

Philp, Horace R.A., 1936: *New Day in Kenya*, London and New York: World Dominion Press.

Piaget, Jean, 1971: *Structuralism*, London: Routledge and Kegan Paul.

Pruen, S. Tristram, 1891: *The Arab and the African*, London: Seeley and Co. Ltd.

Ray, Benjamin C., 1976: *African Religions*, Englewood Cliffs: Prentice Hall.

Rigby, Peter, 1968: "Some Gogo Rituals of 'Purification': an Essay on Social and Moral Categories", in Leach, E.R. (ed): *Dialectic in Practical Religion*, Cambridge Papers in Social Anthropology No.5, Cambridge: Cambridge University Press. Reprinted in W.A. Lessa and E.Z. Vogt (eds): *Reader in Comparative Religion: an Anthropological Approach*, 3rd Edition, New York: Harper and Row.

——————— 1969a: *Cattle and Kinship among the Gogo: A Semi-Pastoral Society of Central Tanzania*, Ithaca and London: Cornell University Press.

——————— 1969b: "Pastoralism and Prejudice: Ideology and Rural Development in East Africa", in R.J. Apthorpe and P. Rigby (eds); *Society and Social Change in Eastern Africa*, Nkanga Editions No.4, Kampala: Makerere Institute for Social Research.

——————— 1971a: "Politics and Modern Leadership Roles in Ugogo", in Turner, V.W. (ed): *Profiles of Change: African Society and Colonial Rule*, London and New York: Cambridge University Press.

——————— 1971b: "The Symbolic Role of Cattle in Gogo Ritual", in Beidelman, T.O. (ed): *The Translation of Culture*, London: Tavistock.

——————— 1972: "The Relevance of the Traditional in Social Change", *The African Review*, 2, pp.309-21.

——————— 1977a: "Local Participation in National Politics: Ugogo, Tanzania", in L. Cliffe, J. Coleman and M. Doornbos (eds): *Government and Rural Development in East Africa*, The Hague: Martinus Nijhoff. An up-to-date version of this paper was published in *Africa*, 48, pp.89-107.

——————— 1977b: "Critical Participation, Mere Observation, or Alienation", in Swantz, M-L. (ed): *Jipemoyo* 1, 1977. Uppsala: Scandinavian Institute of African Studies for Ministry of National Culture and Youth, Dar es Salaam, and the Academy of Finland.

——————— 1978: "Introduction", in Marguerite Jellicoe: *The Long Path*, Nairobi: East African Publishing House.

——————— 1979: "Olpul and Entoroj: the Economy of Sharing among the Pastoral Baraguyu of Tanzania", in Équipe écologie et anthropologie des sociétés pastorales (eds): *Pastoral Production and Society*, Cambridge: Cambridge University Press.

——————— 1980: "Pastoralist Production and Socialist Transformation in Tanzania", in A.O. Anacleti (ed): *Jipemoyo* 2, 1980. Uppsala: Scandinavian Institute of African Studies for Ministry of National Culture and Youth, Dar es Salaam, and the Academy of Finland.

——————— 1981: "Pastors and Pastoralists: the Differential Penetration of Christianity among East African Cattle Herders", *Comparative Studies in Society and History*, 23, pp.96-129.

——————— Forthcoming: "Pastoral Societies and Colonialism in Kenya".

——————— Forthcoming: "Pastoral Praxis and the Symbols of Kinship and Affinity among Pastoral Ilparakuyo Maasai".

Rossi, Ino, 1974: "Structuralism as Scientific Method", in Rossi, Ino (ed): *The Unconscious in Culture*, New York: Dutton.

Rotberg, Robert I., 1968: "Introduction" to J. Thomson (1855): *Through Masai Land*, 3rd edition, London: Frank Cass.

Russell, Bertrand, 1972: *Logical Atomism*, London: Fontana/Collins.

Sahlins, Marshall, 1972: *Stone Age Economics*, London: Tavistock.

———————— 1976: *Culture and Practical Reason*, Chicago: Chicago Press.

Saibull, S.A. ole, 1974: "Social Change among the Pastoral Maasai in Tanzania in Response to the Ujamaa Vijijini Policy of TANU Since the Arusha Declaration", M.A. dissertation, University of Dar es Salaam.

Salzman, Philip C., 1971: "Comparative Studies of Nomadism and Pastoralism", *Anthropological Quarterly*, Special Issue, 44, 3.

———————— 1980: "Is 'Nomadism' a Useful Concept?" *Nomadic Peoples*, 6, pp.1-7.

———————— 1981: "Afterword: on Some General Theoretical Issues", in J.G. Galaty and P.C. Salzman (eds): *Change and Development in Pastoral Societies*, Leiden: E.J. Brill.

Sandford, G.R., 1919: *An Administrative and Political History of the Masai Reserve*, London: HMSO.

Sankan, S.S. ole, 1971: *The Maasai*, Nairobi: East African Literature Bureau.

Sartre, Jean-Paul, 1960: *Critique de la raison dialectique*, Paris: Gallimard. Trans. Alan Sheridan-Smith, ed Jonathan Rée, *Critique of Dialectical Reason*, London: New Left Books (1976).

———————— 1968: *Search for a Method*, trans. intro. Hazel Barnes, New York: Vintage Books.

Schneider, H.K., 1957: "The Subsistence Role of Cattle among the Pakot and in East Africa", *American Anthropologist*, 59, pp.278-300.

———————— 1959: "Pakot Resistence to Change", in Bascom, W.R. and M.J. Herskovits (eds): *Continuity and Change in African Cultures*, Chicago: Chicago University Press.

———————— 1970: *The Wahi Wanyaturu*, Chicago: Aldine.

———————— 1971: "Review" of Peter Rigby (1969): *Cattle and Kinship among the Gogo*, in *Journal of Asian and African Studies*, 8, pp.110-11.

———————— 1979: *Livestock and Equality in East Africa*, Bloomington: Indiana University Press.

Scholte, Bob, 1972: "Introduction: Structuralism and Marxism", *International Journal of Sociology*, 2, pp.115-31.

Schutz, Alfred, 1964: *Collected Papers II: Studies in Social Theory*, The Hague: Martinus Nijhoff.

———————— 1970a: "Concept and Theory Formation in the Social Sciences", in D. Emmett and A. MacIntyre (eds): *Sociological Theory and Philosophical Analysis*, London: Macmillan.

———————— 1970b: "The Problems of Rationality in the Social World", in D. Emmett and A. MacIntyre (eds): *Sociological Theory and Philosophical Analysis*, London: Macmillan.

Sebag, Lucien, 1967: *Marxisme et structuralisme*, Paris: Payot.

Seddon, David (ed) 1978: *Relations of Production: Marxist Approaches to Economic Anthropology*, London: Frank Cass.

Sena, Sarone ole, 1981: "Schemes and Schools: Two Agents of Change among the Maasai of Kenya", paper presented at a joint seminar of Temple University African Studies Committee and Department of Anthropology, 15 April, 1981.

Sève, Lucien, 1972 [1967]: "The Structural Method and the Dialectical Method", *International Journal of Sociology*, 2, pp.195-239.

———————— 1976: *Man in Marxist Theory and the Psychology of Personality*, Atlantic Highlands, NJ: Humanities Press.

Simonson, J. David, 1955: "A Cultural Study of the Maasai to Determine an Effective Program of Evangelism", Master of Theology dissertation, Luther Theological Seminary, St. Paul, Minnesota.

Skinner, B.F., 1953: *Science and Human Behaviour*, New York: Macmillan.

————— 1957: *Verbal Behaviour*, New York: Appleton, Century, Crofts.

————— 1972: *Beyond Freedom and Dignity*, New York: Knopf.

Smith, M.G., 1960: *Government in Zazzau 1800-1950*, London: Oxford University Press for International African Institute.

Sorrenson, M.P.K., 1968: *Origins of European Settlement in Kenya*, Nairobi: Oxford University Press.

Southall, Aidan W., 1953: *Alur Society*, Cambridge: Heffers.

————— 1970: "Rank and Stratification among the Alur and other Nilotic Peoples", in Tuden, A. and L. Plotnikov (eds): *Social Stratification in Africa*, New York: Macmillan/Free Press.

Spencer, Paul, 1965: *The Samburu: a Study of Gerontocracy in a Nomadic Tribe*, London: Routledge and Kegan Paul.

————— 1973: *Nomads in Alliance: Symbiosis and Growth among Rendille and Samburu of Kenya,* London and Nairobi: Oxford University Press.

Stenning, D.J. 1957: "Transhumance, Migratory Drift, Migration: Patterns of Pastoral Fulani Nomadism", *Journal of the Royal Anthropological Institute*, 87, pp.57-78.

————— 1958: "Household Viability among the Pastoral Fulani", in J. Goody (ed): *The Developmental Cycle in Domestic Groups*, Cambridge Papers in Social Anthropology No.1, Cambridge: Cambridge University Press.

————— 1959: *Savannah Nomads*, London: Oxford University Press for International African Institute.

Swantz, M-L., 1977: "Bagamoyo Research Project 'Jipemoyo': Introduction to General Aims and Approach", in Swantz, M-L. and Helena Jerman (eds): *Jipemoyo* 1, 1977, Uppsala: Scandinavian Institute of African Studies for Ministry of National Culture and Youth, Dar es Salaam, and the Academy of Finland.

Taussig, Michael T., 1980: *The Devil and Commodity Fetishism in South America*, Chapel Hill: University of North Carolina Press.

Temu, Arnold, 1972: *British Protestant Missions*, London: Longman.

Temu, Arnold and Swai, Bonavenure, 1981: *Historians and Africanist History: a Critique*, London: Zed Press.

Terray, Emmanuel, 1972: *Marxism and "Primitive" Societies*, New York: Monthly Review.

Teeffelen, T. van, 1978: "The Manchester School in Africa and Israel: a Critique", *Dialectical Anthropology*, 3, pp.67.-83.

Thompson, E.P., 1967: "Time, Work-Discipline, and Industrial Capital", *Past and Present*, 38, pp.56-97.

Thomson, J., 1885: *Through Masai Land*, London: Sampson, Low, Marston, Searle, and Rivington. Third edition with an Introduction by Robert Rotberg, London: Frank Cass (1968).

Thornton, Robert J., 1980: *Space, Time, and Culture among the Iraqw of Tanzania*, New York: Academic Press.

Tignor, Robert L., 1972: "The Masai Warriors: Pattern Maintenance and Violence in Colonial Kenya", *Journal of African History*, 13, pp.271-90.

Tucker, A.N. and Tompo ole Mpaayei, J., 1955: *A Maasai Grammar*, London: Longman Green.

Turnbull, Colin, 1961: *The Forest People*, New York: Simon and Schuster.

—————— 1965: *The Wayward Servants*, Garden City, NY: The Natural History Press.

Turnbull, Colin (ed) 1973: *Africa and Change*, New York: Knopf.

United States Agency for International Development (AID), 1980: *Program Evaluation Report: The Workshop on Pastoralism and African Livestock Development*, Washington DC: AID.

Vierkandt, A., 1949: *Kleine Gesellschaftslehre*, Stuttgart: F. Enke. Reprinted, New York: Arno Press (1975).

Vossen, Rainer, 1977a: "Notes on the Territorial History of the Maa-speaking Peoples: Some Preliminary Remarks", University of Nairobi Department of History Staff Seminar Paper No.8.

—————— 1977b: "Eine wortgeographische Untersuchung zur Territoriale Geschichte der Maa-sprechenden Bevölkerung Ostafrikas", M.A. dissertation, University of Cologne.

Waller, Richard, 1976: "The Maasai and the British", *Journal of African History*, 17, pp.529-53.

—————— 1978: "The Lords of East Africa: The Maasai in the Mid-Nineteenth Century (c1840-1885)", Ph.D. dissertation, University of Cambridge.

Watson, J.B., 1925: *Behaviourism*, London: Kegan Paul, Trench, Trubner.

Waweru, M.K., 1971: "African Missionary to Cattle People", in Parsons, R. (ed): *Windows on Africa: a Symposium*, Leiden: E.J. Brill.

Waxman, C.I. (ed) 1968: *The End of Ideology Debate*, New York: Simon and Schuster.

Welbourn, F.B., 1961: *East African Rebels: a Study of Some Independent Churches*, London: SCM Press.

Wilson, G. McL., 1953/4: "The Tatoga of Tanganyika", *Tanganyika Notes and Records*, 33/34, pp.34-47, 35-56.

Wolf, Eric R., 1966: *Peasants*, Englewood Cliffs, NJ: Prentice-Hall.

Wolpe, Harold (ed) 1980: *The Articulation of Modes of Production*, London: Routledge and Kegan Paul.

Worsley, Peter, 1956: "The Kinship System of the Tallensi: a Revaluation", *Journal of the Royal Anthropological Institute*, 86, pp.37-75.

Zein, Abdul Hamid M. el., 1974: *The Sacred Meadows: a Structural Analysis of Religious Symbolism in an East African Town*, Evanston: Northwestern University Press.

Index

Note:

(1) Since a number of Maasai words appear frequently in this book, and have crucial significance for the understanding of certain theoretical issues, I have provided basic translations in parentheses after each Maasai listing. The following serves therefore as both index and glossary.

(2) These words appear in the text with their gender/number prefixes. They are listed as such and not, as would be linguistically more correct, by the first letter of their word roots. Thus, *olpul* appears under "O" (masculine singular) and "I" (masculine plural) and not under "P". Words in Kiswahili are marked (Sw).